ENCOURAGEMENT
FOR YOUR LIFE

TOUGH LOVE MEMOS TO HELP YOU
FIGHT YOUR BATTLES AND
CHANGE THE WORLD

DEB SOFIELD

ISBN: 978-1-64184-478-9 (Paperback)
ISBN: 978-1-64184-479-6 (eBook)

Firefly Printing Press - lighting your world one word at a time

Encouragement for Your Life is a collection of insightful thoughts, stories, and quotes that offer a great perspective about life for those in need of a new direction and a bit of hope to get there. These tough love memos are from Deb Sofield's weekly radio show and podcasts.

To learn more about Deb Sofield visit www.debsofield.com

EPIGRAPH

One small crack does not mean that you are broken; it means that you were put to the test and you didn't fall apart.

~ Linda Poindexter

DEDICATION

This book is dedicated to my Mom ~ Mary ~ who believed in me and always has. And to my radio listeners who asked me to find encouragement in the world and share it. Thank you ~ this work has changed me for the better.

CONTENTS

ATAP

Recently I was helping a client with his presentation. As we were beginning to work, I noticed he wrote *ATAP* at the top of his page. Thinking that was odd, I asked, "What does that mean?"

He replied, "When I was in high school, I had to give the valedictorian speech for my school. I was very nervous about it until a friend gave some advice to me. He wrote *ATAP* on my paper to calm my nerves. Ever since, when I have to speak, I write these letters at the top of my start page because when you think about it, *All Things Are Possible*— ATAP."

Wow. **A**ll **T**hings **A**re **P**ossible. What a great thought!

And who says things aren't possible? Is it the voice in your head or, maybe, the voice of others? Is it *your* voice? If we stop and consider the options, we might find our way to all that is **P**ossible.

The skeptic might scoff at such a simple thought. But I wonder why it couldn't be true. I'm not saying it will all be wine and roses because it might be beer and daisies. However, on just the right day, ATAP might be all you need to get by. All things are possible, and only you can make the choice to believe.

DON'T BORROW TROUBLE
FROM TOMORROW

I am watching a friend sell their house, and this is not a great experience (even on the outside). They live in an old, strong, secure, well-kept house that looks like other houses on the street, but inside, it's different. Inside, it stands out. It has been decorated beautifully with richly painted floors, fine molding, solid wood doors, and hardwood floors throughout. It is a lovely home.

Years ago, I had my real estate license long enough to know that everyone thinks their house is perfect, so I get it, but with an over-50-year-old home, the buyer has to fall in love with the features that a 50-plus-year-old home has.

The trouble with the sale of my friend's house started because the buyer's realtor sees and fears things that are a reality in many old homes. When someone is looking for trouble, they often find it. I think the phrase that best expresses the oddity of it all is, "They are borrowing trouble from tomorrow." I like that phrase because it explains what I see a lot of folks doing. They are so worried about what could happen that they hesitate and hem and haw and can't move because, in their mind, something (mind you, they don't know what, but something) could happen, so they stop. And then something happens to reassure them that all is well, and once again, they get started. But this fear will stop them again and again.

From all outside appearances, it seems the potential buyer of my friend's house simply wants to move in and call the beautiful, old place home, but outside influences can't be sure because of something, anything, but ultimately nothing, stops them. As I watch, I want to tell all involved, "Don't borrow trouble from tomorrow. I'm sure when tomorrow comes, you'll have plenty to do. But for today, get started and stop listening to those who *borrow trouble.* Obviously, they don't have enough to do and don't want to be stopped alone, so they stop you also. Your best bet is to walk away and begin anew."

I'M GORGEOUS INSIDE

"Are you gorgeous inside?"

Every day, I deal with clients who, on the outside, seem to have it all: the big job, big title, big house, big car, beautiful clothes. And yet, if I were to ask this simple question, they'd be stuck.

For some reason, we equate gorgeous to an outside phenomenon and not to what's on the inside, where many tend to believe that one's business brain should rule for power, money, and prestige. Goodness knows, I am not against power or money or prestige, but I believe to be a whole and healthy person, we need to learn to balance the outside and the inside.

The fact is that most of my clients are gorgeous on the outside, from my perfectly coiffed businessmen and women to my politicians (we don't elect ugly people...*usually*). But gorgeous on the outside is not the same as gorgeous on the inside, and you know what I'm talking about.

I remember once while campaigning door to door, I came to a small home; it was gently loved but worn close to disrepair from years of neglect. As I knocked on the broken screen door to introduce myself and ask for the vote, I noticed the inside was very much like the outside of the home where time had taken its toll. But once the door opened, the lady who came to greet me, although worn by age, was stunning in spirit. In her day, I am sure she was the belle of the ball, and even time and life couldn't take that away from her. Ah, yes, she was gorgeous inside, and although brief, our time together, on the front porch a few years ago, has left a lifetime impression on me.

At this stage in life, most of us can't change what we look like on the outside, but we can be a work in progress on the inside, and that will lead to our headline where we can comfortably say, "I'm gorgeous inside."

WHO SETS YOUR BOUNDARIES?

As I walked along the fence, I came upon this marker: ***Boundary of the United States***. It's an imposing marker set into the fence line between America and Mexico. One can easily scale the fence or swim around the jetty in the ocean, but whether you cross over willingly or not, you've now crossed a border, a boundary line that either keeps you in or keeps you out.

It makes me wonder, "Who set your boundaries? Have you limited yourself? Are you on the wrong side of the fence?"

The concept of boundaries frustrates me. Who gets to set them, and who ensures they are abided by? Is it first-come, first-serve by purchase or by war? Is it simply the victor who gets the spoils and the *boundary line?* Many times, boundaries in business are bumped up against until someone calls their lawyer. Boundaries in relationships cause great angst. Boundaries to one's abilities are hard to acknowledge until the obvious is apparent.

What I often find with my clients is that they have adhered to boundary lines that were set for them by someone else, and their unchosen and unintentional boundaries are closing them in and shutting them out and limiting their hopes, their dreams, and, in an odd way, their future.

It's the voices in their heads that say things that are simply not true, and yet, they have heard those words for so long that they are now ingrained in their soul.

Boundaries for safety and security make sense. Boundaries for limiting your abilities and dreams because of the dysfunction of others does not and must be erased so you find your place to grow and thrive and be your best and, just maybe, climb the fence and swim around the jetty.

Think about who sets your boundaries.

WHY YOU GOTTA BE SO MEAN?

"Get your big, fat a__ in here!" Those are the words a client of mine recently heard from her grandmother. I can only assume the grandmother didn't measure the damage of her words. I'm sure Grandma thought she was being funny. She wasn't.

Weeks later, my client can repeat that stinging phrase that hurt to the bone, and the worst part is that now every time she looks in the mirror, she will hear those words from the person who is supposed to show unconditional love, her grandma. We all know that people say things to hurt someone on purpose, to prove their myopic point, or to put someone "in their place," and they claim it is for fun and that they really didn't mean it. But they do. What I have found is that they do it because deep inside, they are mean, angry, and frustrated that life didn't give them what they thought they deserved or they feel a need to lash out over some past hurt, hidden by a false smile.

Pathetic as that sounds, it's the truth. I see it every day. Hurting people hurt people, and they use the one thing that shows no outward scars: words. Ah, but friend, your words *do* scar inside and out, and for some, those scars last a lifetime.

I spend hours begging people to turn off the voices in their heads. Those voices are skewed and mean and are not reality. Hear me, friends: YOUR WORDS MATTER. They matter today, tomorrow, and the rest of your life.

Daily, I see the power and destruction of words that weigh on the soul, the heart, and the mind. Let me remind you that once your words are spoken, the record cannot be erased. Good-hearted, healthy, good-willed people don't say hurtful things to prove their point. People who love you will build you tall from where you stand. And, friend, if your life is not what you had hoped for, stop taking it out on others. You're better than that.

"IF PLAN 'A' FAILS - REMEMBER YOU HAVE 25 LETTERS LEFT."

—Chris Guillebeau

I like options and to know that if my A plan doesn't work, no worries, I'll move on to B, C, or Z. The key to my success has been to have a plan not only to be successful but also to know where I'm going next. With a plan, I'm able to better weather the storm because, no matter what life throws at me, I can ride that wave knowing the ultimate goal is the shore. Sometimes my plans are about work, sometimes financial, but I am always focused on moving to the next level. I consider myself an optimist, and I think most people do, but even in hard times, we're wired to be hopeful. I find the word hope to be a double-edged sword. On the one hand, it is a weak word because sometimes you find yourself sitting around hoping without taking any action, and on the other hand, it is a powerful word of trust. You're trusting that you've done the right thing to reap the reward given. You trust that you've done all you could to make something happen, and you trust that, ultimately, God is in control of your life today, tomorrow, and forever.

I have always loved this quote by Winston Churchill: "Success is not final; failure is not fatal; it is the courage to continue that counts."

The courage to continue is a powerful force especially when you know that you have 25 letters left to make a go of it.

- "Success is the culmination of failures, mistakes, false starts, confusion, and the determination to keep going anyway. Failure and success have been momentary stages in my life; for me, success is the process of not accepting failure." *Jay Peterman*

- "Failure is a detour, not a dead-end street." *Zig Ziglar*

- "Failure is not fatal, but failure to change might be." *Coach John Wooden*

- "Time is precious; mediocrity is a sin; work is a privilege; failure is a comma, not a period; can't is a word that does not exist." *Bonnie McElveen-Hunter*

FORGIVENESS

My dad had a business here in my hometown for years. We had a recycling plant where they would recycle newspaper, cardboard, and sometimes glass and rags.

It wasn't a pretty business. With all the dust and paper scraps, it was downright dirty, and honestly, I did not enjoy having to work in the office in the summertime. My brothers had what I thought was a better job of picking up bales of paper in the truck in their free time to make their own spending money. Since I was a girl, my dad was not going to give me a truck and send me on my way to pick up bales of paper on the backside of buildings, so I got stuck in my boring office job. My job was to weigh the trucks on the scale full of paper and then weigh them empty and pay the difference.

You wouldn't think that would be a big deal, come in loaded, unload, and get paid. But of course, it couldn't be that easy. I'm a pretty quick study, and it didn't take long for me to learn the signs from the guys in the plant. The guys would give me a high sign that something in this truckload wasn't right, so I would have to go outside in the sweltering heat (and funky smells, and I am *not* good with smells) and "talk" with the folks who were trying to cheat the system. I could never figure out how people had the energy to cheat at a recycling plant. What they would do was soak the cardboard and newspapers with water a few hours before they came to the plant so the paper would weigh heavy. They would then cover up the wet paper with dry paper, so it looked like it came right from my air-conditioned office. But when you watched them unload, it was easy to tell what they had deliberately done to cheat the system.

The oddest thing I remember from those years of working at the plant was how it was always the same people who tried to cheat. These folks made it a daily or weekly habit, and then I had to make it a habit to call them out and adjust their check. In hindsight, more important than the cheating and my learning how to josh with those who got caught without putting myself in danger was that as a young person, I saw what happened when people chose to lie, steal, and cheat.

Every day, they made a choice to fill the truck and water down the paper and then cover it up. What I have found in life as I speak and listen to clients is that many times people purposely fill the truck, water it down, and act like they did nothing wrong. Those are the people who cause such hurt in life, and yet, they lie to themselves and others and continue down a path without respect for the damage they've done.

Some people do wrong and seem to never pay the price. I know when I started my first business, there were a couple of guys who always seemed to cheat the system and never got caught. And that would frustrate me. I liked the guys; they were very friendly, looked nice, and rich (cheating does that for you for a time). I can remember expressing my frustration and anger to my parents about how it was unfair, and they reminded me that I didn't know what their life was like or how it would end up. Unfortunately, I now know how they ended up not nearly as well as they started out in a lot of ways.

I used to struggle with a Bible verse that says it "rains on the just and unjust alike." Really, how do those awful, rotten people get the blessing of rain in their lives?

I'll never know, but I also know it is not my worry. I am not in charge of this world, and I am not going to waste emotional, physical, and mental energy on someone else. When all is said and done, I am responsible for myself, and the same is true for you.

I could have ripped those people who kept trying to cheat us at the plant, but ultimately, they were the ones who paid the price in ways I'll never know.

Friends, I know it hurts. I hear it all the time from my audience, clients, and you, but let me encourage you today that you need to make it a daily habit to forgive and forget and move on. I know a lot of people forgive but will not forget (they love hanging on to the pain), so those people are halfway there. Hopefully, they will grow enough to let go so they can fully live.

Please, do what it takes to move past the hurt and into freedom, the freedom you deserve, to go and do and be your best self.

Benjamin Franklin said, "The best thing to give to your enemy is forgiveness; to an opponent, tolerance; to a friend, your heart; to your child, a good example; to a father, deference; to your mother, conduct that will make her proud of you; to yourself, respect; to all men (and I'll add women), charity."

Desmond Tutu said, "Forgiveness is the grace by which you enable the other person to get up, and get up with dignity, to begin anew."

Finally, Mahatma Gandhi said, "The weak can never forgive. Forgiveness is an attribute of the strong."

THREE RULES FOR SUCCESS

Lately, I have thought about writing another book; it would be about a sideline business I had for years as a rock-star pageant interview coach.

I know, I know, you're probably surprised to know that at one time I was one of the Southeast's top pageant interview coaches for Miss America, Miss USA, Little Miss, the Rodeo Queens, the Hereford Cow Queens, Watermelon Queens, and the list goes on. For years, I had more winners on the stage than any coach in the Carolina's and probably the Southeast.

What's interesting, as I learned early on, is that it's not me, but by coaching my clients to dig deep within themselves to learn to speak without fear and be true to themselves means they win every time.

The reason I think I should write the book for parents of pageant girls is that I've had to lay down a few truths that pageant parents know but don't want to be reminded of, and what is interesting is that the rules apply to all endeavors in life *with or without a crown.*

Most people know me as a coach for presidents of corporations to political candidates to sales teams, but trust me, business, politics, and pageants have a lot in common!

I want to spend a few minutes on three areas that can make or break you in business, politics, or *pageants:*

1. **Always tell the truth**

2. **Don't degrade others**

3. **Be careful of what you say**

In the pageant business, probably the most important lesson a kid must learn is that it's not the questions but the answers that win. And to that point, you must **always tell the truth.**

You must give answers that are true and honest to what you believe.

I know most people think that there is a right "pageant" answer that the judges want to hear, but the fact is, the answer that wins is the one that is true. When you speak your truth, you don't have to think too hard because, in most cases, you've already thought it through, and now, it is a part of your thought patterns for life.

Just like in your everyday life, if you'd simply say what you mean, you could bypass a lot of heartache. It's not about answering with what is easy or will get you by this time; instead, you must answer with the truth. The old saying is right; the truth will set you free. I'm not suggesting you ever be mean or unkind in your words, as we know that "a soft answer turns away wrath." Remember, you never have to overthink if you tell the truth the first time.

It's hard to convince people that speaking truth to power is the best way to go. We live in a society that seems to value double talk, and it is a Southern tradition to say one thing and mean another. For example, the saying, *"Bless your heart,"* really means you're not the brightest light in the harbor or the sharpest tool in the shed. Wouldn't it be better if we dealt with one another in the most honest and caring way we know how? I have found that the one way you do that is by **always telling the truth.**

Another lesson I'll be writing about is **don't degrade others.**

One must be very careful about what they say in front of others, and this is twofold. I had a mother who dropped off her daughter at my office, and from the minute she pulled into my parking lot, stopped the car, and rolled her window down, she told me everything wrong with her kid from her point of view. In the fifteen steps from getting out of the car to my office front door, that kid was destroyed, and it took me twenty minutes to put her back in the right frame of mind for success.

I know the mother wanted me to "fix" a few things (after all, she was paying me to work with her daughter), but after that happened, I called the mother and told her to never do that again. It wasn't productive; it wasn't helpful, and it added an unnecessary burden to her kid.

Let me add that from where I stand, a lot of kids have it hard nowadays. I know that it doesn't seem that way, but the pressure that social media is placing on our kids is more than anything we ever had to deal with (so much for whispers on the school bus), and an email blast can ruin the best of kids.

I see the degrading of people in business a lot. Someone gets angry and lets loose, and the damage is done. Oh, you may not see the result for a while, but trust me, one day you will. And it will be so overblown by their bottled-up reaction because they took it until they decided they wouldn't take it anymore, and then they blow their stack, and you're left wondering what caused that. Well, buddy, you did. You picked and picked and pushed and pushed and most likely embarrassed them. They probably felt shame. Shame is hard, and when someone feels shame, all they can do is hold back until one day they punch back with such force, it will take your breath away… if you live through it.

You need to be an ally to your kids, your family, and your employees. Be their protector. You need to have their back **every time**. Just as family needs to protect family, you need to claim your people, build them up, care for them, be their advocate, and remember: **Don't degrade in front of others.** In fact, how about you don't stoop so low as to degrade them at all? It's not worth it, and the damage could be lifelong.

Another point is to **be careful of what you say.** You need to understand that when your daughter hears you bellyache about the money this pageant is costing (and they do cost a lot of money the first time), she begins to think she is **not worth** it.

Silently, she may even do something to not win to avoid causing her family grief. Unfortunately, I see it a lot as a coach. And what is interesting to me is you are given an opportunity to be the rock on which your kid stands, the people who cheer her towards success, the one group who is supposed to have her back, and all many families do is complain about money, time, and ad page sales. I tell parents that if they hate the program that much, they should have never let her enter because now they're **proving that your love and acceptance has a price.**

Imagine that your parents insinuate that you don't have value. And friend, let me tell you, when that happens and the silver thread is broken, it will be a lifelong battle for that young person to find hope. They will always struggle to believe that they are worthy of love and acceptance.

You'll pay for the boys to play sports with all the various equipment that they need and want but argue over a single dress that makes her feel like she just might be beautiful? **Be careful of what you say.**

I see it in the business world every day in my professional coaching as well.

I am sure there are many reading who can remember with clarity the time when a comment or off-handed remark left the deepest scar. I understand this is a two-way street. Some folks don't have the extra resources that they would wish for their kids. I get it, but I ask, is there something that can be done? A truce that still values that young life but is a fair acceptance of limited resources, a fair trade-off for what you can afford?

I'm just asking.

The pageant business is not the only business where this is a struggle. I have a friend who has a business in a perilous time, and every time I see him, he is talking about how bad everything is and how bad the economy is. He complains about the time of year, his employees, and his ex-employees. And because he says it so much, his current office staff is on pins and needles because they didn't cause the trouble but are paying the price due to his constant chatter about all his woes.

When your staff lives on the edge, you are not being the leader of the pack; you're being the weak link. Don't think you can fake it. They *always* know. **Be careful of what you say.**

Your responsibility as a parent, leader, coach, and boss is to guard your words, even in hard times. Realistically, every word you say is being magnified, cut, and quartered with kids, family, and staff reading into it what they perceive the truth to be through their eyes and limited understanding. You have a responsibility to **be careful of what you say.**

When all is said and done, here is my wish for you. I hope your name is called; I hope the crowd will cheer, but most importantly, I hope you were the people's choice.

THE ONLY THING THAT RELIEVES
PRESSURE IS PREPARATION

Awhile back, I saw this phrase and had to laugh because it is so true. No matter what you do, whether it is singing or speaking or dance or performance of any kind, once you pull back the curtain and see the bright lights and all the people sitting in the audience, the pressure is on. But if you have done what you should in preparation, you should feel a sense of assurance that you've done your best and now is the show, so let it shine.

Of course, this assumes you've done your part in preparation. For years, I was the interview coach for many young ladies in the various pageants, and it was reassuring to hear from them that all we had been studying in our interview practice came up for questioning, and they did great. Why? Because they were prepared!

Pressure, if not moderated, can make the sanest person blow.

Universally, the key to success is preparation, not only for your job or family but also for life.

Did you ever see the billboards from the group Values.com? They had great photos with a great byline, "Pass it on." One of my favorites is the one about the plane landing in the Hudson River with all the people standing on the wing waiting to be picked up, and the billboard says, "Cool under cabin pressure," and the highlighted byline was, "Preparation—pass it on."

On January 15, 2009, after taking off from LaGuardia airport in New York City, an Airbus 320 struck a flock of birds and was forced to land in the Hudson River. The remarkable calm and skills of the pilot and crew have become an inspiration to people around the world.

With the loss of both engines and only seconds to make critical decisions at 3,000 feet above the river, all the training and preparation of everyone involved came into play. The pilot, copilot, and crew had logged many hours of flight time, and it was their steady demeanor that helped the passengers remain calm during an intense situation. The remarkable result was that all 155 people on board survived with reports of only relatively minor injuries.

Additionally, the first responders from the ferry boats nearby acted quickly and employed their extensive training to make sure everyone got to shore safely.

No one involved had ever experienced anything quite like this, and yet, their countless hours of experience combined to achieve an inspiring and successful rescue that will serve as an example of the value of **preparation** for years to...**pass it on**.

I trust you will never find yourself in a situation like that, but I wonder, what are you preparing for?

You're not preparing for anything? Let me rephrase that; other than taxes or retirement, what should you be preparing for?

Goodness, please tell me you're working towards some goal in life!

What I find is that, too often, people will not step up to an opportunity because they have not done the required work that would put them in the spotlight of success.

So, they let the most amazing opportunities go by because they aren't ready.

Folks, the flood is coming. Build an ark. Do your part.

For many, a little work and preparation on the front end will allow them to reap the bright lights, big city, applause at the end if they'll simply put in the time, do the work, and be prepared.

Let me close with a few of my favorite quotes.

"Success is the culmination of failures, mistakes, false starts, confusion, and the determination to keep going anyway." *Nick Gleason*

"The most common trait I have found in all successful people is that they have conquered the temptation to give up." *Peter Lowe*

"You were born to win, but to be a winner, you must plan to win, prepare to win, and expect to win." *Zig Ziglar*

MOST PEOPLE ARE DOWN ON WHAT THEY'RE NOT UP ON

I heard this phrase and could not agree more. Think about it. How many times have you had a great idea, concept, or story that you wanted to share? And after you do, someone threw cold water on it because 1. They didn't understand, 2. Didn't like the fact you were thinking big, successful thoughts, 3. Just decided to be down on what you're up on.

Usually, people do this because they can't stand to see another person be successful. Oh, they would never admit it, but it's true. No one likes to think that someone else might get the upper hand, go and do something spectacular, or even change the world.

Now, this does not apply to everyone. There are a lot of amazingly kind, loving, and supportive people in the world, but unfortunately, it applies to a high percentage of people.

For many years, I have worked as a consultant in politics and can't even begin to count how many times I would counsel someone as to what would happen to their circle of friends when their spouse announced that they would run for public office. Inevitably, someone would say, "Not *my* friends. We're close; we're supportive; we're wonderful and will beat the odds." Sure enough, a few weeks later, they would come back and be distraught that I was right; their "friends" had pulled away, had not been excited, had even said things like,

"What makes you so special that you think anyone would vote for, support, or work for your spouse?" Why is it that it seems to be so hard to be supportive if you think someone else is going to get ahead?

Because people are down on what they're not up on.

So, Deb's standard advice is to **walk away** and find new supportive friends who will build you up and not sweetly tear you down. I know that I seem to give that advice a lot, and you're probably thinking, *If I do that, I won't have any friends.* You're right; you won't have any mean, unsupportive, selfish friends, so what you're going to have to do is find a new network.

I harp on this because I see too many people not living to their fullest potential as a result of being held back by others, and sometimes, it is well-meaning people who don't know your heart. Sometimes, it's not big things; it's the small things. For some, it's the guilt of leaving to find a job in another town or leaving a church (heaven forbid) when they change the color of the carpet or parents who don't want their kid to go away to college or move out of town. It could be any number of things, but in the end, it stops you, holds you back, and keeps you in one place, standing still when you were meant to fly.

Many years ago, I decided that I wanted to run for public office, and I remember thinking that if I chose this new path, some of my friends wouldn't like me as much, and I'd probably lose a few. I can remember mulling over my options, but the pull to be the change I thought was needed was greater than the comfort of staying in place. Sure enough, I had friends who were not happy with that decision for many reasons. One told me I wouldn't win, so why waste my time? Another told me I was throwing away my chances at a job opportunity that we were looking at because she wasn't going to run the company while I was out "having fun" (walk a mile in my shoes going door to door in the SC heat, and *fun* is not a word I'd use). Someone else said I would not succeed without her help in my campaign. Then I heard from another person that it would mess up our occasional routine of going to dinner and movies and fun things on Saturdays. It was during that time that a few friends I knew casually let me know that they would be a part of my new network, a new group of friends who would provide support and help and campaign hours for my election. And they did! To this day, they are part of my life; and the others, I don't see. I wouldn't mind being friends with them again, but now we're so far apart, and the things they said would happen, of course, did not come true (except for working on Saturdays).

If I can do it and come out better on the other side, you can too.

For many who are reading this, your best bet is to simply walk away and not engage with people who do not encourage you, support your dreams, or who are not excited about all the possibilities the world has for you.

I used to have the quote on my Pinterest board, "May all your dreams come true, even the ones they laughed at."

Mark Twain said, "There is always something about success that displeases even your best friends."

I'll end with a quote I love: "Friends are angels who lift us to our feet when our wings have trouble remembering how to fly."
— *Anonymous*

IT'S NEVER TOO LATE TO BE WHO YOU MIGHT HAVE BEEN

I was on the road traveling for speaking engagements: three cities, four airports in four days, and renting a car at one point. While I was at breakfast one morning at a legislative meeting where I was speaking, I struck up a conversation with a lady who, a few weeks earlier, had been in my hometown for a conference. As we began to chat about what a great downtown my city has and what a wonderful time she had, I asked how she transformed herself from a music teacher to a state senator. "Easy," she said. "I decided **it's never too late to be who you might have been.**"

I like that thought. First, because it is true, and second, because it is a hopeful sign for those of you who are struggling with what you hope to do with your life. Friends, she's right. It's never too late. Now, let me add the caveat; if you want to achieve your dream, you should start thinking seriously about that new direction sooner rather than later.

At one of the conferences I was speaking at, another speaker told the story of a man who had developed a computer program that he was so proud of. A colleague stopped by his office to inquire about the amazing program he was so diligently working on in his spare time. He gleefully announced to her that he built a computer modeling system that counted down the years, months, days, hours, minutes, and seconds to his retirement from the company. He said that in 13 years, four months, and nine days, he would be free.

Wow! That is a long time to wait and waste when in the interim, you could start on the path of your heart's desire. Friend, let me encourage you to start today, even if you start small, to move you in the direction that you wish to ultimately go. For some, that is moving to a smaller home now to preserve financial resources for later (not to mention less yard work). For others, it's losing the extra weight that is weighing you down mentally, emotionally, and physically. For some, it might be enrolling in seminary or education classes or taking a class a semester until you are able to commit full time to finish. It might even be taking a course you've always wanted to take at a local college.

Several years ago, I enrolled at our local technical college to take a welding class (Yes, I was a certified MIG welder). My world at that time was so full of mental work that needed an outlet and working with my hands and making things out of small square metal scraps with fire made me happy. Of course, I must admit when I went to class, I was the only woman there. I had to wear a special nonflammable jacket and gloves. I noticed all the guys wore doo rags; being a genteel Southern lady, I decided I wouldn't do that until I started working on my project. Next thing I know, I smelled my hair burning and realized that I better ask the doo rag guys to teach me how to tie mine on, so I'd stop burning the hair off my head.

Anyway, back to my theme of **it's never too late to be who you might have been.**

I know that I talk about living your best life a lot, but friend, it is because so many great people tell me year after year after year about their hopes and dreams, and yet, they make no plans to achieve them. It's as annoying as going to your high school or college reunion and the same folks who were loudmouths telling us years ago how famous they would be still have not accomplished anything worthwhile. But bless their hearts, they're still talking about it.

Now, talking is good, and I do not doubt that some of them will ultimately succeed, but for 99.9 percent of others—**stop talking and start acting.**

Every life coach guru out there will tell you to write your goals down, and for some, I know that works, but your dreams only come true if you do the real work of writing with purpose and not about big ideas without measurable goals. Whether it is writing it down and reviewing your goals daily, monthly, yearly or painting them on your garage wall so you see it every time you drive into your garage or simply writing it down and sticking it in your favorite book in a passage that speaks to you or has great meaning, you need to understand the simple truth of success. And that is the most powerful word in the English language. **Start.** Start today to give yourself some time to think and plan, and then, start doing. It is never too late to be **not only who you might have been but also who you are.**

Bruce Springsteen has a quote I like. He said, "A time comes when you need to stop waiting for the man you want to become and start being the man you want to be."

I am a fan of the late Jim Rohn, who said, "You can't change your destination overnight, but you can change your direction overnight."

I'll end with one of my own, "If you'll set your direction, you'll cover the distance." – Deb Sofield

YOU'VE CHANGED

When someone says, "You've changed," it simply means you've stopped living your life their way.

I love that quote. I found it on my favorite waste-of-time website, Pinterest. When I posted it on my Facebook page, I got several likes and responses because I think it resonates with people.

Why? Because it falls into one of those nice Southern sayings that are usually unwarranted criticism dripping with honey. I find you hear this a lot from the church crowd, who often spend more time gossiping about how bad you are and never looking at themselves, but I digress.

Please understand that I am fully aware that many of you live a certain way because you don't want to cause others grief or worry (or even harm), but please know that for you to live your best life ever, some of you need to come into the light.

Now, I fully understand respect; it is a Southern rule of etiquette, and all well-manned people subscribe to that. I am not advocating that you go against the grain of your personal beliefs or standards (never do that), but for many, you're not living your best because you're living your life someone else's way, and still, some of you have been silenced by others. You've been bullied into cowardliness, or for some, you've never let your voice be heard because you have allowed others to quiet you.

I don't know all the reasons why, but I do know that when you do speak or act or dream or hope or wish in a manner that others don't deem suitable *for them*, it angers them because they don't love you enough to let you shine. Or they're worried you'll outshine their dim light.

This phrase, "You've changed," stings when family members use it on one another; the people who are supposed to be on your team are nipping at your heels. I don't know where or why or how that started, but it needs to stop.

Family is the one place you should be free to be yourself, loved, respected, and cared for. By the way, if you're always ripping your spouse (I see this a lot when I travel, talk about stress! I'd probably leave half of them at the airport), don't be surprised when they walk away because, in this case, you probably *have* changed (and not for the better). Why did you turn so mean and angry?

I was talking with a friend the other day, and she said this phrase when we were chatting about life: "It's one thing to forgive, and we all talk about forgiveness, but unless you forget, you haven't forgiven; you're still hanging on."

You know Deb's rule; **walk away.** Find new friends or have a meeting of the minds to set a new direction for your marriage or your relationships with your family or co-workers.

I think many times people say the phrase, "You've changed," to bite you nicely. Really, how mean does it sound when someone says, "Oh, you've changed," but what that implies is you're not living up or down to their expectations?

I wonder who put them in a position to comment on your life, your dreams, your hopes, or your future.

Hold on, the answer's coming...you did. Yes, **you.** So now, you have to walk it back and find another path for your freedom to shine with or without them chattering on about you because their hurtful words don't matter unless you let them.

Leo Buscaglia said, "The easiest thing to be in the world is you. The most difficult thing to be is what other people want you to be. Don't let them put you in that position."

Oscar Wilde said, "Be yourself; everyone else is already taken."

Wallace Wattles, who wrote the book *The Science of Getting Rich,* said, "The very best thing you can do for the whole world is to make the most of yourself."

So, when someone says, "You've changed," smile and tell them you're glad they noticed.

You know the old saying, "Kill them with kindness." I'm sure you'd rather hit them with a brick, but that's not Christian charity, brother or sister. Amen!

STOP SIMMERING AND START BOILING

I f you want to be a speaker, one of the first things you should do is figure out what you're good at. What gift do you have that you feel you need to share? Now, wanting to be famous is not a gift, and it is not what the world needs; that may come in time, but let's focus on the current need.

So, what is your message for the world? What is your message that you have to say, and unless you are able to speak, you will not rest?

I was in Washington, DC, attending an event for The Campaign School at Yale. I served on the board for years and am a past president. I walked into the room and was greeting many of our students, our trainers, and my colleagues. A lady was standing off to the side of the room, and I casually spoke to her and went about my meet and greet, and I noticed that she watched me the whole time. As the evening was winding down, a small group of us were getting ready to go to dinner, but before I walked out, she took me by the arm and said she felt to called to say a prayer for me.

My group was wondering what my hold up was as I was in the corner of the room with a stranger, but I instinctively knew that if it had been laid on her heart to offer a prayer, I should listen. She was very kind, and in that room, she offered a very beautiful prayer of thanksgiving and love, and I was deeply touched. When she finished,

I hugged her and thanked her, and we went our separate ways. A few days later, I got a call from her, but I was busy and didn't make the return call in a timely manner. I mentioned to a friend about what happened and that this dear lady had reached out to me again, and I needed to get around to calling her. "Stop," my friend said. "Deb, you must call her now because when someone feels called to lift you up, you should honor them because **her message had to be said,** and she could not rest until she was able to accomplish that which she felt called to do."

I did call her back, and once again, she was gracious and kind and offered a wonderful blessing on my behalf. I tell you that story because I could see and hear that she was on a mission and didn't care what anyone thought (in that DC ballroom) or that I was a slacker in returning my call to her. She did what she was called to do because **her message had to be said.**

You should not want to be a typical speaker; the world has too many of those. You know, the late-night motivational paid programing or the wannabe speaker or preacher who reads a bumper sticker before they write their speech or sermon. Oh, they build you up and leave the stage with nothing to learn or remember, but you feel good and encouraged until you don't.

Someone recently asked me, "Why do you always talk about living your best life ever? Why not talk about living with the hand that you've been dealt?"

I answered, "Well, you've been doing that for years now, so how's it working out for you?"

They grumbled and shuffled away.

It is a conscious effort on my part to push you to see beyond your current situation. I've been described as a motivational teacher and not a motivational speaker because, every week, I work to have actionable items that you can use today to change your life. Why? Because you have control of one thing no one can take away from you, and that is your thoughts. Your thoughts become actions, and actions become your world.

One of the stories I like to tell is the story of 212 degrees. It is from a small book by Sam Parker and Mac Anderson called *212 The Extra Degree,* and in it, they talk about the difference of one degree.

At 211 degrees, water is hot.

At 212 degrees, water boils.

Boiling water turns into steam, and steam alone can power a train, move ships across the ocean, and force generators to create power to light your world.

The Power of One degree, by simply raising the temperature of water by one extra degree, is the difference between something that is simply very hot to something that generates enough force to move mountains.

A seemingly small thing, one degree can make a tremendous difference in every aspect of your life.

In their book, Parker and Anderson tell us that, "So simple is that thought of one degree anyone can grasp it, anyone can incorporate it in their life and the fact is that you can take that thought right now and with that thought planted in your mind, you can benefit from it for the rest of your life."

If you think about the power of one degree, it could change everything.

I guess I should talk about the number 212 because that is the degree when water is not just hot, it starts boiling. So many times in our lives, we're almost there, but we give up. Realistically, if we held on only one more degree, one more time, one more call, one more door, we'd win.

So, I have to ask, what is simmering in your life that you're not willing to boil over for?

Boiling over has changed the course of history, whether it was heading across an ocean for freedom or pushing west for a place of one's own or refusing to give up a seat on a bus or at a food counter.

There was a time when people of faith boiled over in evangelism, and it changed the world.

Boiling brings change.

I don't want to change your world; I want to push you to change your life. The world changing will come after you bloom where you are.

You must know by now that you are fearfully and wonderfully made. There is no one else like you, no one! There are almost eight billion people in the world, and no one is like you. You are unique, whether you choose to believe it or not. The truth still stands, so it is important to seek and find that which you were born to do.

My friends all know that I love to cook, and I'm pretty good at it because I love food. I love to create and make and try and then taste and add some more.

I'm not a good baker because I don't like to measure. I find it restrictive, but as all cooks know, one of the worst things that can happen in a kitchen is when something boils over because it makes a mess. And if you're not careful, aside from the mess that is made, you might start a fire if hot oil is involved.

But I don't find that to be the case in life for most people. What I find is if we can discover something that lights our fire, we might create something that could change the world or our little corner of it.

Let me *boil* it down to this: **It's your life, and you're responsible for the results.**

I believe if you take hold of the concept of one degree, it could change everything.

John Cleese said, "One of the hardest things in life is to know what you want out of life as opposed to what you feel you ought to want, what your parents and your siblings and society and your spouse and whoever else may expect of you. If you can allow yourself to trust those little movements round your gut that tell you when something is interesting or exciting, they will tell you where to go."

Thomas Edison said, "Many of life's failures are men who did not realize how close they were to success when they gave up."

Ralph Waldo Emerson stated, "Whatever course you decide upon, there is always someone to tell you that you are wrong. There are always difficulties arising, which tempt you to believe that your critics are right. To map out a course of action and follow it to an end requires some of the same courage, which a soldier needs."

You can't start the next chapter of your life if you keep rereading the last one.

I'll make a personal caveat about today's topic; if you are in an abusive relationship, **you do not need to hang on one more time. That time is up!**

You need to get out.
You need to find help.
You need to protect yourself.

It's your life, and you're responsible for the results.

THE MOST TERRIFYING PHRASE
I'VE EVER HEARD

The other day, when I was reading some information for a speech I am working on, I came across perhaps the most awful thing that could ever be said about someone, and it is from the Tartar tribe of Central Asia. They say that prior to battle, the Tartar tribes of Central Asia used to make a pronouncement over their enemies. It had nothing to do with their ability to overpower or wipe out their enemy in battle. Instead, their curse was this: **"May you stay in one place forever."**

Their curse was that their enemy would stop learning, stop growing, and fail to improve. The Tartar tribe was well aware that a person or group that fails to learn is learning to fail.

Wow. That might be the most terrifying phrase I've read in years.

"May you stay in one place forever."

Wouldn't that be a terrible thing to stay in one place forever? It's not about where you live but no personal growth, no movement, no future, no hope, and no options? I, too, would consider that a curse.

I'd be surprised if anyone out there knew a member of the Tartar tribe or could find Central Asia on a map, and yet, so many people seem to have bought into this phrase and placed it on themselves willingly. From what I can tell, that's what some people do with their lives, stay in one place forever. Or to put it another way, they do NOTHING.

They are happy to stay in one place forever.

They are happy enough with the status quo.

Why dream? It might not come true. Let's just stay where we are and be safe.

Some have bought into the belief that you shouldn't live above your raising (a good Southern phrase) and simply accept and learn to be happy with your lot in life. While I agree that contentment is a virtue, movement is the joy of life. The world is big, the sky expansive, and the ocean goes on forever. Why stay where you are?

Helen Keller said it best. She said, "Security is mostly a superstition. It does not exist in nature, nor do the children of men as a whole experience it. Avoiding danger is no safer in the long run than outright exposure. Life is either a daring adventure, or nothing."

One of the great joys I have is my job, where I get to travel, and time after time, I meet wonderful people who have succeeded beyond anyone's expectations. Some say to me, "I had to get out of my dead-end job to do what I was born to do," or, "I had to leave my little town so I could explore the world," or, "I had to leave my not-so-nice friends and find a new network who encouraged me to dream and be my best and not tear me down."

Now, I am sure that some of you are thinking, "Staying in one place forever is a choice, and I like my choice." To that, I say fine; you can stay, but for your success, I encourage you to grow, to learn something new, to keep your mind active and engaged, and allow your imagination to be open and wide and hopeful. It's not about physical movement. For some, it is their joy to stay (and that's okay), but for others, it is their joy to go on about dreaming, hoping, wishing, doing, being, and becoming.

I hope you don't stay in one place forever because the world is big, and I think you have a responsibility to explore, dream, and discover so you can find your sliver of light in which to stand and shine brightly.

I hope you don't stay in one place forever because you might miss opportunities that are down the way that you'll find if you at least step out and search.

I hope you don't stay in one place forever because even the shyest person can read a book and allow their mind to take them to faraway places. That's why reading is so important, not only for your kids but also for you as an adult. And it's not about your job requirement kind of reading, but learning to read for pleasure allows you to cultivate an expansive imagination.

When you think about all the inventions that have made our lives easier, those were not created by people who stayed in one place forever. No, creators and inventors are people who dreamed big dreams and then made them come true.

- The Wright brothers dreamed of flying.

- Marconi imagined that voice could go over a wire to be heard on the other side.

- Thomas Edison is known for his work with light bulbs, electricity, film, and audio devices.

- George Washington Carver was an agricultural chemist who invented three hundred uses for peanuts, soybeans, pecans, and sweet potatoes, and he changed the history of agriculture in the South.

- Eli Whitney invented the cotton gin, the machine that separates seeds, hulls, and other unwanted materials from cotton.

- Benjamin Franklin invented the lightning rod, the iron furnace stove (or "Franklin Stove"), bifocal glasses, and the odometer.

- Alexander Graham Bell invented the first working telephone.

- Henry Ford popularized the gas-powered car with the Model-T.

- Alexander Fleming was a scientist experimenting with mold that became the basis for penicillin, which is the most widely used antibiotic to date.

- And the current list includes Steve Jobs, Bill Gates, James Dyson and goes on...

These are people who did not stay in one place forever because they heard a call to go, to create, to move.

To have more, we have to grow more.

If you are serious about getting unstuck and moving from "staying in one place forever," it's not going to be a quick fix. What it will take is you seriously stopping your world for a bit, sitting down with a blank piece of paper and pen, and writing your dreams, hopes, and wishes on that sheet of paper and then allowing your mind to start the process of finding ways to make it happen.

So, once again, I am asking that you take a long, hard look at your current self, and understand that for the most part, you are where you are because you chose to be there. If you want to move ever so slightly, start by accepting personal responsibility and commit to a lifetime of self-improvement and learning.

Personal responsibility and personal action result in growth, freedom, and progress toward your goals.

Unless we commit ourselves to learning, growing, contributing to the improvement of ourselves, our families, and others, and being better today than we were yesterday, we will relegate ourselves to the fate of the Tartar's enemies: to be in one place forever. And you know what I say to that? It is *not* acceptable for your amazing life!

ASPIRE TO INSPIRE BEFORE
YOU EXPIRE

Recently, I was sitting with friends, and we were chatting about our morning rituals. What is the first thing you do in the morning when you get out of bed?

Some folks head straight for the coffee pot or put on their running shoes and go for a quick run. Some stay in bed and read emails or hit the snooze button. I head straight to the shower so I can get dressed to be ready for the day. Being self-employed for more years than I can remember, I learned early on to get up and get going and get ready for work so I can be in a work mindset. Otherwise, I'd spend the day in my pajamas and never get ready.

My friend told the gathering that before she gets up, she reads about five to seven websites that offer life advice on dating and marriage and kids and food, diets, love, loss, recipes, and bacon, all before her feet hit the floor. I was rather intrigued, so I asked her to name some of the sites that she so faithfully reads every morning, and she told me she reads Dear Abby, Dear Prudence, Dear Annie, Dear Amy, Dear Ellie, Dear Carolyn, and Dear Margo, and a few other sites like Aspire to Inspire. Then she visits other sites to learn the news of the day.

Aspire to Inspire sounds like something I would like to read, but not before I've had my shower and coffee, so I Googled the phrase.

I found myself reading not Aspire to Inspire, which was a fun site about going back to school, but the next option on the Google listing was **Aspire to Inspire before You Expire.** Now we're talking.

That seems like a great life goal. Come to find out, the quote is well known on church signs across America to remind the "flock" that one day it will all come home to roost.

The more I thought about the saying, the more I was motivated to think deeply about **what I aspire to do in life,** how I **inspire others,** and am I ready (when the time comes) to **expire with grace? Aspire to inspire before you expire.**

It's a catchy phrase, so I can see why it has staying power. It reminded me that *I still aspire* to get going on my *bucket list* of things I want to do in life and get going sooner rather than later, such as visit the Great Wall of China, see Aurora Borealis (northern lights from Norway), go fishing in Alaska, and drive the island of Ireland. All my dreams are doable; I simply need to make time and get a plane ticket and find a friend with free time and extra cash.

What about you? What do you aspire to do? Is there a place you'd like to visit or a restaurant you'd like to try? Would you like to plant a garden, write a book, go skydiving, learn to snorkel, or trace your family tree? Just don't do what the famous comedian Jeff Foxworthy did; he said when he traced his family tree, he realized it was a wreath.

The second part of that phrase is, *what am I doing to inspire others*? I feel my work is inspirational for many who find their voice and learn to use it. I also find great joy in coaching, speaking, and training. There is no greater joy for me than to see a client change before my very eyes in only an hour or two in our sessions. Whether it is the president of a corporation or a medical school interview, that's when I not only inspire but also am inspired myself. It is my hope and prayer that this book and my podcasts or my online training are an inspiration to others as they go about their daily lives. I hope and pray that my speaking will help others find their place in the light and shine for all to see. I know what I am doing, to the best of my ability, to inspire others.

How about you? What are you doing to inspire others? Have you thought about it? Keep in mind that they're watching you.

I came across a great inspirational story online recently by Lisa Jo Baker, a blogger, and she posted a blog titled, "When You Think Your Love Story is Boring." It was in response to a teenager's post of the week on the Huffington Post. The silly kid wrote, "My love life will never be satisfactory until someone runs through an airport to stop me from getting on a flight."

Lisa Jo Baker responds in her masterful way about her husband and life partner; "He drove us all home 18 hours over two days. Three kids and hundreds of miles and potty breaks and princess pull-ups, the car covered in the markers *I'd bought for window art*. Turns out the soft beige ceiling of a minivan makes a perfect canvas. Rainbow swirls color the door panels, and there are goldfish crackers crushed so deep into the seats that they will likely be there come next summer and this same road trip.

"He's unloaded a hundred loads of laundry and put the dishes away. He is patient and kind. He always protects, always trusts, always hopes, always perseveres. This ordinary unremarkable love walks slowly every day alongside. One step, one day, one T-ball practice at a time. One permission slip signed, one Lunchable, one school play, one art project, one Lego box, one more nighttime cup of water delivered at a time."

Talk about inspiration. I loved her post about her husband. Inspiration can be found in simple things that matter most to you. So, what inspires you to do things, great and small?

Now to the final count, the expiration part. In one of my presentations, I talk about what will be on your tombstone because I believe it is relevant to stop and think about the legacy that you're leaving behind.

There is a story about an old preacher who said at a funeral that on your tombstone are two dates: the day you were born and the day you died. And in between those two numbers is a dash, and that dash tells the world how you lived. That dash is your legacy. It's who you are and how you will be remembered.

Friends, what are you doing in the dash? Now, some people rephrase that saying by adding the line, the day you were born, and the day you realized what you were born to do.

Either way, it is a sobering thought to know what you were born to do and how you're going to answer that call.

I saw an interesting quote recently: "He was born mud but died marble." Wow, I hope that is said about me. To know that in the end, I would stand taller than while I was here because of the legacy I am leaving behind.

So, dear reader, how do you aspire to inspire before you expire?

LISTS

I like lists. I'm not sure why because I don't always follow what is written down, but maybe, it is the process of writing it down and crossing it off that does my heart good. It would feel like accomplishment even if I was going to do it anyway like get gas, go to the post office, or go to the store.

Now, lest you think that I don't follow through, there are some days I start at the top of my list and work my way down to completion, but for the most part, I get half of it done and start creating another list. I'm sure they have an official-sounding name for people like me.

A while back, I heard a story on NRP about a guy who collected random lists from the grocery store. I looked the information up online, and sure enough, my memory served me correctly. The book is called *Milk Eggs Vodka: Grocery Lists Lost and Found* by Bill Keaggy. He is a featured photo editor at the *St. Louis Post-Dispatch*.

The book is a compilation of abandoned grocery lists that have been discovered in grocery carts, on market floors, and parking lots across the country.

If we are what we eat, then this book reveals deep truths about the average American (not to mention more mundane truths like a surprising number of people enjoy onions, and, for most people, banana and mayonnaise are very, very difficult words to spell).

When looking online at some of the lists, I had to laugh not only at the bad spelling (hope I never lose my list now) to the type of lists, some on a back of a napkin, or a Post-it Note, or on a dollar bill, or the back of a greeting card. No matter where they wrote down the info, it was an entertaining read.

I seem to find lists online a lot, and I've given you a few in the past, but recently, I have come across more than the usual number of good things I need to know that showed up on someone's list.

Three Ways Nice People are Sabotaging You
Five Habits of Very Smart People
Eight Things Very Successful People Do
Ten Ways to be Less Awkward
Fifteen Things You Should Give Up to be Happy
Thirty Things to do Before You Die

And one of my favorites was written by Regina Brett, 90 years old, of the *Plain Dealer*, Cleveland, Ohio. Her list is filled with wisdom, insight, and advice on how to live the most successful, fulfilling life. She says, "My odometer rolled over to 90 in August, so here is the column once more:

1. Life isn't fair, but it's still good.

2. When in doubt, just take the next small step.

3. Life is too short – enjoy it.

4. Your job won't take care of you when you are sick. Your friends and family will.

5. Pay off your credit cards every month.

6. You don't have to win every argument. Stay true to yourself.

7. Cry with someone. It's more healing than crying alone.

8. Save for retirement starting with your first paycheck.

9. When it comes to chocolate, resistance is futile.

10. Make peace with your past so it won't screw up the present.

11. It's OK to let your children see you cry.

12. Don't compare your life to others. You have no idea what their journey is all about.

13. If a relationship has to be a secret, you shouldn't be in it...

14. Take a deep breath. It calms the mind.

15. Get rid of anything that isn't useful. Clutter weighs you down in many ways.

16. Whatever doesn't kill you really does make you stronger.

17. It's never too late to be happy. But it's all up to you and no one else.

18. When it comes to going after what you love in life, don't take no for an answer.

19. Burn the candles, use the nice sheets, wear the fancy lingerie. Don't save it for a special occasion. Today is special.

20. Over prepare, then go with the flow.

21. Be eccentric now. Don't wait for old age to wear purple.

22. The most important sex organ is the brain.

23. No one is in charge of your happiness but you.

24. Frame every so-called disaster with these words 'In five years, will this matter?'

25. Always choose life.

26. Forgive but don't forget.

27. What other people think of you is none of your business.

28. Time heals almost everything. Give time time.

29. However good or bad a situation is, it will change.

30. Don't take yourself so seriously. No one else does.

31. Believe in miracles.

32. Don't audit life. Show up and make the most of it now.

33. Growing old beats the alternative — dying young.

34. Your children get only one childhood.

35. All that truly matters in the end is that you loved.

36. Get outside every day. Miracles are waiting everywhere.

37. If we all threw our problems in a pile and saw everyone else's, we'd grab ours back.

38. Envy is a waste of time. Accept what you already have not what you need.

39. The best is yet to come.

40. No matter how you feel, get up, dress up and show up.

41. Yield.

42. Life isn't tied with a bow, but it's still a gift."

My list, although long, comes down to a few words of wisdom by the preacher John Wesley; "Do all the good you can. By all the means you can. In all the ways you can. In all the places you can. At all the times you can. To all the people you can. As long as ever you can."

What's on your list?

ACT AS IF

Recently, a friend who was on my show used a phrase that has stuck with me. In the course of our conversation in talking about how to keep your spirits up even when it seems like life has thrown you a curveball, she said that every time her spirits started to wane (in her job search), she would **act as if**. She would act as if it was going to be okay, act as if she had the courage to do the job, act as if she were in the job of her dreams. The mindset alone can change the way you currently feel about a situation. I like it because it is memorable, hopeful, and positive and gives me a sense of moving forward.

How about you? Instead of seeing everything that is wrong with a situation, what if you were to act as if it will go right or better in the direction you were hoping for?

When you don't feel well, act as if you do.

When your heart is broken, act as if you can get by. Take it one day at a time.

When the dark thoughts of depression start to cloud your judgment, act as if you're on the other side of the depressed state.

For some reason, I woke up thinking about Gretchen Rubin's book, *The Happiness Project: Or, Why I Spent a Year Trying to Sing in the Morning, Clean My Closets, Fight Right, Read Aristotle, and Generally Have More Fun.* Gretchen Rubin is considered one of the most thought-provoking and influential writers on happiness. Her books *Happier at Home* and *The Happiness Project* were both instant *New York Times* bestsellers, and *The Happiness Project* has spent more than two years on the bestseller list. She writes about her adventures as she test-drives the studies and theories about how to be happier.

The book cover says Gretchen Rubin had an epiphany one rainy afternoon in the unlikeliest of places: a city bus. "The days are long, but the years are short," she realized. "Time is passing, and I'm not focusing enough on the things that really matter." In that moment, she decided to dedicate a year to her happiness project.

In this lively and compelling account, Rubin chronicles her adventures during the twelve months she spent test-driving the wisdom of the ages, current scientific research, and lessons from popular culture about how to be happier.

Among other things, she found that novelty and challenge are powerful sources of happiness. Money can help buy happiness when spent wisely. Outer order contributes to inner calm, and the very smallest of changes can make the biggest difference.

You can buy her book on Amazon, or you can go online to **happiness-project.com** and take some of her quizzes and sign up for a dose of daily happiness. I like her 21-day projects because they are good mind-benders to get you to think differently about your life.

On her site, she has a section called Tips and Quizzes. In glancing over some of the things she talks about, I love her quiz "Are You the Kind of Person Who Divides the World into Two Kinds of People – Or the Other Kind?"

She asks: "Are you an alchemist or a leopard?" An alchemist seeks ways to change or redirect our fundamental natures. When we are dissatisfied with ourselves, we're often tempted to behave and make choices that don't comport with who we truly are.

Leopards, on the other hand, don't try to change their spots. They know who they are, and they don't worry about everything they aren't.

Another one I liked was "Are you a radiator or a drain?" She says, "More and more, it seems to me that energy is an enormously helpful clue as to whether a person, activity, or place is a happiness-booster, or not."

She goes on to say, "I find it's useful to ask, 'Does this person make me feel energized?' or 'Does this activity, though intimidating and frustrating, make me feel more energetic in the long run?'"

Perhaps counterintuitively, in her experience, some low-energy people nevertheless act as radiators because it's not their personal verve that matters but their level of engagement and quality of their ideas. And some people who are very high-energy and gung-ho end up being drains because they somehow make things harder instead of easier or put a damper on other people's observations and ideas.

Another one I like is: "Are you a Tigger or an Eeyore?" If you're a Tigger, you say things like:

"Happiness is a choice."
"Look on the bright side."
"Smile!"
"Fake it 'til you feel it."
If you're an Eeyore, you say things like:
"No one can be cheerful all the time. It's fake."
"Thinking the glass is always half-full isn't realistic. It's self-deception."
"If someone asks me, 'How are you?' I'm going to tell the truth, even if people don't want an honest answer."
"Authenticity is important to me. I hate phonies."

Gretchen Rubin's advice for the Tiggers out there is to remember that you can't *make* someone happy. Let your happiness naturally rub off on the Eeyores, but don't exhaust yourself trying to jolly them along. Telling Eeyores to cheer up or refusing to acknowledge anything negative won't make them cheerier. Your effort will drain you, and it will irritate the Eeyores. In fact, they'll probably hold more stubbornly to their worldview and may become even more intensely negative to counterbalance your positivity. And that's the opposite of what you want!

Her advice for the Eeyores is to remember that when you believe you're being realistic and honest, the Tiggers may find you gloomy and critical. Because your downbeat emotions are catching (a phenomenon called "emotional contagion"), they dread being sucked into your negativity.

Remember, too, that while you believe that some Tiggers are fake, their extreme cheerfulness may be in reaction to *you*. Yes, you may be inciting the very Tiggerness that is driving you crazy! As a counterbalance against your attitudes, their extreme cheerfulness may be in reaction to some major happiness challenge elsewhere in their lives. Cut them a little slack.

She goes on to say, "Research and experience show that the 'fake it 'til you feel it' strategy really does work. People who act happier, friendlier, and more energetic will help themselves feel happier, friendlier, and more energetic (the opposite is also true)."

Ms. Rubin could not have said it better: act as if. I hope you will for your sake and those around you who are looking to you for leadership, hope, friendship, and love.

STRIVE TO CLIMB HIGHER

Recently, a client called me about entering a competition. She was not sure that she wanted to go through the hard work, early mornings, late nights, or the stress, pain, and hassle of it all, so she called to ask me what I thought.

Realizing that she would have a lot of work to do to win the race, I was tempted to let her off the hook this time, to focus on her work, to build her career, to push her to the top. But then I realized, looking back over our last year together, how far she had come in just the first year of working towards her goal.

So, I told her to sign up again and work through it.

What I saw in her a year later was incredible; she had a rebirth of self-confidence, a new vision of herself, and the ability to be the best at what she did. What I saw through the tears and pain was a discovery of her true self, and I knew that if she could find the courage to love that person, she was on a path for life success.

Why did I push her? Because I knew through the tears and pain, she could do it, and over time, she would learn the skills, routines, programs, and production that would build a foundation of success even if she didn't feel like it at that moment.

I know that is not what she wanted to hear, but just call me *tough love Deb,* and I'll be by your side as you move to the next level. I have found that too many times, people ask friends for advice hoping to hear what they want to hear and not what they should hear. I'm as guilty as the rest, but in my life, my friends tend to be just as bold and blunt as I am.

A few years ago, I asked three friends to give me constructive feedback about my personality, my demeanor, my manners, my graciousness, and my leadership. I strive to go to the next level, and I wanted to be sure that I had done or was on a path to do what I needed to do to be successful.

So, three friends who I knew truly cared about my well-being were going to be my judge and jury. I am fortunate to have people in my life who have my back.

I can remember that all three letters back to me started the same in that they were very cautious about what they were critiquing me on. But as they progressed, they got the courage to speak truth to power because I had requested it and was willing to make changes. They said things I knew were not up to par in my life. Then they offered advice about things I needed to work on from my loud and booming voice and personality (inside and out) to my forcefulness when gentleness would have worked as well, to my chatter about a few folks who had done me wrong, and I continued to ruminate about it years later (and they were tired of hearing me bellyache). It was an eye-opening and humbling endeavor, and I still have their letters, which I occasionally read over every once in a while, to make sure I am still working on me to be my best.

What about you? Would you ever consider allowing someone who loves you to write you a letter about your personality, demeanor, manners, graciousness, and leadership? It's a good thought for those of you who strive to climb higher. Pick the traits that you'd like to develop and focus on who you're working to become.

I picked those five areas because they are the places in my life I wanted to develop; you may have others.

Personality: Am I consistent, even-keeled, and kind?

Demeanor: Does the look on my face reflect my heart? Do I carry myself with grace?

Manners: I grew up with four brothers, and we could finish a meal by the time my dad had finished saying the blessing. Eating that fast in a social setting is not good manners; bless my mother, she hammered social grace and manners into all of us, hoping it would take hold. Do my eating quirks distract from my conversation? Proper manners show class and status. Am I living up to my upbringing?

Graciousness: For me, it is about being thankful and kind, slowing down to smell the coffee, and letting others shine in their light.

Leadership: How can I take my lifetime goal to the next level?

It's a lot easier to climb the ladder once you've let go of the bottom rung, but to let go, you must learn to trust yourself.

It's a lot easier to keep moving once you leave the safety of the shore and get into the boat and rock along with the waves to find your path.

It's a lot easier to grow your circle if you seek out likeminded and grounded friends who want you to succeed and are proud to call you their friend—those who build you up rather than tear you down.

It's a lot easier to develop your true self by listening to that small voice within you that speaks words of kindness.

It's a lot easier to go farther with the guidance of others to gently pull you back onto the road from the rut that you've been living in.

It's a lot easier to live your best life once you commit to doing the hard work to better yourself for your future.

It's a lot easier to read a book from the library than spend hours wasting time on the internet with nothing to show for it.

It's a lot easier to rest when you've done the hard work on yourself, for yourself, to stop and be grateful for all gifts you've been given by your creator, and to reflect to others the joy in your life.

I know that I say it all the time, but I'm blessed in the work that I do. I was very pleased to receive a nice note from one of my favorite young people (and for the record, they're all my favorite young leaders).

In my training sessions, I ask the typical question, "What is the greatest gift you can give another person?" The standard answers are love, time, and kindness.

But one day, when I asked that same question, I was surprised to hear "Tumbler Cups!"

"What?" I said.

"Tumbler cups. I just love them, and they are so useful."

I burst out laughing so hard at that answer that I had to let it go; her honesty and sweetness were not to be denied. Yesterday, when I went to the post office, I received a box, and inside was a large tumbler cup with my initials on it. There was an accompanying note that said, "Ms. Deb, thank you for always building me up. I look up to you so much. I couldn't ask for a better coach! Love GG"

You and I have the opportunity to touch a lot of lives every day, everywhere. We make a difference whether we realize it or not.

I want to encourage you to continue through the hard work, early mornings, and late nights. Work through the stress, pain, and hassle of it all because if you start today, one year from now, you will have a rebirth of self-confidence, a new vision of yourself, and the ability to be the best at what you do.

When you fight through the tears and pain, you will discover your true self and find the courage to walk your path for success.

MAY ALL YOUR DREAMS COME TRUE, EVEN THE ONES THEY LAUGHED AT

I recently came across a phrase that made me smile when I thought about it because the truth it holds can be life changing.

May all your dreams come true, even the ones they laughed at.

There is something about this phrase that captures me. Maybe it's because I've had thousands of dreams, thoughts, and ideas that I've tried to pursue or have pursued, some to success, some that are still in my attic, and a few that are just sweet memories. But let the record show that at least I tried.

I hear a lot of polite snickering when someone verbalizes their dreams to go higher or to better themselves. What's funny is that others, due to their limited imagination, cannot fathom the idea of dreaming big and striving for continual improvement, so of course, it couldn't work for you since it never occurred to them.

But let me encourage you, dear dreamer, that the sky is the limit if you'll let your imagination go with what you think might work. Until you try, you'll never know.

It's been said that dreams are not those that are seen while you're sleeping, but those that don't let you sleep.

I found a great quote that said, "Tell me my dreams are unrealistic, and I'll tell you yours aren't big enough."

It's also been said that if you are not living your dreams, you are living your fears.

I believe most dreams are crushed (or at least dented) by those who have other ideas of what you should be doing. Maybe it's a parent who wants you to be a doctor or lawyer, both great and honorable professions, but if your heart is set on being a chef, there is going to be a clash of ideals.

I'm not saying that you shouldn't listen to those who love you and want what is best for you, but sometimes, we all have to step out and see if the ice will hold. My grandfather used to say, "A whole lot of learning happens if we can make it across the lake or if we break through and go under."

When I was in school, I wanted to be a coach for sports, and my best path forward was to major in physical education. "Whoa!" My dad said. "I'm not paying for that major." So, I chose my second-best field of study, which was communications and public speaking. It's funny how that has now become my life's work! It has also become my first love, and the irony is that I do coach but in a different way.

One Saturday morning, after I graduated from college, I was reading the newspaper when I saw an ad that said, *Make a lot of money, learn to be an auctioneer*. I thought to myself, *Whoa, this might be my new calling*. Once again, my dad was not impressed, but this time, he suggested that if I wanted to pursue my "new calling," I could, with my own money. I did take my leap of faith and became the 42nd woman in the state of South Carolina to earn my auctioneers license (not being grandfathered into the system).

I was hired by a local auction company and traveled the state and learned a lot about life, hard work, and crazy nutty people who steal at auctions. After a few years of calling bids from the back of a truck, I decided that I needed a new direction

After my vision of being a Sotheby auctioneer came to a screeching halt in a scrap metal yard in 101 degrees (and not as I had hoped; my lofty dream to auction fine art, furniture, and silver), I told the boys I had my fill of 12-hour days calling bids in rain, heat, and humidity. I was tired of looking through box lots of towels to pull out the silver candlesticks and start all the cars for the SLED auction. Yup, I wanted to go back to what was more in my comfort level, so I applied and went to law school. I'll stop right there. Let's just say that was not my best idea. In fact, in hindsight, what was I thinking? I wasn't a good student by any stretch of the imagination, and at law school, they expected me to study, *really* study, and that wasn't going to happen!

I have probably embarked on 15 to 20 different roads to see which one would lead me to my passion, my heart, and my home, and I am thankful that I did. Each job prepared me in some way for the next adventure or for something bigger, something unusual, something life-changing, or simply a redirection of the path I was on. In some cases, I had to stop doing things that I was interested in but not talented at.

I'm sure that many of you can retell some great stories of first jobs, grand adventures, and dead ends that oddly prepared you for something else in your life, and although it didn't make sense, it helps you now.

I hope you will take to heart this concept of wishing all your dreams come true, even the ones they laughed at. Allow your imagination to wander back to those days when you did dream. Laugh about the silly things you tried that didn't work and reflect on the things that did, the things you were excellent at.

Think back to a time when life might have been a little easier, when you had the luxury to think and hope and plan without restriction or consideration of responsibilities that you may have today.

Remember, it's your job to make your dreams come true. Don't quit your job!

The great Earl Nightingale said, "Never give up on a dream just because of the time it will take to accomplish it. The time will pass away."

NEVER LOOK DOWN ON SOMEONE UNLESS YOU'RE HELPING THEM UP

I know that most of us don't "think" we look down on others, but many times, we compare and contrast and then make a judgment, whether we're right or wrong.

For many, it is not a matter of arrogance but thoughtlessness. We fall into thinking of or being so consumed with ourselves that we don't stop to realize that as a member of the human race, we have a responsibility to help others. Where does that responsibility come from? Hopefully, it comes from your core, your goodwill, your fundamental life beliefs, and the basic concept of kindness no matter what your situation.

I'm speaking to myself today. I sit in planes, trains, and automobiles, and usually, due to being tired, I rarely engage in conversation with my seatmates because I have been talking for the last few hours, and my voice is tired. But as life would have it, nine out of ten times, my seatmates tend to want to talk and talk and talk, and I usually end up enjoying the conversation. In my case, it's not about looking down. What I have come to learn is I have a responsibility to help others up, allowing them to be seen and heard as they brag about grandkids, jobs, and vacations, giving them space to help them up.

I'm sad to tell you that I wasted a few years before I learned the secret to success. In my opinion, the real secret to helping others up is allowing them to step into their light.

There is nothing wrong with wanting to be seen and recognized for your accomplishments. Over time, I realized that I'd shine just as bright or brighter when I reflect the light of others if I simply hold back and let them have their day in the sun.

Now, don't get me wrong; I still have to work at it, so I watch and learn from others who are wiser than I am. I'm amazed at how this concept still needs to be reinforced or taught and how often we need to be reminded of it for our success.

I was speaking at a conference recently, and after a wonderful time with the audience, many were coming forward to shake my hand after my presentation. An odd thing happened as a fellow speaker decided to stand next to me so they could interject themselves to be a part of the conversation. Mind you, their presentation had not gone so well, and since no one had sought them out, they decided to stand in my light to be seen. Although it was odd, I realized what was happening and decided it was okay. I really didn't mind, but it did make me stop and think about how I show respect to others.

It's been said that even the most introverted person will influence 10,000 people in his or her lifetime. Some will be a good influence, and others will receive the wrong message and be negatively impacted. So, the question is not whether or not you will influence others but *how* you will influence others. Our acts of kindness can inspire a chain reaction of others doing the same.

I looked up the phrase "random act of kindness" on Wikipedia. It said, a random act of kindness is "a selfless act performed by a person or people wishing to either assist or cheer up an individual person or people." The phrase may have been coined by Anne Herbert, who wrote, "Practice random kindness and senseless acts of beauty" on a placemat at a Sausalito restaurant in 1982 or 1983.

Encourage random acts of kindness, it is an excellent reminder to never look down on someone unless you're helping them up.

BE A LAMP, A LIFEBOAT, OR A LADDER

I came across this saying a while back, and it made me stop and think about who in our lives have been there as a lamp, a lifeboat, or a ladder.

I'm sure that for most of us, it would be easy to choose someone who is a lamp in our life; someone who believed we'd come into our own one day and be the person we were born to be. That one person who, against all the odds of human reasoning, liked us, loved us, and believed in us. Today, we reflect their light as we go about our daily business.

I wish I could say that it is always family that is the lamp, but many times, it's not. Although that is hard, you can still be okay.

It is odd, I know, since family is supposed to be the rock wall of support for most of us. But with life's stress on families with financial issues, troubled relatives, and relations, health issues, etc., it often cuts off the light to those it should burn bright for.

Time and time again, I see that lamp is a true friend, a teacher, a coach, or even a friend of the family. It often is a family friend who can see into the darkness of the family dysfunction and hold a candle to light the way for one of the kids to find their path.

I encourage you today to dust off your lamp, trim the wick, add the oil, and burn brightly because, for someone out there, you may be the only light they see.

Next, let's talk about being a lifeboat.

I love the water, so the concept of a lifeboat resonates with me. As I speak to audiences from all over the world, the stories are all the same. At some point in life, many people have simply needed a lifeboat, a safe place to drag themselves onto and hold on until the storm passes.

In the safety of the boat, we can survive being buoyed by the waves of life because we can hold firm to the sides of the boat and pray we're not tossed overboard. I like the concept of a lifeboat because no matter where you are in life, you have an option for safety if you'll reach out, grab hold, and hold on tightly until the storm passes.

Many a sailor prayed for a red sky at night (sailors delight) vs. the red sky at morn (sailors forlorn) to get through the storm.

I hear stories of those who lay their head down at night with little to no hope for tomorrow, and yet the sun comes up, and in the night, the waves of life have stilled, and they can finally see over the bow to scout the safety of the shore with renewed strength that they will row towards another day.

Ah, to be a lifeboat, what a gift it is to be a place of refuge and safety.

To be a lifeboat is different than being a lamp because a lifeboat holds you, and you can choose to get in or stay out.

Life is about hard choices. I wish it were easier. But the choices you make will chart your course. It's always my prayer that those I work with find the safety of the shore and are protected from the rocks.

Finally, let's take a look at the ladder.

I don't know about you, but I am not fond of heights. When I moved into my new home, I threw away my rickety ladder and bought a nice, sturdy stepladder with side rails.

At my old place, I had two giant water oaks in my front yard. They made a mess, so once a year, I would have to get my brother's 18-foot slide ladder and clean the gutters on the front of the house.

I can remember being up near the top of the ladder cleaning with one gloved hand in the gutter and weaving my arm through the ladder while holding the gutter to steady myself for dear life.

I learned to clean the gutters early on a Saturday morning because I noticed if I did it in the afternoon, all my friends who drove by my house would see me up there and honk the horn to say hi, and it scared me every time and made me worry I'd fall. Finally, I got a leaf blower with a long wand so my wonderful yardman could blow out the leaves from the rooftop, and we'd just clean up the mess from the plant beds below.

I'm not a big fan of ladders, but I do like the concept of climbing the ladder for success. And not only for myself but also for my friends. Many years ago, I decided to surround myself with people who were on a life path for success in their personal and professional lives, people who were positive, joyful, loving, kind, and caring. People who understand the concept of helping others up the ladder and not pulling up the ladder once they had reached the top.

Far too often, I see that happen in the business and political world. Someone is helped up a ladder to great success, and instead of reaching down to help another climb, they pull the ladder up so they will be the only one, the only woman on a national board, the only man on a nonprofit board, etc.

If you were to ask me, I'd say you do damage when you play those games. A ladder is meant to help people climb, so they should get the chance to see if they can. If they can't, at least the option was there. In order to help others be successful, we need to help them climb up, not hold them down or keep them off altogether.

How about you? Can you think of those you've helped climb the ladder? Have you had to push or pull someone up so they, too, can see the view? I hope so. I hope your arms hurt and your muscles are strong from all you've done to help others climb.

Friends, we all have choices in life. You can be a lamp, a lifeboat, or a ladder. What's so great about this concept is that *you* get to choose which one. *You* get to make the decision on what your legacy will be. *You* get to make your corner of the world a better place.

You can be a lamp, a lifeboat, or a ladder—or all three.

George Washington Carver, one of my heroes, said, "How far you go in life depends on your being tender with the young, compassionate with the aged, sympathetic with the striving, and tolerant of the weak and strong. Because someday in your life, you will have been all of these."

I'm sure you've heard the story of the ship and lighthouse. (Just for the record, there is no proof that this ever took place, but it is a great analogy nonetheless.)

The captain of a major Navy ship radioed what he thought was the ship ahead. Into the radio, he said, "Please divert your course 15 degrees to the north to avoid a collision."

Crackling, the voice on the other end of the receiver said back, "Recommend you divert *your* course 15 degrees to the south to avoid a collision."

The captain barked back, "This is the captain of a US Navy ship. I say again, divert *your* course."

"Sir, with due respect, I say again, you divert *your* course."

"This is the aircraft carrier *USS Lincoln*, the second largest ship in the United States' Atlantic fleet. We are accompanied by three destroyers, three cruisers, and numerous support vessels. I demand that *you* change your course 15 degrees north that's one-five degrees north or countermeasures will be undertaken to ensure the safety of this ship."

Through the darkness came this response; "This is a lighthouse. Divert *your* course for the safety of your ship."

"YOU ARE WHAT YOU SETTLE FOR."

—*Janis Joplin*

I hate it when I come across a quote that hits me full-on. Really, I am what I settle for?

This quote makes my mind immediately jump to a thousand excuses. *What about my circumstances? What about my age? What about my job? What about my family? There's got to be a reason, and it's not me. It can't be me! Okay, fine, it's probably me.*

How about you?

Have you settled for a small network of friends because you're too lazy to reach out and meet new people? Is it hard to know who to trust nowadays? Are these people who seem nice really who they say they are? Do they care about your success, or do they want to hang on? Instead of taking people at face value, have you set up roadblocks?

Have you settled for being a few pounds overweight because you love to eat and try new things? There's a picture at my gym of the cookie monster surrounded by cookies sitting on the couch watching TV, and as he is scarfing down cookies, he says, "I don't know why I can't lose weight. Must be my personal trainer's fault!"

Have you let yourself go just a bit? Have you settled for a mediocre income because you won't push yourself, because you're tired, and you feel like you work all the time? Have you settled?

Life takes twists and turns, but you can't allow those twists to become your excuse for not trying, not working, not planning, not doing. Have you settled because it is comfortable, because it's easy, because you're tired, because you don't think anyone cares or will notice? Quite likely.

What can I say to get you off the couch and working on the tasks you have been putting aside until another day when you have more time, when the kids are gone, when your spouse is out of the house, when you pay off the credit cards, or when you get done listing all your other excuses?

Recently, I was speaking in Georgia, and during the presentation, I was encouraging my audience to take small steps like clean out the garage and attic to give their minds a place to begin and rebuild.

A lady in my audience hollered out and asked, "Why?"

"I'll tell you why," I replied. "It's because when your life is so full of stuff, you cannot make room for anything new. When you can't walk through your garage or park your car in your garage or are embarrassed to open the garage door or the attic or any other place you have filled to the top with stuff you will probably never use again, you've blocked out opportunity. You have shut the door to newness. You've closed off an opening. All because you couldn't find the time, make the time, take the time to clean out so you can clean up."

I see people in my coaching business who have settled for where they are because they have thrown up all these self-made roadblocks. Why? Because working through it is hard work. And, isn't it supposed to be easy? We all say *do what you love, and the money won't matter* until it does because you have to pay the bills.

Unfortunately, for many, it is hard work. But once you begin and get into the project, it becomes easier because, in short order, you can see progress. Oddly, that is exciting enough to move you forward, and then you can see a flicker of light at the end of the tunnel to finish. And then you're done, and even if it was hard, you finished, you succeeded, you won, and you didn't settle!

What I find is many people think they can get by with being good enough. They're not striving for greatness; it's all just good enough.

They have a major presentation for their company, and their attitude is, *Well, if I can just get by, I'll be okay*. Okay doesn't move you up the ladder. You stay where you are, and then you wonder why you don't get ahead. I know it takes time to research and plan and study, but to be great, you have no other choice.

It's the weekend, and it's probably football season where you are. Do you think the coach told the team, "Hey guys, we're good enough. No need to study the plays, no need to stretch and work out, no need to watch what you eat before the game." Come on, you know that no coach in America says that to their team! To be a well-oiled machine, you have to work at it, and settling is not good enough. *Ever.*

As a speaker, my friends in the speaking business and I are always amazed when a group calls and asks about availability and our speaking fees. Once they hear the fee, sometimes they'll say, "Well, we can get XYZ for this amount, and he is *good enough*." And I say, "Wow, good enough? Then you better call him because your audience is waiting for good enough. That will move them from where they are to where they want to go. *Good enough*."

Sometimes, they laugh; sometimes, they don't, but you know from where I sit if all you want is good enough, don't call me. My job is to move you from where you are to where you want to go, and I take my job seriously.

For some unknown reason, it's been laid on my heart to care about your success. As I've gotten older, I look around and think, *I don't want to live in a community of average. I don't want my elected officials to be average. I don't want my neighbors to be average. No, I want to live, work, and play with people who are doing good work, being a part of the community, and helping others achieve their potential.*

Good enough in the speaking business makes you feel good for that one hour, but by lunch, when you ask the group, "Hey, what did you learn?" The answer is, "Well, nothing really, but I feel good." To which I respond, "Well, how long will that last? Hmm, not long, I'm afraid."

How is it you think it's okay to settle? What goes on in the mind of a smart, well-reasoned, intelligent person who thinks it's okay to be mediocre, to be average, to be just okay?

It's not, and you know it!

Stop being lazy. Argue all you want, but you know I'm right (and for the record, I don't want to be right. I want you to be rock-star amazing).

Weekly, I tell you stories of those who fought through and succeeded on the other side. In one of my podcasts, I told the story of Stephen King and his frustration in his writing that was thankfully saved by his wife who encouraged him not to give up on his dream. Or I'll tell the story of Scott Hamilton. No one ever considered the physically small guy able to achieve greatness until he did, against all odds.

History is full of those who didn't settle, who got up every day and went forth and prospered; people who instinctively knew that they fearfully and wonderfully made and understood that it was time to step up and own it.

I have a quote that I write on my desk calendar every month. I'm not sure who said it, but it goes like this; "Our father does not inspire us to do that which cannot be done." I believe that my heavenly Father *does not inspire me to do that which cannot be done.* Whatever you believe, understand that I do not think you've been inspired to do that which cannot be done. No, if it's been given to you, you can do it.

So, friend, don't settle for less than what you've been given. Today is the day to get up, get going, and make progress because if you are what you settle for, I hope you settle for nothing less than rock-star amazing.

ADD A WORD, GET A THIRD

I have a client who is going to be a country music star. I'm working with her on interview skills so when her time comes, she'll be ready for the bright lights, big hair, and big city.

One day, while we were working together, I was looking at her CD cover. I asked who the other people on the CD were since they were not backup singers, and I knew they didn't write her songs. She told me how she learned some very hard lessons by being so young, innocent, and trusting in Nashville.

She said, "Deb, don't you know the phrase *add a word, get a third?*"

"What does that mean?" I replied.

"In the music business, everyone wants a piece of success, so if someone can 'add a word' to a song, they can then claim some sort of ownership and be paid *for life*."

"Really? That is ridiculous! I say brilliant things all the time to help others out, and I don't get paid any more than my coaching or speaking fee at that time." We decided that I should move to Nashville.

"Add a word, get a third." Isn't that interesting? The more I thought about it, the more it really bothered me, and then I realized I see that happening in business all the time. Someone adds just a little something to a project and then takes full credit. Someone changes a color on a brochure and then tells the world that they are the art director. Someone adds or deletes a few words on a paper and then claims ownership, and who is there to stop them? Except you should hear the words of your mother ringing in your ears to stop taking credit for others' work. It is wrong, and if you're doing that, stop before it catches up with you.

Why don't you do it on your own and then be the owner of the idea or concept, without having to resort to stealing other people's work?

Just because you run in front of the parade, it doesn't mean you are leading it. To be a leader, you must have followers. No one follows a dishonest person for long, and if they do, you're in bigger trouble than you thought.

The reason this is important is not only because it's wrong (although that is a big deal) but also because if you're not that clever, bright, or verbal, over time, people will find out. Eventually, others will see that you can't turn a phrase, or your design skills are limited to computer graphics, and your writing skills are average. Then you've condemned yourself to the role of cheater, liar, or thief. And nobody likes those people.

On the circuit, I speak about how careful we must be nowadays because no matter what we say, someone can bring it up on an iPhone and do a fact check and then tell the world that your numbers are not true, and your concept is not your own and that is not your design. At that point, your days are numbered; although many people will forgive, they won't forget.

Years ago, when I was working on a project to take to market, I had a company that made a Christmas stocking that looked like a little mink coat. (Don't worry, it was fake fur, but it looked and felt amazingly real; they were beautiful.) I fell in love with it and thought it was a brilliant idea. Why hang an old sock when you could hang a little mink coat? It made sense to me. I needed a seamstress to help me with my pattern design, and as she was handing me the final product, she informed me that since she had made it better, she was now a partner in my company.

"Hmm, I don't think so," I said. "You were a work-for-hire, and you signed that piece of paper that said non-compete. If you think that's the way I do business, you might want to hire a lawyer."

She wisely backed off, but isn't it a shame that so many try to get by when they have no standing, no ownership, and no skin in the game? Yes, she did work for me, but the contract stated that it was work for hire and nothing else. Whenever anyone asks me about who can help with pattern ideas, I never give her name because she can't be trusted. Her dishonesty overshadowed her talent. I found plenty of other great seamstresses who did beautiful work for a fair price without trying to claim ownership.

I have to tell you this quick story. I had developed a number of different patterns and animal prints for the coats. I was in Tennessee looking for a production house, and the owner of one of the shops we were in talks with asked to keep a coat for review. A week later, when I went back to pick it up, she claimed she didn't have it. Now, we knew she did; she fell in love with it like everyone else, and instead of making a version of one for herself, she took mine. That one petty theft of one coat killed our desire to hire her firm to do our work; a $120 theft cost her tens of thousands of dollars of work in a depressed area of Tennessee where the people needed to work. She did damage not only to me but also to herself and her community.

How you treat others will come back on you or to you tenfold, so let's make sure you're doing the right thing so you can walk that path of success. Hold your head high and do business honestly and fairly.

How you handle and guide others can make a big difference in their life to put them on the right path for success if you're willing to speak up and be a leader (just know that sometimes it will hurt because you're shining a light in the darkness, but it is the right thing to do).

To paraphrase Zig Ziglar, who said it best, "Remember, the only taste of success some people have is when they take a bite out of you."

For those of you who spend your time taking a bite out of others to taste success, you could do it on your own. It takes hard work, but you can do it. If you can't or won't or are simply too lazy, I'm pretty sure most folks don't like you anyway, so don't add to your troubles by taking credit for other people's work.

If someone is taking credit for your work, you might want to step up and confront them in private at first and in public if you have to because if they are bold enough to steal in private, they'll take you for all you're worth in public. So, stand your ground.

I had a person tell me once that if he was going to steal, he would steal big because when you steal little, people find out, but when you steal big, folks are so shocked by it they can't wrap their heads around the fact that you walked away with billions. I guess Bernie Maddoff taught us that.

I remember saying to that guy, "How about you not steal at all?" After a very uncomfortable silence, he backed up and said he was joking. To that I say, the body will go where the mind has been, so be careful.

I love this quote. "Watch your thoughts; they become words. Watch your words; they become actions. Watch your actions; they become habits. Watch your habits; they become character. Watch your character; it becomes your destiny." — Unknown

James Allen said it best when he said, "You are today where your thoughts have brought you. You will be tomorrow where your thoughts take you."

I have a friend who told me he lives his life with these three rules: "Honesty, Loyalty, Compassion." Those are his rules for a good life.

And to those who are doing well by doing right, keep up the good work, and don't worry, we can see the difference. True talent cannot be hidden; it always shines through. And no one can take that away from you.

SOMETIMES YOU'VE GOTTA ASK

I'm not one to ask for help. It's not that I want to do it on my own (goodness knows I do way too much on my own), it just seems to me that everyone is busy with their own world, and I hate to ask in case it might be a bother, which it usually never is once I get around to asking.

I had a dear friend say to me one time, "You know, Deb, you can ask for help. It's not a sign of weakness, and in your case, it might be a sign of strength."

I know I looked at her like she had two heads. "A sign of strength to say that you need help? I'm a little slow on that concept. You're going to need to explain."

She proceeded to tell me that as much as I like to help others and find a sense of community or friendship or joy from my time well spent, others feel the same. I knew she was probably right. I do enjoy helping others get on their feet and make a go of it and be successful, so it would only make sense that there are others, just like me, who also enjoy the opportunity to help. Now, you would have thought I could come to that on my own, but no, I'm embarrassed to say it took me a while.

Recently, I took my own advice. I had just come through an election, and if you've ever run for office, you know that you need the help of others. So, today, in honor of all those who gave of their time and talent, allow me to send a shout of thanks to you.

I'm sure you've heard the quote from Jim Rohn, "You are the average of the five people you spend the most time with."

If you check out that phrase online, you will see thousands of articles and commentary on the meaning of it. Some use it to talk about weight, wealth, and walking. Others use it to discuss family, friends, and frenemies. Still, others use that phrase to chide, correct, and cajole others into being what they want them to be. Well, no matter what you choose the meaning to be, it is an interesting concept. *You are the average of the five people you spend the most time with (outside of your family).* You need to stop and look around and see who is sitting next to you. And I hope it is one of your dearest, truest, kindest, and most caring friends.

You know the one that the greeting card says:

- We'll be friends until we're old and senile, and then we'll be new friends.

- A good friend will come and bail you out of jail, but a true friend will be sitting next to you saying, "Wow, that was fun!"

- Best friends know how crazy you are and still choose to be seen with you in public.

- And I say to my friends, "You will always be my best friend... you know too much about me."

I love the old African proverb, "Alone, I may walk fast; together, we'll walk far." Isn't that great? Often, *together* makes the journey more interesting and seems to go by much faster.

It's been said, "Show me your friends, and I will tell you who you are."

How true! As many of you know, I work with a lot of young people, and it seems to me that a quick glance at their friends on their Twitter feed or Facebook page is a great insight into who they are and where they're probably going.

Sometimes, it pays to ask for help when you're going through a hard time. Many times, the person I sought out may not be the most popular or well connected, but their heart is in the right place, so their advice is solid. That is a gift we can all hope for; someone who is willing to hear you out and either offer advice or simply by being there provides a sense of comfort.

I'm not always verbal and witty, and there have been times that I say silly things and realize I need a rest. I do have a quiet side, and I have come to learn that sometimes just being there and being a rock or shelter is more valuable than any training or coaching or talking I could ever do. Sometimes, when asked, I just listen. I've learned that there is no need to talk when others need to talk something out. There's also something about speaking out loud. It seems to put the words and world in order.

So, how about you? Can you or will you slow down enough to ask for help? Can you sit quietly with a friend and just be there (without your cell phone)?

I recently saw a commercial online of a young lady who was dating a guy. Every scene of the video, he or her other friends were on a cell phone, at breakfast scrolling through the feeds, at the park talking on the phone, at lunch watching a video, at coffee with friends while everyone was staring at their phone. And the last scene was her boyfriend at his own birthday party taking photos of his cake and friends with his phone. Not until he shut out the light did the phone go away, but the screen lit up again as he was scrolling for news.

Will you be a friend who offers a hand of help when you see a need and not wait to be asked? I hope so. It is more blessed to give than receive but what is so cool about that is you do receive a benefit when you give, and nothing can take that away from you.

As a coach, I know it is hard for people to come to the place in their career where they realize that they probably need a little help to get to the next level. Asking for help is not easy when you're the president of the company or the super sales star or the leader of the pack who is supposed to have all the answers or is assumed to have all the answers, but believe me, many a successful person took the time to find a mentor, a friend, a coach, someone who they could reach out to and ask.

If you are part of the faith community, we have an invitation to ask and ye shall receive, seek and ye shall find, knock and the door will be open unto you. So, *asking* is a foundational part of our makeup, our desires, our opportunities, and for some, our success.

You will be asked the same question over and over by your little one or your elderly parent; consider it a gift to answer all 21 times. It's not easy, I know, but it is the right and proper thing to do, to teach, to nurture, to show your love unconditionally, and at all times, whether you feel like it not.

It's okay to do the asking. In fact, sometimes friends and family wish for that so they can show their love and concern.

Wow, what a gift it is to be able to support each other. I hope you'll take opportunities to give and receive help today!

ALL TOGETHER...

Right outside my window, I have the most amazing birdbath. What makes this resting place so beautiful is the many visitors that come to drink and wash and play.

When a bird lands on the rim of the bath, I stop what I'm doing and watch them peck at the water, jump in and wiggle, flex their wings, and groom themselves. It's a good thing the bath is not near my office window; goodness knows, I'd get nothing done!

I wasn't always a bird person. The little creatures never crossed my mind until my dear friend gave me a magazine subscription for Christmas one year called *Birds and Blooms.* I tend to read cooking magazines, news, and foreign affairs. But a magazine about birds? I wasn't sure that I was going to like it; wow, was I wrong! I love this magazine, and I have learned a lot. It is one of the magazines I look forward to reading because I know it is going to be interesting.

And it is because I never gave it much thought about what birds eat, how they eat, and what they need to sustain themselves in summer and winter. I am by no means a bird expert, but I do find great joy in their assembly.

It's funny how things come to mind when you're mindlessly watching birds take a bath, like how a few different types can be at the bath together, wait their turn, and not seem to mind the other birds waiting. Sometimes, a few birds want the bath all to themselves. Most birds don't like the occasional pigeon that comes by for a drink, and bluebirds don't like anyone in their bath. The cardinals, wrens, and finches don't seem to mind each other.

My lesson today is simply this. Do you let anyone come to your table? Do you welcome them or tolerate them? Do you treat them with kindness or let them fend for themselves? Do you make a space for them or crowd them out?

Believe it or not, birdwatching reminds me a lot about how people treat each other.

I attended a committee meeting the other day. The blue jays were not happy to see others at "their" table. It wasn't an issue of race or political affiliation but of ideas, perceived intelligence, and social standing.

It became very clear that not everyone was welcomed at that table, and since I struggle to pay attention anyway (and the meeting was boring), I decided I'd watch the body language of each of the cast of characters. It was my real-life version of watching my little birds at the bath, and I'll admit it became a source of joy and sadness for me to observe.

Since I wasn't in charge, I could only smile and nod at the other guests at the table. I offered water and coffee and a few jokes to help break the ice and asked the guests their thoughts on the issue at hand in hopes of bringing them into the fold.

Sometimes, they spoke in hushed tones. Other times, their tone for the conversation seemed to be edgy, probably because they instinctively knew how a few at the table viewed them, so my attempt to bring them to the table and make sure they were part of the team didn't work as well as I had hoped.

I didn't have much luck for two reasons from what I could tell.

1. They allowed the posturing of the blue jays at the table to mess with their heads, and thus they "kept their head down."

2. Those who didn't want them there would not make eye contact or help them carry the ball, so to speak, when they made a comment.

So, it was a two-way street; they did not feel welcomed by a few at the table. The rest of us tried to make up for it by adding them to committees and seeking their input, which, in turn, made those blue jays unhappy with those of us who were helping them. They didn't like the addition of, let's say, the pigeons.

In my opinion, the pigeon is not the most loved bird. They make a mess, walk funny, and they're gray; there's not a beautiful color in their plumage except for the occasional shimmer of their feathers.

As in life, the odd ones stood on the side, waiting to be invited, but no such offer came from leadership. They let them sit there and watch. It doesn't take a rocket scientist to know when you're not wanted, when you've been pushed to the side because you don't look like the others.

And as with life, if that is how you treat people, shame on you! It's hard enough out there without those few mean, self-absorbed people who make life harder just because they can. But trust me, if that's you, you'll survive for a season (maybe), but your day's coming, and it won't be good. Then *you'll* feel what it is like to be on the outside.

Back to my birds. it seemed to me that others at the table were like my chickadees at the bath. They sit on the rim and drink and then fly off to the feeder then come back and do it all over again. They'd hop into the conversation and hop right back out, never being sure about their standing or safety. Like the ladies at the table, some wanted to join in, but due to self-esteem or other issues, they couldn't bring themselves to stay for the duration and let or make their voice be heard.

And still, others were like my blue jays or crows—all or nothing. Just like at the bath, no other bird is allowed to sit on the rim waiting for them to finish. They get the bath all to themselves, which is very similar to the person who always sits at the head of the table or speaks the loudest or acts like they are in charge with or without a position of authority. They simply seem to take it, and everyone else moves away. If that's your authority model, remember one day that's going to hurt if you don't learn how to show cooperation and goodwill.

I like the cardinals because they like to come to the bath with their mate, and both can sit and watch and play and drink, and they don't seem to care who else is at the bath because they get along with everyone.

My favorite birds are the robins, chickadees, and titmouse. They don't care who is in the bath; they will all line up and wait their turn to wash, drink, and splash. They are like so many good-hearted people I know, who welcome everyone to the table regardless of race, color, creed, perceived intelligence, or social standing.

Like most of us, we can allow others to our table. It does not diminish my position of power or strength to have others around, but what I do expect is that if you're going to take a seat at the table, be a part, join in, let your voice and ideas be heard, and participate. Others want you there and want to hear what you have to say. For those who think the space is just for them and those like them, remember what it was like when you started out and how grateful you were that someone allowed you to the table and then encouraged you to bloom where you were.

Nature and life are similar, and how we react is similar to what I see daily at my birdbath.

So, my message is twofold. Get a birdbath for your yard. You'll thank me later. The joy of watching is a blessing, and I really do mean that.

Think about how you treat others—people who are not like you, people who don't have what you have, or believe the way you believe or care about the things you care about.

Recently, I was on a 12-hour flight overseas, and I got stuck with, perhaps, the most obnoxious seatmate in my twenty plus years of flying. He was the worst! His self-important attitude reflected in everything he did. Everyone who came by our seat and accidentally knocked into him was stupid, the stewards were idiots, and the food was awful. As he sat there sleeping, his sleep was jerky, not calm. His mannerisms were harsh, and his face revealed someone who, in my opinion, spent his time trying to keep up and surpass everyone he knew. (I was right; he ran to the customs counter ahead of everyone.) Being first, being right, being selfish played out in his face, his actions, and his attitude. During the course of the flight, he spilled his drink, and as I offered him my napkin, he grunted, as he had been a real jerk to me at the beginning of our flight. I just smiled. My world is too big to worry about someone so mean. He could have learned a lesson at the birdbath; being the only one in the water is fine until you need someone to help and you find yourself alone. It isn't all that fun, even if you are first to the customs counter. You still have to wait for your luggage.

Treating people how you want to be treated is one of the golden rules. It makes sense. It is the right thing to do, and you'll leave a lasting legacy when you do it correctly. You'll be a fading memory if you do it wrong.

The table is big enough to hold all who come.

I'll see you at the birdbath.

WHAT'S YOUR BALANCE?

I don't mean your physical balance, although that is important. What I am asking about today is your "credit" in the accounts of worthy organizations such as your volunteer activities, your kid's school, and your place of worship. What I find is that for many of you, you make great deposits and have a lot of credit with good organizations, and although that is a worthy endeavor, I want to make sure that those who need you the most are not shortchanged.

Suzanne Bates wrote in a recent column that "if you already have credit 'in the bank' with volunteer events and community organizations, you don't need to keep making deposits."

I completely agree, and I'll take it one step further. Instead of making deposits in things and organizations that will forget you over time, would you consider making deposits in the lives of those you claim to love and are responsible for?

Yikes! This is going to be a tough-love lesson, but don't worry if you'll get it right. If you simply try, you'll find more lasting joy and make memories for a lifetime. It all depends on where you choose to make your deposits.

(Quick note: I am not denigrating good community organizations. I fully understand that volunteers are needed and appreciated, but my message today is that we all reconsider the deposits we make.)

If you were to be completely honest with yourself, you'd have to admit that you get a great deal more personal joy and a sense of satisfaction when others compliment you and cheer you on than if you do what you're expected to do for your family. Rarely does family say thank you and job well done and we're proud of you.

Although family is supposed to be grateful, the saying is true that familiarity breeds contempt, and family usually doesn't give you high fives and back slaps. Why? There are three main reasons:

1. They think it is your job to do what you do (bring home the bacon, fry it up in the pan, etc.).

2. They've gotten lazy.

3. You've stopped saying thank you and job well done and we're proud of you to them, and since you don't say it, they have little to no guidance on how to say the words or praise or how to do the right thing.

Now, we have a dilemma.

I get it because I see it a lot in the speaking business. When you're on the road, the speaker is important, loved, and sort of famous. People stand in line to shake our hands, buy our book, and have a photo taken.

But then we come home, and all our family wants is for us to take out the trash or pick up the kids or change the oil in the car. It's not so exciting with the family.

So, how do we reorganize for balance? That's a great question.

As you are coming into the holiday season, these days can be the most exhausting, lonely, and financially snug and stress-filled time of the year, if you're not careful.

But it doesn't have to be that way. Ah, friend, let me give you permission to slow down, sit quietly, and don't spend money or time you don't have to the well-meaning organizations that will take all you're willing to give, mentally, emotionally, and physically.

I don't blame charity organizations for asking you to do more; I do appeal to you to consider the credit you have racked up "in the bank" with all your volunteer events and community organizations, and since you've given so much this year, you don't need to keep making deposits.

Your family and friends need you now more than ever.

I sit on a board in my town, and our plan is simply that we only give time, money, and staff for three years, and then we're done. The organizations will survive. (Since they know in advance, we only give for three years.) And then, we can help others.

If we choose to.

And that is the key to balance: having choices.

So, are you in or out of balance? Only you know, but I'm sure your friends and family can tell you.

It's not easy when it seems that all you do is work, and no one says thanks, so I have an idea. *You* say thank you. *You* think about what you're grateful for when you look at your family, your home, your car, your stuff, your life, and let it encourage *you* to stop what you're doing and restore balance to your life, your family, and your commitments. Let's start making deposits in the right places.

Let me level with you that at first, it will be awkward.

In fact, for some, it will be so awkward that your significant other will wonder what you're up to, so be ready with an answer that you need to slow down and take stock in where you are and where you want to go, and that maybe this year, you reconsider how you'll spend your time.

Another reason this will be awkward is because no one knows what to say back to you, so if you can say something nice as you're walking out the door with the trash or as you pass in the kitchen, say thank you for keeping such a great place that we call home or just want you to know how much I appreciate all you do.

By the way, guys, your sons will treat their wives the way they see you treat their Mom (or your wife), and daughters will watch and file away the thought that is what real men do to show love.

Friends, you already have credit "in the bank" with volunteer events and community organizations. You don't need to keep making deposits.

You need to start spending your time for you and those you care about.

I ask that you consider making a deposit that will last a lifetime and that is with those you love and care for. I guarantee it will improve your balance.

THE POWER OF A NUDGE

I don't know about you, but I sometimes struggle to get moving on projects, book writing, speech writing, and radio show writing. You name it, and I'm usually dragging myself to get it done.

What's odd is that it's not that I don't want to do it, but I find so many other "worthy" things to do instead of my work, like clean the house, vacuum my car, read my emails, and do my laundry (I'm odd like that), but I still have to get to it. I still have a responsibility to my editor, my team, and others to do my work, so sometimes even I need a nudge.

I like the word "nudge." It sounds funny, and the spelling doesn't look correct, but the concept is powerful.

I found this great article by Rebecca Clark of Nudge Village that resonated with me, and I wanted to share parts of it because maybe you're a lot like me, and you "need a nudge."

So, here we go. Have you ever had a family member, a friend, a co-worker, or even someone you barely know make a suggestion or comment that made a monumental difference in your life? It may have been a simple remark, but it had a lasting impact on the choices you made moving forward.

We call these "nudges."

These little ideas, comments, and suggestions have the power to increase our self-confidence, encourage us to change direction in our lives, educate us on new possibilities, and instigate a new business, adventure, or idea.

How can small, seemingly unimportant interactions hold this much power in our lives?

I think the power of a nudge is that instinctively we know what we could or should do. We simply need the validation of it, someone on the outside who sees what perhaps we don't, and they offer a nudge to help us move along.

Now, a lot of people offer nudges, some good, some not so good, so you have to know where you stand and be willing to accept it or reject it according to what is best for you.

Years ago, I had an offer to go to Vietnam for an extended period of time. I wasn't enthused to go; I know that sounds odd, but at that time, I was very busy and had a lot on my plate to up and leave town to tour the world with seven people I didn't know. It was at that time I had a friend who nudged me and said, "Deb, hello, where is your head? You'll still have the work to do when you come home, but this opportunity is once in a lifetime, so start packing."

I accepted her nudge because I trusted her opinion. I also knew that she knew about my heart's desire to travel the world and see things, eat things, and do things that others usually don't get to do.

And speaking of eating things, here's a quick aside. I was with a political delegation, and we dined at some very nice places, and at one dinner, I noticed the offering didn't look like anything I had ever seen on a dinner table. By this time, I was pretty sick of eating fish for every meal. (I'm not a big fish eater unless it is Long John Silvers, which I'm not sure is really fish but tastes good.) I was down to rice with some vegetables and a few other things by this time on the trip. So, I politely asked, "What is this interesting dish?" My host said, "Oh! Ms. Deb, this is a specialty. This is the webbing of ducks' feet." Yeah, that's not going to happen. It was a translucent congealed duck foot shape in a sauce. So, I smiled and had another cha gio (similar to an egg roll). I am an adventurist eater, but I simply could not do that.

Suffice to say, food choices and all, I am very glad I went. It was a wonderful experience, and I had the added benefit of seeing where my parents' apartment was when they lived in Saigon (now called

Ho Chi Min city) for a time due to my dad's job. It was a grand adventure, and I went because of a nudge.

Back to the online article, the act of accepting a nudge is important. But what may be even more important is taking the time to become "a nudger." You can practice this by sharing small tips that might help a friend, suggesting that someone ask for that raise, and expressing confidence that a person will be able to attempt and achieve a goal.

Sometimes, it is only to be helpful, and sometimes, we will truly be inspired to say something that will help someone completely change direction in their job, their friendships, and life goals.

We all have the power to nudge and be nudged. It gets easier with practice, and as we become more aware of these interactions, we also start to notice when we might be unintentionally nudging people in the wrong direction or becoming a detriment to their growth. But those moments will be rare.

So, friends, try nudging someone today. You'll see the power of a nudge. It might change you too.

I think I get nudged a lot more than I know. The problem is that sometimes I don't comprehend the gentle touch. My lack of comprehension is not only because I'm hardheaded (although that's embarrassingly true) but also because I bump up against the wall so much that I'm not sure when I've hit the wall or have been nudged into action.

I've had to slow down to become more aware of my surroundings; it's kind of like getting in touch with my intuition and gut and allowing it to speak to me rather than ignoring the warnings or the good ideas.

And that is probably the same for many of you. Life is hard, and you get batted about by work, family, and friends, and at the end of the day, if anyone touches you, it could be a bad day for them. Should you be so inclined, let me encourage you to notice the nudges, the gentle thoughts that fill your mind (when you're not really thinking about anything), or the words from others (who have your best interest at heart). The reality is that sometimes those words, said in kindness, might hurt, but sometimes, they are a cool drink of water on a hot day.

Many years ago, I had a friend who had a drinking problem, and I was the one who was selected to say something to her about it and tell her how many of us had noticed that it was getting out of hand. She was at the point where she was driving impaired, which was wrong and certainly not fair to the innocent ones who might be on the road when she was driving. We wanted to express to her that we were worried about her, her family, her reputation, her job, and her life. It's not an easy conversation, but I had a responsibility to nudge her into a conversation about her truth because the consequences of her choices were damaging her life. Even though that was hard (*and it did cause a break in our friendship*), I decided I'd rather nudge a friend than go to her funeral or give her eulogy. My nudge was well taken at the time. It was received with tears and promises to get help, but over time, embarrassment took over, and she drifted away.

What I like about the concept of a nudge is that it doesn't have to be a long, drawn-out conversation, as with my friend. I had invited her to lunch, we had a great time, and as we were leaving, I mentioned that I needed to say one more thing. I had planned to do it in the parking lot, so she had an escape that was easy so as not to cause any more embarrassment than the situation already did.

I tell you that story to simply say that sometimes we need to step up and nudge those we care about to get on the right track, nudge them to see the truth (no matter how hard it is), nudge them to walk away if someone is causing them harm. The power of a nudge could save a life. It could also give someone the freedom to live the life they've imagined, to do what they were born to do.

Nudges are given all the time. But, sadly, not all are followed.

It's been said that a nudge is, "A whisper of confidence. A suggestion to pursue a different path. A recommendation. A simple act of gratitude."

Trying nudging someone you care about today.

IF OPPORTUNITY DOESN'T KNOCK, BUILD A DOOR

I grew up with the idea that when opportunity knocks, you open the door and let it in, but what do you do when opportunity doesn't knock, and you are looking for a new opportunity? I agree with the funnyman of yesterday, Milton Berle. If opportunity doesn't knock, you need to build a door.

Yes, sometimes you need to pull out the hammer and saw and make things happen. Ideally, I wish it would appear on its own, but you and I know that isn't always the case, so now is the time to get going to put on our work clothes and get to work.

Is there an opportunity that seems closed for you? Is this something you need or simply want to happen? Once you have looked at all the options, can you see a way through? Maybe or maybe not, but if it is something you feel passionate about or know you have the skills and proficiencies to do the job, maybe you need to pull out your toolbox and start building your own opportunity and future.

What I find is that many people want it to be easy. I don't blame them, but that's not always an option. Sometimes, we've got to get our hands dirty to create an opportunity or build a door.

So, if opportunity is not knocking, what door do you need to build?

Have you stopped long enough to think about what doors you might need to build? There's no better time than now when many are thinking about new directions and opportunities. Is there a door with family members who have, in a sense, locked you out that you can build? Or do you need to rebuild a door?

Is there a door with a work colleague that you need to create?

Is there a door with your friend or spouse or partner that you need to build or at least repair?

I understand that there are some realities here. I've been a coach long enough to know that people who are hurt or who perceive they've been hurt will often not allow you or anyone to make things right. Strangely, they love to hang on to their exquisite pain, as bizarre as it is. It makes them feel powerful to hold others at arm's length and to punish them, in a sense, which is heartbreaking because no one is being punished but them. Trust me, everyone else has moved on, and as the lady on the YouTube video is famous for saying, "Ain't nobody got time for that!"

I find that a lot of people who have closed others out think they are doing it to protect themselves from further hurt or shame, but mostly, I find that they want to retaliate in the one way they can, and that is to close themselves off from others.

It makes me want to ask how that is working out for them as they sit there all alone, wondering why they have no friends or company or someone to go to the movies with.

Well, I can tell you the answer. They become more bitter and angry and alone, and unfortunately, they stand on the other side of the door, unwilling to answer the knock of opportunity or restored friendship or love. The simple fact is nailing it shut only hurts them, which is the exact opposite of their intended desire because most people who are on the receiving end of the silent treatment (or no engagement treatment or acting like they don't exist treatment) will simply go away and find other friends and other things to do. They will find, or create, other *opportunities*.

Unfortunately, we can't fix the wallowers, the ones that have a skewed view of their justice or pain, but we can, for many, provide an opportunity to unlock the door or build a door to let the sunshine in and healing begin.

And that's an opportunity that a rational person would like to see happen, and a healthy person might even help build that door from the other side instead of boarding it up to hide from their truth.

So, if you're so inclined to try once more, then good for you to reach out and begin building that door. And if you're rebuffed, at least the door is built, and they now know they can walk through at any time. You've created the opportunity, and that is all anyone can ask.

Some will say if the door is closed, it's closed for good reason, but that may or may not be the case; people do change. Incidents that seemed big in the past might appear smaller now, and sometimes, the reason for the disagreement dulls with time. You've got to weigh the pros and cons and make a decision that is best for you or your family.

I have long believed that if a door is closed, maybe you should open a window or, in my case, break a window and get through. (It has worked to my advantage at times, and others not so much.)

I'm not one to sit and wait. If I make a decision, I usually go for it. No moss grows here. But as I get older, I tend to mull over my decisions before I act in haste. I'm getting too old to do things twice. I like the line from Abraham Lincoln, "I may walk slow, but I don't walk backwards."

When I see opportunity, and it seems to be the right thing for me, I'll make a run at it and give it my best to see what comes of it. Occasionally, I've had to review the situation and form a plan before I begin again.

That's a pivotal part of opportunity; you must *begin*. Staring at a closed door is a waste of time. No one is going to open it for you (at least not usually). You've got to put your hand to the task and either push or pull, saw or chop to make something happen.

If opportunity doesn't knock, I encourage you to pull out your tools, your skills, your best ideas, and go ahead and build a door. Because sometimes, the best-laid plans are missing an important ingredient: you. It is you who are called, you who are ready, you who are willing to go the distance.

If you see an opportunity, go for it. You found it. You can make it right or better because you stepped up. You took the initiative, and with hammer in hand, you began to build. Since you're not a quitter, you can finish the job.

I like the thought of building a door and not a window or a cubbyhole because we want to build something that allows as much opportunity to flow through as possible as fast as possible so we can get to work building our future, repairing our past, or living fully in the present.

I had to laugh when I realized that this quote—"If opportunity doesn't knock, build a door"—is from the comedian Milton Berle (or Uncle Milte, as he was called). He's a guy who started on the stage and did silent movies, Broadway, vaudeville, radio, motion pictures, and television. He was also the first major star in television to have the nickname "Mr. Television." And that's not all, here are a few more fun facts about Mr. Television:

- NBC signed him to a 30-year television contract in 1951.

- He held the Guinness Book of World Records for the greatest number of charity performances.

- He was a lyricist for over 300 songs.

- He had a collection of five to six million jokes.

His career lasted over 75 years; he was king of TV for many years until his style faded with the viewers. Talk about living a life of opportunity!

He was known as a joker, and some of his best lines are:

- "Laughter is an instant vacation."

- "I live to laugh, and I laugh to live."

- "Radio, that wonderful invention by which I can reach millions of people who fortunately can't reach me."

- "You can lead a man to Congress, but you can't make him think."

- "A committee is a group that keeps minutes and loses hours."

Here is my favorite joke of his:

He found it impossible to make a date. He'd start to talk to a girl, and his tongue would twist up like a pretzel. He went to a bookstore and looked for a book that might help him overcome his timidity. On a non-fiction rack, he saw a book titled *Ways to Women.* Blowing his whole allowance, he bought the book, rushed home, and discovered that he'd bought volume ten of the encyclopedia!

He's a guy who was ahead of the game of opportunity. When one door closed, he built a door and opened another, and he did this for 75 years. That's impressive.

If opportunity doesn't knock, build a door.

I CHOOSE

I came across the quote below online the other day. I like it because it puts in place what I consider the realities of life, the simple facts that are true for so many of us. Another thing that I like is as you read through the list, you'll come to understand the proper steps for our success, meaning that you (and I) *choose*.

I Choose
To live by choice, not by chance.
To make changes, not excuses.
To be motived, not manipulated.
To be useful, not used.
To excel, not compete.
Self-esteem, not self-pity.
To listen to my inner voice, not the random opinion of others.

And I'll add, *"who don't have your best interest at heart."*
We choose every day. We make choices for ourselves, our families, our loved ones, our colleagues, our friends, our pets, and the list goes on.

Every day, I meet people who have made choices, large and small, to better themselves or their loved ones because it finally hit them that they get to choose.

They choose to live by choice and not by chance. Living life according to their expectations, hopes, and dreams is so much better than living by chance, allowing someone else to make your decisions, or not engaging fully in what is happening around you.

Living by choice is a blessing, an opportunity to redirect your life if you so choose or being able to sit still since your life is on the path you chose. Friends learn to live by choice. It frees you to be your best and do what you were born to do.

I choose to make changes, not excuses. Change is always hard, but if you're in the driver's seat, it's a great ride. I know I often speak about this subject because I fully believe that at any time, we can choose to make changes. Jim Rohn is famous for saying, "You can change anytime; you're not a tree."

I won't sit here and tell you that I don't make excuses. Believe me, I do, but you and I know that excuses only lead to more excuses, and then little to nothing gets done.

I grew up with all brothers. I'm pretty sure I heard every excuse in the book for not doing things, but that didn't make the problems go away. Ultimately, they had to do the work. Excuses weren't accepted at my house, action was.

Don't make excuses for things that you know need to be done. Don't put off tomorrow what you can do today; don't prolong the pain by waiting. If getting things done now would be a help to you, get to it. You have the power to make changes that you choose to make, so don't waste your valuable 84,400 seconds today…times a wasting, get to it!

Choose to motivate, not manipulate. Isn't it funny that those words are so close in concept and worlds apart in action? I've always thought it is a silly idea that someone else can motivate you to action, and I say that as a motivational teacher. But what I know is that I can lay the idea before you to learn to live your best life ever, but until you can see your new future, you won't pick up the baton and run. Motivational speakers are great in the moment, but what happens when the lights come on, and you walk out of the conference and into your current situation? That's where the rubber meets the road. You have to find your spark of motivation that moves you.

Now, let's take a detour and talk about manipulation. Manipulation is never a good idea; in fact, it's psychotic! Nobody should be manipulated into doing things that are not right. When that happens, if you can, by all means possible, you need to extract yourself and get away from those types of people. They are damaged, and it isn't healthy. It is selfish and mean, and you don't have to put up with it. Remember, you can choose to walk away.

I understand that it will not always be easy, but if it is the right thing for you to do, then walk away. Manipulation is evil, in my opinion, and has no place in a healthy relationship.

Choose to be useful and not used. There are many good people who need a helping hand, and you might be the right person at the right time to be useful, to be kind, helpful, generous, and good. There is no better feeling than when you know you were useful, and it was a blessing.

So, the other side of that coin is to be careful that you are not used, that you don't let others take advantage of you or your goodwill. Only you can make that choice.

Choose to excel and not compete. Excel at doing your best, against yourself. You can set your bar and jump over it, set your time and surpass it, set your direction and accomplish it. That is so much better in your personal life than competing. I understand that in business, it is competition, but in your personal life, stop competing with your brother and sisters for attention. Stop competing with your friends to prove your self-worth. Stop competing with everyone else to show off or to show that you've made it; most don't care and never considered themselves in the race with you to begin with (hard, I know). We seem to think that everyone is running against us. I have friends in the speaking business who think they are competing with me for speaking jobs, but I've got to tell you; I don't waste a minute worrying about their ability compared to mine. I work hard, do great work, and don't worry about the others. I'm not in a competition, except against myself to be better, to reach a larger audience, to work to make sure my words match my message.

Choose to excel and not compete. You don't need to compare yourself to others. They don't have what you have; they don't know where you're going, and you don't need to waste time worrying about them. Let them worry about *you*!

And to that point, I encourage you to choose self-esteem, not self-pity. Friends, you are fearfully and wonderfully made, so I have to ask; why are you standing in the shadow when you were made to stand in the light?

When I am on the road speaking, self-esteem is one issue that repeatedly comes up with people. I have never seen so many damaged, hurting, broken people like I see nowadays, and part of it is they spend so much time competing against others who don't even consider them a challenge. They are fighting windmills all by themselves. That is exhausting work, and it is shocking to them when they realize no one is watching.

Self-esteem comes from one's understanding of their self-worth, their core, their being. The idea of self-pity is so repugnant, exhausting, and ridiculous to most people that they won't even give it the time of day (nor should they). Self-pity is a waste of energy for you and everyone you come in contact with. We are not a society that recognizes self-pity. We move on and find someone else to do the job, which causes the pitiful one to be even more upset, but it is by their own doing.

Don't do it. Self-pity is not becoming; it's not professional, and it's not for you. You have so much to be thankful for that engaging in sad-sack behavior is beneath you, and no one is impressed by that type of behavior.

I choose to listen to my inner voice, not the random opinions of others. That is my wish for you as well. Listen to your gut; listen to your inner core, your good voice inside your head that says you're amazing, you're a rock star, you're wonderful, good, kind, loving, and smart. All those good things are who you are if *you* choose to be.

Some folks will want to tell you something "for your own good." Listen, smile, and **reject**. If the information is not being given with the right intention, you'll know it. Don't listen and don't take it to heart.

Smart-aleck comments to "put you in your place" are only given by weak, self-absorbed people. Don't listen. Remember, deep inside, they are talking about themselves and not to you.

Comments about your weight, your house, your cooking, your car, your clothing, and your kids. You know the drill; **don't listen**. Those words are meant to hurt and not help. If they were to help, they'd be your walking partner, your house cleaner, your dishwasher, your car mechanic, your personal shopper, or babysitter. Random opinions from others don't mean a thing unless they are said by those who love you and truly have your best in mind, and your spirit, gut, heart know the difference.

Carefully weigh the words of others.

I choose
To live by choice, not by chance.
To make changes, not excuses.
To be motived, not manipulated.
To be useful, not used.
To excel, not compete.
Self-esteem, not self-pity.
To listen to my inner voice, not the random opinion of others (who don't have your best interest at heart).

I'll leave you with these sayings that I really like:

- A can of worms won't open itself.

- Spend your time on those who love you unconditionally. Don't waste it on those who only love you when the conditions are right for them.

- The tongue has no bones, but it is strong enough to break a heart; be careful with your words.

- Be sure to taste your words before you spit them out.

Poem by Miranda Marrott

"WRITE IT ON YOUR HEART THAT EVERY DAY IS THE BEST DAY IN THE YEAR."

—*Ralph Waldo Emerson*

As I was thinking about what to give as a word of encouragement this week, I wanted to share something that would be uplifting and not just educational, or a training session. When I found the first part of this poem by Ralph Waldo Emerson, I knew I had landed on my thought for this week.

Friend, this year, "*Write it on your heart that every day is the best day in the year.*" That means that every day, all 365 of them, you have a chance to write a different story, sing a different song, and play a different tune since this will be the best day in your year. You can create and be and dream and become the person you always wanted to be, the person we all knew you could be.

Nothing holds you back, but only you can change that voice in your head to hear the new words for a new year of opportunity. This year, you're going to write it on your heart that every day is the best day in the year.

This year, you're going to **grow** through life and not just **go** through life. It's been said, and it is a great reminder that you can do it, you can be it, or you can become it when you set a path forward.

Put things in order by cleaning out, reorganizing, setting up files, and cleaning out drawers, and then taking some time to think about milestones you need to plan for and accomplish on your timeline for success as you grow through this next year.

Continue to write it on your heart that every day is the best day in the year. This will give you a new perspective about the year ahead.

I like to get my planning done in the lull between Christmas and New Year's, so when the first of January comes (and goes), I am already set to begin afresh and anew as I start over in another exciting year.

When I think about the process of writing on my heart to believe that every day is the best day in the year, I am hopeful. I am hopeful for many reasons. One reason is that this past year, although a good year for me, is closing out, and once again, I have an opportunity for another 525,600 minutes (in a year) to make a difference in my world and the lives of others, and that is exciting.

Following this advice, I am going to do a few other things this year with regard to my heart. Yes, I'm still going to drag myself to the gym so I can be physically healthy, but I have a few new thoughts to make sure that every day is the best day—not only for me but also for others.

I have been mulling over the idea of PAS to pass the love, caring, and sharing along.

P stands for physical. I have come to believe that people need physical interaction, and study after study will back me up on this, meaning that people of every age need to feel the power of touch; kids and spouses need to be hugged; parents and grandparents need to feel the power of human touch. I'm not talking about the side half hugs, but the full-body bear hug (when appropriate). People need to know that they matter, especially seniors who may not have many kind, gentle, and loving people to hug them due to age or infirmity. The idea of touch in the proper way is very healing for both the giver and the receiver, so this year, become consciously physical when appropriate. Whether a hug, a handshake, a pat on the back, any kind of proper physical touch is good and, in some cases, healing.

A stands for affirmations, meaning I am going to say, more than I already do, to clients, friends, and family that they are doing a good job, that I appreciate them, and that I can see they have been working hard. I will speak with kindness so I can help them move to the next level. Affirmations that are honest and true and helpful are good for the mind, soul, and body. You know that I am all about speaking up and letting your voice be heard. This year is the year to allow that to happen. Speak up and speak often. Remember, you might be the only voice that someone will listen to, so you have a duty to speak and try to do so without fear so you can do what you were born to do.

S stands for safety, meaning that in the sea of life, I find that a lot of people need to know that when the wind blows and the rains hail down upon them, at least one person will be there for them to either pull them out of the rain or help them adjust their sails to set their course for safety. Many of the young people I work with have a level of fear that makes them unstable; they need a sense of security and safety in their home, with their extended family, and with their friends. They need to know that they have people who will help them in their lives. By the way, it's not just kids who feel this seismic shake from the world; husbands and wives feel it also when the world comes dangerously close to crashing down. A sense of safety is one of the most blessed gifts that we can give one another this year.

The idea of safety crosses every aspect of our lives, from physical to mental to emotional safety. The understanding that you can find at least one other person to feel a sense of security can make the difference as you step out in faith to do what you are called to do.

Unfortunately, in America (and around the world), we've become a violent society, so the need for safety and security is, perhaps, the one gift that, if provided, can change a life.

Kids thrive when they feel safe; marriages grow when they feel safe, so consider what you can do to add a level of safety to your home, your family, and your life.

My thoughts simply come down to the acronym PAS. Be properly physical, give honest and kind affirmations, set up boundaries for safety and security for yourself and those you love—and serve others.

Write it on Your Heart
Write it on your heart
that every day is the best day in the year.
He is rich who owns the day,
and no one owns the day who allows it to be invaded with fret and anxiety.
Finish every day and be done with it.
You have done what you could.
Some blunders and absurdities, no doubt, crept in.
Forget them as soon as you can, tomorrow is a new day;
begin it well and serenely, with too high a spirit to be cumbered with your old nonsense.
This new day is too dear, with its hopes and invitations, to waste a moment on the yesterdays... ~ Ralph Waldo Emerson

"SHE STOOD IN THE STORM, AND WHEN THE WIND DID NOT BLOW HER WAY, SHE ADJUSTED HER SAILS."

—*Elizabeth Edwards*

Let me be the first to welcome you to the New Year a few days early. I am excited because I fully believe this is going to be a good year, despite all the predictions, politics, and pundits. At this time, in the lull between the holidays, it is a good time to survey your life, and if needed, let's adjust your sails so every day is the best day in the year.

One of my favorite quotes is, "She stood in the storm, and when the wind did not blow her way, she adjusted her sails."

Wow, how great is that thought! Sometimes, we've got to adjust our sails when the winds blow against us, and they will. You and I must decide to continue to fight the wind and inch along, regroup, adjust our sails, and go.

I have a quote on my work-wall that says, "Deb, ride the wave, instead of fighting the current." Even in my work, I have to stop many times and redirect, so I am not wearing myself out fighting something that could be so easy with a small adjustment.

I love the water. I am drawn to the ocean, lakes, streams, pools, baths, and showers. I find water calming, but I can tell you, in vivid detail, about the storms I have seen crash upon the beach or how we had to fight against the coastal waterway change in tide to make it to safety or watched a calm lake churn into a force to be feared.

Now, I'm not much into sailing because I prefer a motor to do the work, but I have seen and been around enough sailing vessels to admire the dexterity of the controls for the mainsail.

I speak and train in Boston, and I love to watch the kids in sailing school on the Charles River from the safety of the shore. It is fun to watch the little boats go in circles until a good wind adjusts the sail, and then they sail to the shoreline, all smiles in their success in harnessing the wind by simply adjusting the sail.

How about you? As you reflect on last year, did you make substantial progress in your journey, or did you go around and around in circles?

Did the wind catch your sail and bring you into a bountiful shore, or were you sailing on a hope and a prayer to make it anywhere safely?

Either way, it is my hope for you that this year that with a positive mindset, a workable plan, and an eye for opportunity, you will find your wind, adjust your sail, and sail to outrageous success.

I'll share a few tips for adjusting your sail for a good new year. Sometimes, we have to make allowances for others, meaning we need to unload the extra weight that is harming us by their actions and attitudes, and when we do that, it can make our lives easier to do what we were born to do.

To make the sailing vessel lighter, we need to throw some things overboard—things that are weighing us down, things that feel like an anchor around our neck dragging along the bottom of the seafloor, things that take up valuable space on our ship and in our lives.

Allow me to suggest a few things that I have seen from my speech-coaching business.

The questions I like to ask my audience are, "What can you do to help others?" and, "What will ultimately help you?"

Only you can answer that. I know it seems odd to help others when you have your hands full with your own life but allow me to encourage you to consider doing these three things.

Now, on this first one, I want you to be careful because it can be messy, and some folks are so full of vim and vinegar, bile and hate, and seething anger that you need to protect yourself mentally, emotionally, physically, and spiritually. Please note that this will not work in every situation, so use your common sense.

Would you consider giving others specified, timed freedom to speak their mind? I know you don't want to hear it; it's the same old chatter they've been bellyaching about for years, and for some people, you're opening a door for all their pent-up hurt and anger to come spewing out. I know it's ridiculous, and you know it's ridiculous, but if you can (meaning you have protected yourself and your feelings in advance), allow it to be said. Listening might allow you to put an end to an ongoing, exhausting situation.

Allow them the freedom to speak their mind, to have their say, and then cut it off and be done. Make sure they know that you'll listen with an open mind this one, final time, so say your piece and put a lid on it.

I happened to witness a situation where a conversation between a couple went from friendly to irrational verbal sparring, and instead of fighting back, one person let the other vent until it was over, and then, it was over. It had all been said. It wasn't easy, but by setting a guard and a shield around them, knowing this was coming, they withstood the firestorm until the flame went out.

Nothing haunts some people like the things they didn't say, and for them to heal and **set you free**, sometimes, you've got to let them speak their mind one final time. Remember, I'm trying to clear your path of these weights so you can set your sail and go.

Second, listen more. A lot of people do not listen with the intent to understand; they listen with the intent to reply.

Leo Buscaglia is famous for saying, "Too often we underestimate the power of a touch, a smile, a kind word, a listening ear, an honest compliment or the smallest act of caring, all of which have the potential to turn a life around..."

I talk a lot about your voice being the only voice that someone might listen to or hear. At times, the only person they want to hear them out is *you*.

Listening is not easy, but your encouraging silence will allow others the space to find and set their sail and then set out for a new course. This year, would you consider listening more? Would you allow others to stand in the light and shine on their own? Remember, whether they shine or not is not your problem. You moved out of their way so they could find their space. In my speech coaching, I have a saying about the value of your words. It is, "Allowing someone to finish a sentence is a form of self-esteem." I've come to believe that listening to what is being said also provides a sense of self-esteem by my silence, and in allowing their words to flow, I've given them a gift.

It's been said that meaningful silence is always better than meaningless words.

Third, help others forgive. I saw a great quote; "If you carry the bricks from your past relationship, you will end up building the same house."

How true! Many people would like to absolve a situation but won't, out of respect or deference to you. They're your friend first and foremost, and if you were hurt, they are hurt and will hold your grudge, but you have the power to allow them to remove themselves from the situation since it is not their issue.

I have a friend who is divorced, and she wants all her friends to carry the weight of her hurt and anger for the other woman and her friend because the mutual friend did not step in to help stop the behavior of her now ex-husband before it got out of hand.

I understand that she is hurt. And no doubt, she has every right to be, but to ask all of her friends to maintain a grudge for years afterward is rather silly. And most of her friends are done with the exercise in futility since the ex is remarried and moved out of town. And to top it off, he is now divorced from the "other homewrecking woman," so karma happens.

Asking others to hang on to your grudges, hurt, and anger is not being a true friend. It is showing your immature, selfish side, and as my favorite internet sensations says, "Ain't nobody got time for that!"

Forgiveness doesn't excuse their behavior. Forgiveness prevents their behavior from destroying your heart.

This year, consider adjusting your sail to help you glide across the waters of life at your pace, at your command, on your journey, without the baggage of last year.

"She stood in the storm, and when the wind did not blow her way, she adjusted her sails."

NOT LOOKING FOR FLAWS,
BUT FOR POTENTIAL

Ellen Goodman said, "We spend January 1st walking through our lives, room by room, drawing up a list of work to be done, cracks to be patched. Maybe this year, to balance the list, we ought to walk through the rooms of our lives...not looking for flaws, but for potential."

I like the idea that, this year, we look forward not at the work to be done or cracks to be patched or for flaws. Let's look for potential.

Isn't that what a new year is all about, potential?

I believe so, and I want to focus on that concept today.

Webster defines potential as "existing in possibility."

I spent a lot of time last year talking about getting up and going forward in your amazing life because I believe a spark of potential exists in each us; we need to fan the spark to turn the flame into a fire.

Recently, I met with several wonderful people who had reached out to me to ask how to move forward in their lives or how to find their passion or how to forgive themselves enough to breathe again.

Good, honest, kind, loving, amazing people who focus so much on their flaws that they couldn't see their potential, and some went to so far to sadly tell me they had no potential, to which I laughed and told them in the nicest way possible that they are ridiculous.

Of course, you have potential. Everyone does. What you do about it is your responsibility. Yes, this takes work on your part, but the work is worth it.

A friend, coach, or mentor can help you pull back the curtain to see what could be, but you must actively engage in changing your life, reset your direction, and map out a new plan. Friend, you have some homework to do this weekend.

For so many, it's like helping you dig through the closets of your life and finding and pulling out that dream that you put on the shelf, whether by anger or frustration, time or talent, family, or work responsibilities that makes your heart glad. It is the dream that enlivens you to the thought of doing something about it. Let your potential shine through, and let's see if we can make it work. It's worth a try.

The potential is there; you know it, and others see it. But you have to trust the step will be there as you walk forward. I can assure you that many times the step is there; it's just hidden under years of neglect.

I grew up in an area of my town called Paris Mountain; it's just a big hill. It was a wooded area, and our home had trees all around it, so as a kid, when I was playing in the woods, I had to be careful because of the years of leaves that had fallen that would cover a hole or root base or limb that could trip you up in a skinny minute.

But what I learned from growing up in the woods is that no matter how deep the duff is (that's what we call the leaves, branches, bark, and stems, existing in various stages of decomposition above the soil surface but on the forest floor), there is always a forest ground floor on which to stand. You couldn't always see it, but you knew it was there.

I had the good fortune to meet up with a friend this past week and walk around his family farm looking for arrowheads. Once we dogged the cows and goats (and one very protective dog guarding the goats against coyotes), we found ourselves by the stream and soon discovered that we were sinking in the soft sand. We had to steady ourselves on a few rocks and jump and climb and balance ourselves to the stream bank and then hang onto the roots of the trees as we scaled to the top to safety. The potential of getting soaked in the creek was not a good option on such a cold day.

When we think about potential, what usually comes to mind is what *could* happen or what *might* happen down the road. I wonder if you're able to put the concept of potential in the present for today, this week, this month, this year. Meaning, the decision you make today, right now, is the right decision for you. Step out in faith, and since you have seen it in your mind's eye, you know it could work.

A number of years ago, some clients informed me that because of the work I do as a talent strategist, I have expertise helping develop men and women for success in business and politics by coaching my clients to the top of their particular mountain. Whatever mountain they have to climb, we'll do it together. I just happen to use the skill of public speaking to help them find their voice so others will listen.

So, as your "talent strategist," let me suggest that this year we walk through the rooms of your life not looking for flaws but for your amazing potential and meaning, existing in possibility.

Now, I can hear a collective sigh of some of you saying out loud, "Deb, it's impossible because I have too many mistakes," or, "You just don't understand my situation," or, "I really don't have the potential you're talking about. I can barely get through each day." Believe it or not, I have heard every excuse in the book, and I still think that the decision to focus on the potential of what could be is stronger than your limited expectation of who you think you are. Remember the phrase, "Act as if."

- Act as if potential is yours for the taking.

- Act as if your success is right around the corner, so keep working towards your goal.

- Act as if everything is going to be all right.

I struggle not to yell at people when they tell me that it's impossible for them to move forward because of all they have in their background or mistakes of their past or the pressure of their current situation.

I saw a great quote many years ago, and it is applicable here. "Impossible is just a big word thrown around by small men who find it easier to live in the world they've been given than to explore the power they have to change it. Impossible is not a fact. It's an opinion. Impossible is not a declaration. It's a dare. Impossible is potential. Impossible is temporary. Impossible is nothing." — Muhammad Ali

This year, we're going to walk through the rooms of our lives not looking for flaws, but for potential.

YOU'LL NEVER BE THE SAME AGAIN

Steve Jobs said, "When you grow up, you tend to get told the world is the way it is, and your life is just to live your life inside the world. Try not to bash into the walls too much. Try to have a nice family, have fun, save a little money. That's a very limited life. Life can be much broader once you discover one simple fact: Everything around you that you call life was made up by people that were no smarter than you and you can change it, you can influence it, you can build your own things that other people can use. Once you learn that, you'll never be the same again."

This year, "You can change it, you can influence it, you can build your own things that other people can use. Once you learn that, you'll never be the same again."

So, how is your life? How are you doing? How do you feel today? Every once in a while, we need to stop and talk to ourselves and ask the questions that roll around in our heads, and hopefully, we can give true answers.

I ask the question from the thought that Steve Jobs states that when it comes to life, "You can change it, you can influence it, you can build your own things that other people can use." How cool is it to build for others once you've found your place in this world?

Most people live in a very controlled world; your friends live that way; your family lives that way; your boss lives that way. So, if you venture too far from the farm, you're going to scare some folks. The truth is when we were growing up, we were told the world is the way it is, and your only option is just to live your life inside that world.

But that's not true, and I have a serious problem with that worldview not because I'm a rabble-rouser but because that is too small a way to live in such a big world.

I worry for so many that when the controlled world crumbles away, they fall apart and hit the ground and then realize the only way out is up. But that is actually a great day because you'll never be the same again.

I know you have responsibilities, but I also encourage you to do the extra work to build things other people can use. Build a life that leaves a legacy; build a future for the next generation, and build a firm foundation that can stand strong against the storms of life and shelter you and those you love.

So, what big idea do you have that would help others?

What opportunities have come to you that you're weighing the pros and cons about?

What actions can you take to make your life better?

Only you can answer those questions, but I encourage you to think, hope, and dream about leaving the small box that you call your life, and with your family safely in place, consider doing some of the things on your bucket list.

My job is to remind you that, "Everything around you that you call life was made up by people that were no smarter than you and you can change it, you can influence it, you can build your own things that other people can use."

I am inspired by the lives of many who do something in life they felt called to do.

Theodore Roosevelt said, "Far better is it to dare mighty things, to win glorious triumphs, even though checkered by failure... than to rank with those poor spirits who neither enjoy nor suffer much, because they live in a gray twilight that knows not victory nor defeat."

I recently saw the TED talk by Ric Elias. He had a front-row seat on Flight 1549, the plane that crash-landed in the Hudson River in New York in January 2009. In his talk, he shares what went through his mind as the doomed plane went down towards the Hudson River with no jet motors running. A stunned silence filled the plane, and then three words came across the plane's loudspeaker from the pilot, "Prepare for impact."

Ric Elias didn't think about his work or his car or his golf game. No, in those few minutes, his world was made very clear, and if he survived, he would get going in his life with his wife, his kids, and his dreams. He ends his talk saying that he hopes that no one in the audience would experience what he did, but he hopes you and I will stop waiting for tomorrow and stop living the limited life that others have put upon us. Stop thinking that we cannot, at any time, change our lives. I love the Old Spanish Proverb, which states, "Tomorrow is often the busiest day of the week." I'm here to remind you that today needs to be your busiest day. Today should be the day you make your move, your decision, your promise to yourself that you can change. You can influence, and you can build whatever life you choose.

You know that I'm not big on new year's resolutions because no one keeps them past January 15th, but from all my coaching and speaking to people, I know that when they were younger, they tended to follow the crowd only to become older and wiser and realize the crowd never had their best interest in mind, and they should have set their own direction for their own life.

I know this is hard, especially because our parents had hopes and dreams that they wanted us to follow and to do things they didn't do.

My parents wanted me to be in real estate. They knew I was good with people, so they thought that would be a good business for me, but after I got my RE license and started selling homes, I realized I was not cut out for that business. I could care less where you put your washer and dryer and outdoor furniture because I have little to no ability to see a blank space and fill it with stuff. It's not my gift.

Through trial and error, I had to find my own way. I have failed and I have succeeded, but I've rarely been bored. I've also had the good fortune of having a grand time along the way; no doubt, I have been blessed.

Our lives take different paths. You can see this clearly when you connect with past schoolmates on Facebook, and although many put their best face forward, it doesn't take a rocket scientist to see that many settled for a safe life where they don't bash into the walls too much. Try to have a nice family, have fun, save a little money, and live their very limited life. And if that is what they felt they should do, then good for them. No judgment here. But it is exciting to read about those who discover one simple fact; "Everything around them that we call life was made up by people that were no smarter than they were, and they went about to change it, influence it, and build their own things that other people can use. Once you learn that, you'll never be the same again."

RUNNING AWAY FROM YOUR PROBLEMS IS A RACE YOU'LL NEVER WIN

As I've gotten older, I've tried to keep myself out of trouble, and I'm doing pretty well at that. It's not that I go looking for trouble, but sometimes, it seems to find me, usually because of something I said or because of something someone said I said or because I was misquoted. So, I have had to be more careful because I don't want to hurt anyone, and I don't want to cause harm. I want to be thought of as kind.

But often, I look around and see that some of my peers, friends, and colleagues seem to look for trouble, find trouble, and jump in with both feet and wonder why they are stymied in finding success in their life.

My thought for today is the idea that running away from your problems is a race you'll never win.

Why? Because your problems will follow you, catch you, and drag you down again just when you start to make positive progress.

You've seen it in your own life and the lives of others. Isn't it amazing to watch someone begin to embark on a great adventure or job or opportunity, and they seem to fizzle out or have to restart or stop completely? It's because the problem caught up with them.

It makes sense to ignore the problem or forget or act as if it isn't real or true or as bad as it may seem, and occasionally, that might work; time does erase many issues. But for your long-term success, you need to consider the old saying; running from a problem is a sure way of running into a problem or more problems.

If you don't fix the problem, clean up the mess, make amends, or work towards a solution, the issue will still be there long after you're gone because the reality is no one else is going to clean up after you. No, they will wait until you pass by again on your way to doing big and positive things for the good of many, and then that old problem will come back and drag you into back into a mess all over again.

We see that every day with politicians, sports figures, and media celebrities. And it's not just the big issues like drugs or alcohol, stealing or lying to a grand jury; it is the little things that will get you tangled up.

The words you said or didn't say, promises made and broken, and commitments you agreed to and then backed out of or walked away from.

It might have been a financial deal you struck that went bad or a lie you told that was found out or you took something and didn't return it or you've not been true to your values or your word.

Friend, if you've ever wondered why you haven't progressed to where you should be in your amazing life, may I suggest that you're wasting valuable time running away from your problems when you could settle the matter. You could leave it behind and keep going without the weight of the burden dragging you along.

I know for many, the hope is that time will heal or at least reduce the bigness of the problem, but it never goes away until you do something about it.

For your success, I want you to consider how to face the issues or problems that are weighing you down or haunting you or causing you harm as you've tried to move forward. You don't need that extra weight pulling you down when you are on a path for flight.

This is not an issue of blame. The problem exists, feelings are hurt, issues have not been resolved. And it is holding you back and causing you harm.

I am about you living your best life ever and being successful, and that is hard to do when you always have to look over your shoulder and watch your back.

I don't know your situation, but I do know that if something is taking up space in your head rent-free, as my friends like to say, you need to find a way to settle the matter.

Because running away from your problems is a race you'll never win. You must deal with the issue sooner or later, so consider choosing to handle it on your terms with kindness and true humility towards others.

That is key; kindness in the midst of your anger is a tough road to walk. Getting mad and demanding a fix to get this problem off your plate isn't going to solve anything; it's only going to make matters worse for you. And false humility to get what you want won't save you either; everyone can see through a fraud.

No, you might need to take some time to think about the best way to solve the issue, talk with others who may know of the problem, and offer sound advice. Maybe you need a witness to go with you to address the situation. Maybe you need to simply write a check to cover the damage, or maybe you just need to respectfully ask to have a meeting to settle the issue once and for all. (I encourage you to always take a witness because a friend can help keep you calm and add a level head to the discussion.)

I can't begin to tell you all the stories I have about people coming back later in life to solve an issue, ask forgiveness, and try to make right things that should have never started in the first place. However, due to pride and arrogance, they got themselves wrapped up so tightly, convincing themselves they were right or too important, or the person they cheated, offended, or stole from didn't matter. They had to suffer for years under that delusion and still had to come clean so they could get on with their lives.

It would have been so much easier (and wiser) to fix the problem years earlier, but they didn't, and finally, they have come to realize that running away from their problems is a race they'll never win.

I'm reminded of a story I heard years ago about two Buddhist monks. The story is told about a senior monk and a junior monk who were traveling together. At one point, they came to a river with a strong current. As the monks were preparing to cross the river, they saw a very young and beautiful woman also attempting to cross. The young woman asked if they would help her get across the river.

The senior monk carried the woman on his shoulder, forded the river, and let her down on the other side.

The junior monk was very upset but said nothing.

As they both were walking, the senior monk noticed that his junior was very silent and enquired, "Is something the matter? You seem very upset."

The junior monk replied, "As monks, we are not permitted to touch a woman. How could you carry that woman on your shoulders to the other side of the riverbank?"

The older monk replied, "I left the woman a long time ago at the riverbank; however, you seem to still be carrying her."

I like that story because that is what happens when you think you've run away from your problems; you're still carrying them with you. You think your mind is clear, but it isn't, and you know it.

What is interesting is that many times, the person you offended has, to a large part, forgiven the situation since they could not do anything about your actions. For some, they have moved past the hurt and pain because they didn't cause the harm. Oh, they still remember, but like the oyster that finds a grain of sand in its shell, over time, they have put layer upon layer on to cover the pain and get on with their lives. You are the only one still carrying the load.

Friend, for your sake and your success, please make it right. Do the right thing. That's all you can do, and if they don't forgive or they don't react as you would hope for, at least you'll know that you have finally left it at the riverbank.

SOMETIMES, WHEN YOU LEAST EXPECT IT, YOU WILL WIN

Every once in a while, something happens that restores my faith in how the world works.

Recently, I was wasting time online and came upon a story of hope where the good gal had a shot at winning.

I'm talking about the Oscar nomination for Best Original Song sung by Joni Eareckson Tada for the movie *Alone Yet Not Alone*.

The article explained the movie that saw limited release this past year.

A Christian-themed historical drama set in 1755 against the backdrop of the French and Indian War, the film centers on two sisters who are taken captive during the war and subsequently separated, which leaves them clinging to their faith in search of survival. The title *Alone Yet Not Alone* refers to the family hymn they sing to remain hopeful.

The article goes on to say that what makes this nomination so unusual is that no one in the industry knows much about the movie or singer. They go on to say, "It's still common to see A-listers crack the final five. The nods are generally split between show-stopping numbers from animated films and musicals, and contributions from pop-music staples."

This makes the nomination all the more unusual since both the movie and the singer are not on the Hollywood A, B, or C list. I love it when a crack opens, and someone else can slip in.

You might recognize the name Joni Eareckson Tada; she is an inspirational Christian speaker, singer, artist, radio host, and author who has quadriplegia. She is unable to use her hands or legs after a tragic diving accident in 1967. For years, she was a frequent singer/guest with the Reverend Billy Graham on his crusades.

Hollywood is still in shock about this song and singer who, by all accounts, has bested Taylor Swift, Coldplay, Jay Z, and Beyonce in Best Original Song.

What made me cheer is the fact that sometimes, when you least expect it, you might win. Now, even if in the end, this song doesn't bring home the Oscar, but the fact remains, it is a contender, and that is half the battle. We can at least hope for a victory when we're in the game.

What I hope you take away from this is that against all the odds that seem to be in your way, if you still do your best, stay faithful and true, and work harder than the next person, you could win. I'm not saying that you'll always win, but you could win, and in my book, that is exciting enough to get up and get going.

You might remember a few weeks ago, I did a program that I titled "May All Your Dreams Come True, Even the Ones They Laughed At."

I love that because, as a speaker who spends time with my audience, I hear stories of hope and dreams and desires for good things, and every once in a while, the light seems to hit upon the right star and illuminate the person where they stand.

And that is exciting for all of us who love you and hope for your best in life.

I trust you have that in your life, and if not, keep reading because I will be the voice that encourages you to dream big. We've all heard the line, "If you're going to dream, you might as well dream BIG."

That idea needs to be alive in you today and tomorrow. You have a choice to live the life you want. I know you have responsibilities, but you can carve some time to work toward your dreams.

Walt Disney said, "All our dreams can come true if we have the courage to pursue them."

And I'll say to that, "Dreams don't work unless you do."

That means that some of you need to get going on your dreams. Enough with your excuses. William Ward said, "If you can imagine it, you can achieve it; if you can dream it, you can become it."

Do you know what kills that dream you have? Doubt.

Doubt kills more dreams than failure ever will.

Tell me when and where did you allow your mind to think that it is not possible? When did you stop believing that your dreams are doable? You need to banish the doubt from your mind today because occasionally we can win; we can stand in the light and shine brightly.

Another quote I love says, "Don't let someone who gave up on their dreams talk you out of yours."

You know the type. They're the ones who act like your ideas could never take hold, or you're ridiculous. They refuse to hear you, or they tell you to stop dreaming and be quiet because you're imagining things that are unrealistic.

You know what is amazing? Others may not see your potential, but you do. Never let your light be dimmed. Guard your heart, guard your head, and guard your dreams.

I hate to be the bearer of bad tidings, but others who didn't make it don't want to see you surpass them. I know it's crazy, but you and I know it's the truth.

I see it all the time. Big sister could never make the swim team, so little sister shouldn't even try.

Big brother couldn't make the soccer team, so little brother should try basketball or something else that doesn't show up big brother.

Don't go to college because Mom or Dad didn't go.

And the one that slays me is when I hear, "Don't try; we wouldn't want you to fail." What they're really saying is, "We don't want you to succeed because then it shows what we didn't, couldn't, wouldn't do." Don't let someone who gave up on their dreams talk you out of yours.

I'm going to guess that more than half of your friends and family gave up on their dreams (and some for valid reasons), but be careful when looking to them for encouragement; they don't know how to give it. So, stop looking for acceptance; it's not going to happen.

Now, I do know that some who gave up on their dreams still want the best for you, and they will sacrifice for your dreams and future, and if that is the case, you are lucky indeed. Thank them, love them, and bless them for their loving kindness and sacrifice. Those good people are few and far between, so hold on to them.

Tony Gaskins said, "If you don't build your dream, someone else will hire you to build theirs." And that's the truth. If you stop believing, hoping, praying, pushing, planning, and working on your dreams, they will not come to pass. You must be meticulously involved with your dreams, meaning that you have a plan in place and are actively working on it. And if not, at least prepare yourself and get started!

And remember, starting is half the battle. There are other battles as well including, time, energy, and availability, but if you can get yourself started, you become an active participant in building your dreams!

I don't know if Joni Eareckson Tada will take home the Oscar, but I do know that by showing up and doing the work, she's on her way to winning.

Even though she is not able to use her hands or legs, she uses what she has: a voice that rises above any physical challenge. And because she believes in the beauty of her dreams, she has touched the lives of millions. If she can do it, then why can't you?

And if her song wins, then that will simply be another dream come true. Sometimes, when you least expect it, you will win.

GIVE IT A TRY

"It's impossible," said pride.
"It's risky," said experience.
"It's pointless," said reason.
"Give it a try," whispered the heart.

I love the heart, the one muscle that you must use to keep strong when everything seems to be falling apart. At the center of your body is the heart that beats and keeps the whole body in motion.

Call me crazy, but I believe your body hears everything you say about it. That's why it is so important to learn to love yourself and be comfortable with who you are and how you are. Not that you can't seek improvement for health or well-being, but keeping your heart healthy and strong will hold you in good times and bad, success and failure, happiness, and tears.

We're always being told to guard our hearts, or they will break. You will have heartbreak, but it doesn't mean it's broken. It may just be still for a while until it heals or has a reason to beat with joy again.

Keeping your heart closed off from others might cause some of the most damaging tears to your heart if you're not careful. Sure, guard your heart against those who don't value it but don't lock it away, or it might atrophy or worse, stop loving, stop giving, and stop you from living your best life ever or what you are called to do in this lifetime. But if you keep your heart open, it might bring you unspeakable joy, sometimes even through tears.

I'm not sure who came up with this quote, but it is a keeper in my book because it is what our world and environment say. I hear it all the time. *It's impossible, Deb. It's risky, Deb. It's pointless, Deb.* To which my response is simply: *Well, let's at least try.*

As a speech coach, I have a wonderful clientele who are very brave to walk in my doors and say they need help because they know their ability to speak and change lives is important and not impossible.

For some, it is a matter of self-pride that is working against their best judgment and defeating them, so they come to learn how to fight back and speak without fear.

For others, their head says it's risky, and prior experience has confirmed that speaking is not their best skill (yet), but they know they need to fight through so they can do what they were born to do.

After an initial lesson, some will say, "Deb, it's pointless and hard and scary."

"Give it another try," I say. "You'll only get better with practice and a solid direction to speak the words that need to be said, the words that some so long to hear, the words your heart wants to say but might be too afraid. 'I love you.' 'I'm sorry.' 'Can we try again?' 'Will you forgive me?' 'Will you come alongside and be my friend?'"

"It's impossible," said pride.
"It's risky," said experience.
"It's pointless," said reason.
"Give it a try," whispered the heart.

Listen, I know anything you try that is new is going to fall into the pattern of fear, but you've got to push through. With all your might, you need to build your strength and fight through to the finish.

I love this quote from Doug Larson; "Some of the world's greatest feats were accomplished by people not smart enough to know they were impossible."

What are you up against these days? What issue has distracted you from your goal? What problem seems so large that you've come to a stop or simply a fork in the road and don't know what to do or which road to take?

Do you feel defeated because you listened to the mindless chatter of others who say it can't be done, or are you listening to a voice in your head that said it's impossible or risky or pointless?

Remember, "Being challenged in life is inevitable, being defeated is optional." — Roger Crawford

I often talk about turning off the voices in your head that say discouraging things to you and replace those negative words with words of affirmation or by the use of autosuggestion, meaning that you have a go-to phrase that can redirect you back to your path. It could be a phrase, a song, a verse, or a word or promise that you hold on to in hard times. Whatever you need to do to put yourself mentally, emotionally, physically, or spiritually back on track.

What I find interesting is sometimes it's not your head that says these things, but those who you respect or hold in high esteem that might offhandedly say something that causes you to doubt your direction or goals.

Many times, friends and family do not encourage you like you wish they would, and frankly, that is a hard and discouraging place to be. It is painful when the ones you respect or admire or even love don't give you the affirmations that you can do it against all the odds. Despite the pain, don't listen to others. Learn to listen to your heart when it whispers, "Give it a try." That's why you have a heart.

Your heart will not lead you astray. The desires of your heart are your true being, your true self, your core desire, so be careful that your path forward is right and true and honest and fair. Years later, you'll be proud to say you walked the line, came through the fire, flew on wings of eagles, and arrived joyfully at the end.

What do you want to do? Where do you want to go? How do you want to be remembered? Make movement towards those ideas, big and small, as soon as you can so you can start on your plan for personal success.

Don't listen to the naysayers who will harp and say, "Your dreams are impossible, and your pride will be hurt." Remember, for most of us, it's pride that gets us into more trouble than it's worth. When we're so prideful that we don't make movement for fear of ridicule or failure, we've come to a stop, and if you're not going forward, you're not making progress.

Mark Twain said, "Temper is what gets most of us into trouble. Pride is what keeps us there."

Be careful when others remind you of your past failures. Experience is born out of failure, and just because you failed once, it doesn't make you a failure or mean that you'll fail again. It only means that you might need to find a new way. Not trying is the only thing that adds up to failing.

Don't fear failure so much that you refuse to try new things. The saddest summary of life contains three descriptions: could have, might have, and should have.

My favorite quote on trying is from Margaret Chase Smith. At age 67, when she announced for president of the United States, she said "When people keep telling you that you can't do a thing, you kind of like to try it."

I don't know about you, but one of the worst things someone could say to me is that my work is pointless. Believe it or not, some of my reasonable friends ask me why I do a radio show. They say, "Deb, it's pointless because it doesn't really build your business. You don't sell that many more books or corporate speaking engagements, and you don't have the opportunity to meet many of your listeners." And since my friends are businesspeople, they question my return on investment.

To them, spending time writing and producing a show, finding guests, and then crafting a weekly newsletter from this work on the outside seems pointless. To them, this is not a reasonable use of my time. But, *to me,* it is. I started with the station with the purpose of teaching public speaking skills, but I soon realized that many people were writing to me, asking for more life skills. Since I care about my friends and community, I want to do this work. And frankly, it makes me happy. Although I can't put a number on my ROI, I am happy enough with the nice emails and comments that I receive for doing my radio show. So, as I say to them, I will because I can, and I don't worry about the impossible, the risky, or the reason. I listen to my heart, and I always have, and I hope I always will. There's no need to whisper to me. My heart speaks out loud, and I trust yours also does.

"It's impossible," said pride.
"It's risky," said experience.
"It's pointless," said reason.
"Give it a try," whispered the heart.

HEY, GOOD LOOKING...

Whoa, when was the last time someone said that to you? I hope today or at least yesterday and maybe tomorrow. How do you turn those good looks into opportunity, opportunity to do all the things you dream of, opportunity to be the person you desire to become, opportunity to excel in your field of work or study? Believe it or not, it has little to do with your good looks, smarts, and lineage. It has everything to do with the skills you have, the disciplines you have, the personality you've acquired, the character and reputation you have established, and the language and speech that you use. All of that refinement makes you more attractive to your family and friends and the marketplace.

Did you know by becoming an attractive person, you'll attract opportunity? I was reading an article by Jim Rohn, and he was talking about how to bring opportunity into your amazing life. I have used a few of his phrases here in my message for today.

I believe that a lot of us are looking for opportunity.

Webster defines opportunity as, "a favorable juncture of circumstances; a good chance for advancement or progress."

Rita Coolidge says, "Too often, the opportunity knocks, but by the time you push back the chain, pull back the bolt, unhook the two locks, and shut off the burglar alarm, it's too late."

Friends, great opportunity is waiting for you to move, step up, and get going to develop your best so you can be your best.

Louis L'Amour said, "Some say opportunity knocks only once. That is not true. Opportunity knocks all the time, but you have to be ready for it. If the chance comes, you must have the equipment to take advantage of it."

The key to continue making yourself a more attractive person is developing your skills. If you can develop your skills and continue to refine your character, your health, and your relationships, you'll become a more attractive person and you'll attract opportunity.

In fact, opportunity will probably seek you out.

Remember, the concept of personal development is the never-ending chance to not only improve yourself but also attract opportunities to help others, and that is an added benefit of doing the right thing.

The whole concept of opportunity really does center on the ability to use what you have or set out to learn what you don't know.

Think about the skills you have. What do you do? What do you have? What sets you apart?

There was a guy at my church growing up, and he always had a pocket of tootsie rolls for the kids. Every kid in the church made it a habit of finding Mr. Daniel because we knew his skill was attracting kids with candy. Now, I know you have other more important skills, but when you're seven, that's a big deal.

I was doing a skills search online, and up popped a lot of options but one that caught my eye was "Lifehacker: 10 Skills You Can Teach Yourself." Here are a few.

1. **Learn to fix things**. I love Home Depot, and I love to fix things. My friends, on the other hand, are not so impressed with my desire since sometimes my trying does not lead to success. But I love to try! And when I succeed in putting on a new vacuum band because the other one was broken or replacing a light fixture, I am thrilled with my handiwork. The sense of accomplishment is fun, not as fun as eating a box of donuts, but close.

2. **Learn to defend yourself**. I'm heartbroken that we have to learn to do this, but we do. Be careful out there. There's no need to start something that will go off track quickly and cause a fight

or worse. But don't forget to do your part, like lock your doors when you are sitting in your car, install lights around your home on the outside, and take a class to learn how to hit them hard because these seemingly simple things could save your life.

3. **Pick up a subject you missed in college**. Whether it is online or in person, you can go back to school and take classes that interest you now. You can find courses online and learn a lot from teachers at top universities. It's fun, and you can do it on your own time.

4. **Learn to cook**. Stop eating out for all your meals and start cooking at home. It will save you money, and you'll develop great skills that will pay health benefits for years to come. Unless you're making chocolate chip cookies, but you can add oatmeal to make it healthy.

Those are examples of skills. Now, what are your disciplines? I have two I like:

1. **When you get up in the morning, make your bed**. Leaving something undone gives you the subconscious message that this room can be let go a little, so you do. One unmade bed leads to laundry on the floor, dishes in the sink, and then everything goes downhill from there.

   A messy bed tends to give a room an overall sense of chaos, whereas a partly made bed can make even a messy room seem more put together. It's a small but tangible form of control over one's environment.

2. **Keep your clothes cleaned and pressed**. My favorite quote is from Coleman Cox, who said, "Keeping your clothes well pressed will keep you from looking hard pressed." I love that, and it's true.

In addition to skills and disciplines, you know I believe in the importance of a good personality. When my business associate and

I owned an ad agency, she was enthralled with the Meyers Briggs personality test. I thought it was limiting and didn't reflect who I was day in and day out. Whether you are an INFP or ENTJ on the scale of personality tests, all that matters to me is that you have a great personality, and that includes having a great:

- **Attitude** – The capacity to stay optimistic and positive. Attitude is the number one quality for career success.

- **Enthusiasm** – The possession of intense and eager interest in a subject or cause. It is an energy that often inspires others.

- **Ethics** – Do you live by a code of sound moral principles?

- **Goal-Focused** – Do you have clarity on the objectives that you strive for in your personal and professional life?

- **Listener** – The capacity to suspend your own agenda and deliberately and empathically allow others to be heard.

Skills, disciplines, and personality are important, but nothing stands up to character and reputation.

Character and reputation are the most important skills that you must establish in your life to be seen as a leader by others. They say that character is who you are when no one is watching. John Wooden, probably the most famous coach in any sport, delivered a line very similar to the one above. He said, "For your pursuit of being the best basketball player to be possible, you should always assume someone is watching and act accordingly." And he is right. In today's world of NSA and camera phones, know that someone is always watching. It's up to you as to what they will see.

I couldn't close out without talking about the language and speech you use. Friends, your words matter, and they will set you apart from others, make you more attractive to the marketplace, and will take you further than any other skill you could develop. Develop your speaking ability and learn quotes and poems and stories to keep others interested. Remember, for many, your voice is the only voice they hear, and that is your opportunity to change your corner of the world.

WHEN YOUR PAST CALLS, DON'T ANSWER. IT HAS NOTHING NEW TO SAY.

I have this great job to be the speech coach for TEDx Greenville. It is a conference that will be in our area in April. In the course of meeting the presenters, I met one whose mission in life is to help those who have been in prison begin again because, as she says, they've paid their debt to society. Once they're released, it is time to get on with their lives. Her talk is an interesting journey from life to death, prison to freedom and a new life that is filled with uncertainty.

One of the lessons I gleaned from the conversation is how strong the pull of people's pasts is. Change is hard, and even once they have left the past in the past, it is a daily struggle to keep it there because, for so long, it's all they ever knew.

How many times have you fallen back into an old habit or pattern because you answered the call of your past? You know you should not have picked up the proverbial phone, but you did. You said, "Hello," and now, you're dealing with the aftermath.

I'm encouraging you today to say goodbye and leave your past behind you as you move forward.

I think it is interesting that so many people I talk to have this same pull. It's like a spiderweb that seems to draw many back even after they have come so far. It's odd in a way that the stickiness of your past is hard to unglue in the present.

But it wouldn't be if you had not answered the phone. Friends, let me remind you that **when your past calls, don't answer. It has nothing new to say.**

And the reason it has nothing new to say is that you are not that same person. You are not the same person who made those mistakes years, months, days, hours, or even minutes ago. Now, you may be making new mistakes, but that's a talk for another day.

Life is movement forward unless you choose to live in the past.

And some people I have met along my journey do like to live in the past because, for some, it might have been their glory days. You know, when you played football without your knees hurting or could sing without your voice cracking or were student body president and did great things years ago.

For some, remembering your past is beneficial, but don't live there because that is not your future.

And those who have a past that is less than stellar, why have you brought it along with you? Leave it behind, and even if it calls, don't answer. Why? Because it has nothing new to say.

I know that in some circles, it is considered spiritual or healing or good for your soul to keep digging up old bones and chewing on them again, but that is not for me. Hopefully, you will realize that it is not for you or anyone you know because unless you glance back and learn from a mistake, you're left staring at a damaged or empty past, which does you no good.

For those who are of the faith community, once forgiven, you have no need to go back and relive the muddy days. That's an insult to God and grace, and you know it.

If I had a nickel for all the could've, should've, would'ves of life, I'd be a wealthy woman. But since I don't dwell in the past, I'll have to make a living another way.

I had a friend who was wailing about what was done to her by her so-called friends ten years ago, and the darndest thing is that she can remember every jot and tittle even down to the clothes they wore. But the problem is that she is living in the past. Everyone and

I mean *everyone*, else has moved on and moved out and even moved up except her.

A friend of my family went through a divorce. His wife walked in one day and said, "I'm sorry, I don't love you anymore. You've done nothing wrong. I just want out," and she left the car keys on the table and walked out the door. That had to be devastating, and to the best of my ability, I get it, but our friend carries that hurt in his heart, head, and on his shoulders and has now turned bitter, mean, and I hate to say it, but ugly.

He has chosen to let his ex destroy his life forever. He not only picks up the phone to his past but also carries the phone with him and even lifts the receiver to make sure it's working in case his hurtful past comes a-calling.

If someone treats you badly, remember that there is something wrong with them, not you. Normal people don't go around destroying other people. Never let someone with the significance of a speed bump become a roadblock in your life!

Friends, we all have made mistakes that we're sorry for, but if you don't move past it, settle it, forgive it, and forget it, then only you are hurting your soul and spirit.

I know I have spoken about this before, but I keep hearing the same stories of unforgiving past lives and mistakes and how good people keep dragging from relationship to relationship, therapist to therapist as they travel along.

You can't change what you refuse to confront. See your past for what it is and move on. Okay, your past called, and you answered. It told you nothing new, now hang up. You've already confronted those mistakes. You've seen them for what they are, for the millionth time. Now is the time to change. Change your mindset. Only you can do that. Only you can forgive, forget, get over, pass by, move on, and not answer, *only you*. Remember, the other person doesn't care and has likely forgotten already.

I saw a funny quote online that said, "You want to come in my life, the door is open. You want to get out of my life, the door is open. Just one request. Don't stand at the door; you're blocking the traffic."

Friends, I've said this before, and I will say it again. "If you carry the bricks from your past relationship, you will end up building the same house." You will end up in a different location but the same place, and you'll wonder how you got here again. I'll tell you how. You built the same house on a different lot.

On behalf of everyone who loves you, we're sorry you had to go through all that. You didn't deserve it. We know you are hurt, but please know if you look up and move forward, you'll see that you can heal, forgive, and even forget. The choice is yours. We want you to find healing and forgiveness because we want you to be happy.

My favorite song on the radio these days is by Pharrell Williams from the movie *Despicable Me,* and it's called "Happy." This song will make your two left feet move because it is happy.

It's been said that life is like a camera. Focus on what's important. Capture the good times. Develop from the negatives. And if things don't work out, take another shot.

For every minute you are angry, you lose sixty seconds of happiness.

You'll lose your happiness if you're too busy on the phone listening to the voices of the past.

ATTRACT WHAT YOU EXPECT, REFLECT WHAT YOU DESIRE, BECOME WHAT YOU RESPECT, AND MIRROR WHAT YOU ADMIRE

I had an interesting speaking engagement in Pennsylvania and then Maryland recently, and it brought to mind this saying. "Attract what you expect, reflect what you desire, become what you respect, and mirror what you admire."

In Pennsylvania, I was speaking to those who are planning on running for public office. I teach seminars called "Your Campaign Speech" and "How to Engage Your Audience to Listen to Your Message."

In Maryland, I had the wonderful opportunity to speak at the Spouse Program for members of Congress. I must say they were both wonderful groups to spend time with, and my thought for today is a direct result of what I saw that week. Because if you're in public office or would like to be, if you run a corporation or would like to, you need to learn the skills that will set you apart from others, and one of those skills is the ability to speak and be heard and seen in the quiet and the noise. Otherwise, you'll never make it to the finish line in the hard race for success.

Many of the folks I work with figured out that for them to be successful in life or politics or business, they had to *attract what they expected, reflect what they desired, become who they respected, and learn to mirror what they admired.*

When you think about it, that's an interesting thought that you can attract what you expect.

Every day, I expect good things, and I look at the bright side. By changing myself to be more positive (even when I don't feel like it) or to step out of my comfort zone to be perhaps more kind than my usual nature, I have reaped the rewards of being around people who also expect great things with a positive resolve to be better, stronger, kinder, than perhaps our nature would provide. Change is good; it is hard but good for most of us. It is not impossible, but it is not easy.

If you were to attract what you expect, what would happen? This goes to the heart of expectation. What great or small expectations do you have for yourself or others?

How do you see yourself? Not your glorified ego-self but your true self? You know, the one who shows up when you're doing nothing or in your spare time or when you least expect it. If you see yourself as a helper, healer, or hero, that is what you will become.

I believe that it is wise to make a personal list of expectations that are reasonable and doable that you can do in a structured time frame. Your list will serve as a guidepost to your success, whatever that may look like. It's the plan that you can follow in both sunshine and stormy weather.

"Attract what you expect, reflect what you desire, become what you respect, and mirror what you admire."

Not only will you attract what you expect, but the good news is also in parallel with your expectation comes the realization that you and I will reflect what we desire.

When you have a visual, mental, or physical goal in mind, it is much easier to reach. How does one reflect what they desire? There are all sorts of ways. It can be by how you dress or what car you drive or where you live. There is an old adage in politics to get where you want to go, dress the part. Once you begin to reflect what you desire, for some strange reason, the stars align, and you'll be able to step up into the place, office, or position you worked for. It's easy to see that if you start to dress like the CEO or golf pro or fashionista, you'll start to see yourself in that position, and others will take notice of the new you.

When you have a heart for your work or place of worship or even your favorite charity, it becomes you, and people will start to see you in that light of leadership.

If we attract what we expect and reflect what we desire, the old saying says that we'll become what we respect.

Who do you respect? I love the word respect and am disappointed that it seems to have lost its luster in today's ego-driven world. Thank goodness that Aretha Franklin keeps it alive.

Respect is such a wonderful thing because it sets the bar high. I have great respect for some in public office because I know their heart; I also respect a few leaders in ministry because I am challenged by their message. There are some in business who, by being honest and fair, have my respect. I have respect for many in leadership primarily because of the position and often not the person who sits in the seat at the time, but the position is worthy of respect.

We try to teach our kids to respect their elders and be kind to their siblings because if we're going to become what we respect, we need to set the bar as high as we can and encourage those we love and mentor to reach and exceed it.

How do you become what you respect? I believe the foundation is you must be an honest person who keeps their word, even if it costs you money, time, business, or friends. To be known as honest and fair is the most respectful accolade you could ever receive.

I believe that generosity, manners, diplomacy, goodness, fairness, and kindness are born of respect for others, including animals.

Respecting yourself enough to keep you in good stead with your family and friends and community is a worthy goal.

I always find it interesting that, somehow, we all seem to know the person who cheats or steals or lies, and many times, we are not surprised or shaken because that is what we have come to expect from that person. Their negative behavior is often because they don't respect themselves, so keeping their word is of no use. We don't respect them because we know them, and rarely will a leopard change his spots.

When you lose the respect of others, it is very hard to get that back. So, your best bet is to pay attention, repair mistakes, ask forgiveness, pay that debt you owe, clean up your act now, and do right.

"Attract what you expect, reflect what you desire, become what you respect; you'll mirror what you admire."

If you admire good manners, mirror them by learning what fork to use in social settings.

If you admire intelligent conversation, pick up a book and start to read and listen to well-known thought leaders or learn from the many great souls of yesteryear.

If you admire those who keep themselves up and are healthy, push away from the table and get yourself to the gym so you can turn your roly-poly into a rock, and then you'll be strong and feel great.

If you admire those who can sing or dance or paint or speak—get going on your practice! Remember, it doesn't happen overnight, but if you get up and get started, at least you'll be heading in the right direction!

If you're going to mirror what you admire, you have some work to do. The good news is since you now notice what you need, it will make the journey so much easier.

For your success, I encourage you to attract what you expect, reflect what you desire, become what you respect, and mirror what you admire.

"SOMETIMES YOUR ONLY AVAILABLE TRANSPORTATION IS A LEAP OF FAITH."

—*Margaret Shepard*

I have had a lot of different experiences in my life and have taken chances that on the outside might not have seemed so smart. Okay, they probably weren't so smart on the inside either, but who knew? I jumped in anyway because I have this theory about life that you've got to go and do what you want to do in case the world changes and those one-time opportunities disappear. I fundamentally believe that we are not meant to live a boring life. This world is too big, too amazing, and too discoverable for me (or you) to sit at home and not experience it.

I saw a post on Facebook that I put on my page that says, "Travel is the only thing you buy that makes you richer." Isn't that the truth?

And it's not only traveling to other countries but also a new adventure close to home that makes memories for a lifetime.

Growing up, I knew that if I made a mistake that I was young enough to survive the fall—whether it was financial, emotional, or physical. I always figured if my big idea didn't work out, or if none of my ideas worked out, I was young enough that I could start again without much loss of time, energy, or money.

My friend gave me a plaque one time when she sensed I was struggling to decide on an opportunity that had presented itself, and on it was a wild-haired female character jumping over a fire. It said, *This is Faith, and this is a Leap of Faith.* I like that little plaque because it reminds me that sometimes living the life of comfort and ease is probably not going to provide the heart-stopping thrill of landing your first airplane or getting up for the first time on your water skis or riding the world's longest escalator.

The plaque also reminds me that sometimes there are problems or issues that you can't lightly step over. You'd be better off to leap over them.

The fact is, for most of us, the fire will always be there but how we get across is the journey we write home about.

And you know instinctively that once you make that leap, you've now done something big.

Having the courage to take a leap of faith probably is not an everyday occurrence. If you have to do it often, you might need to stop and see what is driving the need to remove yourself from certain situations in such a grand fashion.

I came across a quote from Margaret Shepard years ago, and I have kept it on my computer as a reminder of life. "Sometimes your only available transportation is a leap of faith."

I love that quote because, in my own life, it has been true, and I am sure it has been true for you if you admit that sometimes you've had to jump and pray that there would be a ledge or limb or line that would catch you.

I thought it was an interesting dichotomy that although the fear of the unknown is great, sometimes, the fear of the known is greater.

I work with people all the time who look around their current situation and say to me, "Deb, I've got to get out. If I stay in this job, or relationship, or group of friends, I will miss the calling I believe I have."

Remember, I am not a licensed counselor, so I do not dispense advice on life or love or leaving, but I do help others shake open closed doors so they can see what is on the other side.

For some, seeing with new eyes the opportunities that might await is a big adventure, and it might seem like an enormous leap of faith to take a new job in another country to build a career, to move to another city to find their dream, for some to unload and rebuild.

And even though on the outside it seems like a small step for mankind, for some, it is the gulf wide enough to expose every fear and doubt, and the only way through is simply a leap of faith because sometimes your only available transportation is a leap of faith.

What leap of faith do you need to take in your own life? Is there something you've always wanted to do but have held back because it seems like such a big deal? Is there some challenge that you simply can't walk over due to the size, and if you make a decision, you'll be leaping over mountains? Is there a dream that you have had for years that is on the back burner that is on your one-day list?

One day, when the kids are grown, the house is paid off, the credit cards are manageable, or the job is safe… What are you waiting for?

To find amazing joy in life, it will be a leap of faith to know that you're ready to do the job, to know that you're able to be successful on the other side, to know that what you'll gain is greater than what you will leave behind.

I am not advocating that you do foolish things that would cause harm to you or your family or company; that would be silliness. Nor is acting irresponsibly going to accomplish what you're hoping for. It might close all doors to your dreams if you act without a plan or purpose or provisions for those you care about. No, that's a leap of crazy that will leave you damaged for years to come.

Just remember that sometimes in life, your only available transportation to reach the goals and dreams and hopes is a leap of faith.

I like the idea of leaping – giving it your all, not being extremely cautious, but putting your whole self into the opportunity.

To grow a business, you have to take that leap of faith and hire a few new employees. I know the cost of salary and benefits and training seems like a huge obstacle, but when the fit is right, you'll wonder why you didn't do it sooner. Your output will increase, and your team will grow, and you'll be able to take on new and bigger projects to grow even bigger. I've seen friends wrestle with the struggle and be grateful in the end.

Or how about restoring a relationship? That one is hard but think about it; if you make the call, set up the coffee meeting, go through with it, that unbridled leap of faith on your part for restoration might restore that which was lost, or you'll realize that once forgiven and somewhat forgotten, it's time to move on with no strings attached because you took the plunge to make it right. It's a monkey off your back, and they can wallow in self-pity, but you're free.

Every once in a while, I see big leaps of faiths, and I so marvel at the commitment that it takes, whether it is keeping the baby when it was unplanned or blending a family with a new marriage and being accepting of all the children or opening your heart to a new member of the family.

I could go on and on at the amazing leaps of faith that people take every day, and what is remarkable is that for so many, it wasn't a hard jump because they believed, or they knew, it was the right thing to do. That is what makes this world an amazing place. Everyone doing well by doing good in their corner of the world.

I love today's message because I see the success of it time and time again, and I also see how sometimes, due to fear of the known or unknown, many people leave opportunity behind because they are comfortable in their little world. It's not how I would live, nor would I encourage those I love to live. I'm not an encourager of living small. I hope you dream of more and bigger and better, and I hope you know that there are a lot of people cheering for you, praying for you, believing in you as you take that leap of faith. Sometimes, your only available transportation is a leap of faith.

YOU ARE WHAT YOU DO,
NOT WHAT YOU SAY YOU'LL DO

I don't know about you, but one thing in life that really chips me off is when people tell me they are going to do something and then never get around to it.

I have a friend who offered to take me out for my birthday. That was in October, and I'm still waiting. Well, I'm not waiting anymore because they've obviously forgotten what they offered. As I look back over our friendship, I have to face the fact that they rarely keep their word about things they say or promise. They are not unkind, and they do not mean anything by their forgetfulness, and we always have a grand time when we're together. I have to chalk it up to that they're just busy with the husband and kid and always talking about getting a job. I get it, and now, when they make their big announcements of what we're going to do, I just smile because I know nothing will happen. But it's the thought that counts for me.

A while back, I made of list of things I had promised other people but never got around to, and I had to go and make things right. Some folks moved on, and when I didn't keep my word, they did other things. At that point, I could apologize and move on myself.

If someone doesn't let me make it right when I offer, I am not going to beat myself up over the fact that I made a mistake and then tried to rectify it. It comes down to simply making time, taking the time, and creating a space in time to do what I said I would do.

You might have the same issues in your life. We mean well, but life gets in the way and crowds out our good intentions.

You are what you do, not what you say you'll do.

For being so simple, the saying is profound. There are people who hold on to the promise of what we say we'll do vs. others who just chalk it up to life getting in the way if we never get around to doing it. Good for all of us when our friends don't hold us accountable for our lapses of commitment.

Children actually hold us accountable to this saying. If you say to your kids with good grades, "We'll go eat a cheeseburger and then go to the zoo," a year later, you will be reminded of what you offered when finally, one report card comes home with a good grade.

Kids remember our promises as truths. We said it; we promised it; we must deliver, or according to them, we'll break their hearts.

It is not just kids who keep score. I have found that many of my parents' generation also expect us to do what we say we'll do (imagine that). For many, it's not about a promise but an honest measure of a man or woman's worth by keeping their word.

Rarely does someone ask you to make the promise. You make it whether in haste or with the best intentions. You made a commitment, so you must deliver.

Promises made should be promises kept—even the little ones.

I have learned some hard lessons to curb my tongue on making promises I cannot keep. It's so easy to be generous until you've got to pay the bill. It's so easy to offer other people's time until they tell you they cannot help you out, and it's easy to throw out a big idea but then not have the wherewithal to make it happen.

We all do it with the best intentions, but many of us fail because we never make it happen. Or worse, we don't start at all.

Think with me for a minute. What promises have you made that you have not kept?

- Did you promise to fix something for somebody?

- Did you remember to return things your borrowed?

- Did you repay a loan or pay for a repair?

- Did you promise to clean out the car, attic, garage, closet, storage unit that's costing you a boatload of money monthly, and it's full of stuff you can't remember that you even own?

- Did you promise to spend more time with the kids, wife, husband, relatives, in-laws, and out-laws?

- Did you promise to bring flowers home occasionally or a box of doughnuts? (Okay, I made that up because that is my language of love.)

You are what you do, not what you say you'll do.

The good news is I know there are some who do keep their word in small ways and big ones, and that is great! You have my admiration.

And doesn't it feel good to do what you say you'll do or accomplish what you planned to do or finish the job you started? There is no better feeling than accomplishment.

How can I encourage you to get going again, to start, or finish?

I'll do my part weekly to encourage you. But you have to step up and do your part. Please know I am here cheering you on to do the things you've promised, to be an encouragement to your amazing life.

We all need to do what we said we'd do. Make the call, send the email, and write the letter to finish what we committed to so many years, months, and days ago.

A while back, I was speaking, and a young lady asked me to be her mentor. I should have had the courage to politely say that I don't mentor anyone because I can barely keep myself together, but what did I do? I was the bold, brash speaker who was too weak to be honest with her and myself. I knew as I was saying that I could probably work with her that I would not have the time due to my travel and speaking schedule, so weeks went by and then a month, and another, and I finally wrote her an email apologizing for not keeping my end of the bargain. I offered a few dates where we could meet on Skype. She was going through a transition and was very kind about my apology and offer to connect, but she had found someone closer to her hometown.

I was lucky that she was forgiving, but I made a mistake, and I knew it, and I had to make it right. It is important that my word is my bond.

I'm not asking you to do anything I am not doing myself, so maybe together, we can hold each other accountable and keep our word. Or better yet, here is something I have learned the hard way; I try not to make a promise I cannot keep.

I have pulled back on my over-generous offers so I can be real and reasonable for those times I do offer something to make sure I can keep my word because we are judged by what we do, not what we say we'll do. I have a responsibility to my friends and family, and so do you.

So, we're in a new month with a world of new opportunity to make right that which we promised, to do what we said we'd do, to go where we said we'd go, and to be whom we claimed to be to make our world a better place.

Let's get started!

"RAISE YOUR WORDS, NOT YOUR VOICE. IT IS RAIN THAT GROWS FLOWERS, NOT THUNDER."

—*Rumi*

When I was thinking about doing a radio show, I knew that to be successful, I would have to set a standard that would be consistent for you, my audience. As Americans, we like things in a consistent order, so for this to work, I needed structure with time frames for the various parts of the show. I decided that one thing I would like to do is to add a simple option for consistent learning. I figured the best way to do that was to invite my guests to be a part of the process, so I decided to ask each of my guests to give me a word for the week, a book that changed their thinking or their life, and answer the question of why public speaking skills are important.

You wouldn't think that would be hard, but in reality, most people don't learn many new words, read many books, or stop and think about why their public speaking skills are important – to which I find interesting since those might just be the three things I think about all the time.

As a speaker, I am always interested in words and not only for the meaning but also how others hear certain words and how they react to the word, or perhaps, that word has no meaning to them. I had an occasion to sit next to someone for many months who was book smart, and they would use words I had never heard of, so I'd secretly write down the word (how I thought it might be spelled) and then go home and look it up and add it to my list of words for the week.

One of the reasons I did this is because I know the value of words, and I know how what we say and in what tone can convey a multitude of messages. For me to continue to learn and grow, I figured it was an education I didn't have to pay for, but it would pay dividends for a lifetime, especially in my line of work, if I would pay attention and listen and learn.

I came across a quote by the poet Rumi, "Raise your words, not your voice. It is rain that grows flowers, not thunder."

What a nice way to think about our words and tone and tenor of our speaking voice.

As an interview coach or in my presentations coaching, I come across all sorts of dialects, drawls, and diction.

When you think about your voice and the words you use, how do others hear you? In our time together, I would like for you to consider raising your words or growing your vocabulary to increase your value.

And not only increasing your vocabulary for business purposes, but also for your life and those you love and care for. The Bible says a soft answer turns away wrath, but grievous words stir up anger. That is perfect with our thought for today; "It's the rain, not the thunder, that makes the flower grow."

This was a hard lesson for me to learn when I was younger, as I was all about the thunder. Being the youngest of five and the only girl, I worked hard to be heard.

A friend and I owned an advertising agency many years ago when I was starting out in business. I remember my dad had to drop something by my office, and as he was waiting for me to get off the phone to speak to me, he overheard me raise my voice and yell at a supplier because something had gone wrong. He didn't say anything, but later that night, when I got home, my mom called me and asked about my day. I didn't think much of it until she got around to asking about my yelling, to which I told her I probably yell ten times a day at supplies and printers and the mating squirrels that made too much noise outside. I explained that no one listens or hears, and then we're held accountable to the client for missed deadlines. "Business was stressful," I told her.

Well, my yelling upset my dad (who, by the way, is very quiet) because he had never heard me raise my voice. He was quite surprised at my volume and was upset at my audacity and that I would speak that way in a business setting to which I was reminded that "We don't do that in our family." That is not how I was brought up, and nothing is so stressful that I cannot maintain my calm and demeanor as a lady and a professional – and never let my father hear me do that again.

What a great reminder that I needed to raise my words, not my voice. It is rain that grows flowers, not thunder. Although I am all about thunder, the reality is it is not professional and rarely does it accomplish what you think it will; in many cases, it is the opposite because thunder usually falls on deaf ears and becomes only noise and not words we hear or value.

The Wall Street Journal used to run a weekly column by Erin McKean called "Week in Words"—a field guide to unusual words. Ms. McKean is a lexicographer, which is my new word for the week. I learned it is primarily the art or craft of compiling, writing, and editing dictionaries. Who knew people did this for a living? I, for one, am glad they do.

Words matter. Meanings of words matter, and how you use your words matters whether you think so or not.

I mention this because as you and I grow in knowledge, it's a great practice to build on the blocks of what we already know.

There is no doubt that thunder is more my nature, and I tend to use my outside voice most of the time partly because many of friends don't hear so well and partly because I don't think people listen, so I'll have the loudest voice in the room.

In keeping with my theme for today, how can I help you raise your words?

Just an aside, I gave up asking my guests for their word for the week when 1. They couldn't pronounce it; 2. They looked it up in a dictionary and had never used the word in a sentence because it was not a word in their working vocabulary; 3. They mistakenly thought a hard word was a better choice vs. a word that might have fallen out of favor or not one you hear very often.

I try not to be the word police, but sometimes, I did harass them when it's a word that is not well known.

Okay, let's get back to how we can raise our words. Reading books, magazines, newspapers, and online blogs are the best way. I can remember when I learned the word flummoxed, which means to bewilder, confound, or confuse. I had never heard that word before and had to look it up. Within a week, I saw that word in a newspaper article. Maybe because it was a new word, it popped out at me, or maybe my new word stuck. When I am out speaking, I always ask my audience to give me a new word that they have learned.

Most famous sayings are not made up of words you don't know or understand, and they have withstood the test of time.

"Four score and seven years ago, our fathers brought forth on this continent, a new nation, conceived in Liberty, and dedicated to the proposition that all men are created equal."

"Let us resolve tonight that young Americans will always ... find there is a city of hope in a country that is free. And let us resolve they will say of our day and our generation, we did keep the faith with our God, that we did act worthy of ourselves, that we did protect and pass on lovingly that shining city on a hill."

Remember, "Raise your words, not your voice. It is rain that grows flowers, not thunder."

WE HAVE ALL BEEN PLACED ON THIS EARTH TO DISCOVER OUR OWN PATH, AND WE WILL NEVER BE HAPPY IF WE LIVE SOMEONE ELSE'S IDEA OF LIFE

As I was working with some clients this week, I had an epiphany, a sudden realization, an unexpected intuitive leap of understanding; we have all been placed on this earth to discover our own path, and we will never be happy if we live someone else's idea of life.

I have a diverse client base, and I am thrilled to work with so many amazing people who are making great strides in life to move down the path they feel called. There is such joy in seeing happiness, contentment, and peace when someone finds their right path, their calling, their life's work. And there is no greater joy than seeing someone settle gently in the path of their God-given talents, skills, and abilities.

There is another side that I see, and that is when someone is not following their dream, but the dream of someone else, and that makes for a rough road. I'm not saying it's impossible, and I'm not saying that someone cannot grow to love the path they were told to follow. But from where I sit and coach and speak and counsel, I just find the idea of discovering our path to be the easier weight to carry.

The reason I have come to believe this is because I truly feel that we have all been placed on this earth to discover our own path, and we will never be happy if we live someone else's idea of life.

I am sure one can grow into a bit of happiness and survive, but I don't encourage that because life is to be lived and not just survived. I know that many parents, friends, and bosses do push people to fit the square peg into the round hole because they think that is what is needed, or it fits with what "our family does."

I see kids applying to medical school—not because they want to be a doctor but because it is what Mom and Dad want. We work on law school interviews because Grandpa was a lawyer, so you have to go to law school to carry on the family name. Or you're next in line in the family business, so buck up and be happy because your last name is on the building, and don't worry, you'll learn to love it in time. For a lot of people, that's okay, until it isn't. Would you consider letting your young person, your spouse, or friend discover their own true path?

It is always interesting to me when in mid-life, people up and change direction because as they see the birthdays pass by and the aches and pains kick up or friends pass away, it is a reminder that life is too short not to do what you dream of or love or at least try to make a go of it.

Maybe you know people who have done this and ended up with crazy results, such as divorcing their spouse or buying a motorcycle and riding across the country or joining a rock band...until they come to the realization that was a bad idea. No, I'm not talking about being foolish, but I am encouraging you to consider starting today what steps led you down your path.

What does your path to happiness look like without the influence of someone else's idea of what your life should be or look like?

I don't want you to jump the gun and make a poor decision that would end up costing you. But what I have found is that when a couple honestly sits at the table and shares openly some ideas of what they dream about, when friends feel safe to say what business they have always wanted to open, when young people can show a plan to their parents that prove they have thought something out, opportunities present themselves.

You must have the courage to dream, plan, and work on the discovery of your path. For those of you who are lucky enough to have one special person or a group of friends who believe in you and trust that you will be careful with the plan that has been agreed upon, you should get started today.

Do you remember when you were just starting out? What were some of the things you had hoped to do? Just think of the few things you had hoped to do before what I call the 3 Ms – marriage, mortgage, and munchkins – or after the 3 Ms. What path did you start down that had the potential for great happiness and success as *you* see success?

If it was a good path back and you could continue, and you're doing your life's work now; that is great.

If, on the other hand, you didn't follow your dream, what can you do today to make small movements in that direction, with the blessing of those you care for?

You may have a family or other responsibilities and cannot just turn the ship very easily, but what I have found in my work is if you have a smidgen of an entrepreneurial spirit and attitude, you can incorporate some of your path – your heart's desire, your dream – into a reality. Don't worry about what others have in mind for you. Many well-meaning people do not have a clue of who you are or what you're made of or where you're going. But believe that you still do, and it's that spark I hope smolders into a fire. I see success in small steps happen every day.

When I was younger, my parents thought I'd be good at real estate because they knew I wanted to work for myself and have my own hours and set my own pace and have a job that challenged me. So, I dutifully signed up for real estate school, and although I had a great time in class because I enjoyed learning new things, once I passed my exam, I was quickly picked up with a company and put on the street looking for buyers or sellers. It was pretty obvious to me early on that I was not cut out to show houses. That was 25+ years ago. I didn't like going into empty houses, and I had no interest in looking in closets, attics, garages, or under anything. That's a problem if one plans to be a great real estate agent.

I will never forget Dorethia. She was the one woman who ended my housing career. I really liked her and wanted the right home for her. The one she showed me that she liked had been wrecked on the inside, and I couldn't see her and the kids in this messed-up house. (The previous owner had pulled out the gas fireplace and left it a mess.) So, I encouraged her to look for another home in the same area if she was so inclined. Somewhere in my conversation, my broker was unhappy that I didn't just sell her the one she thought she wanted, signed, sealed, and delivered, so we could all get paid and go home. I decided then and there that I didn't like all the rules around selling houses. I liked selling land because it was more my personality to walk an acre than to waste my time discussing where one would put their washer and dryer. Without a doubt, my parents meant well when they strongly suggested real estate, but in reality, they could see that it was not my cup of coffee. So, as we say in baseball, "No harm, no foul." And I found my way to my next great adventure.

I was lucky, directions were provided and offered, and no harm came to my short-lived stint in real estate. I think instinctively we all know when we're pushed to live someone else's idea of life, even if it is with good intention and not by force. But what I see so often is the reality that many people are living someone else's dream, and their dream slowly dies and smolders in ashes until a breeze comes along and stirs up the embers to relight the fire.

Think of me as a simple breeze to remind you of what you wanted to do before you were told what to do. If we believe that we have all been placed on this earth to discover our own path, and we will never be happy if we live someone else's idea of life, we need to dust off the map, pull out our GPS, and load up the car and get started down the road of discovery.

"BE SOMEBODY WHO MAKES EVERYBODY FEEL LIKE (A) SOMEBODY."

—*Kid President*

Have you ever been around someone who makes you feel like you matter? And it is not dependent on what time of day or night or weekend or if they are with other friends or they find you by yourself or even if you don't see you for a while. When you reconnect, the way they treat you is with respect, kindness, gentleness, graciousness, and sheer unbridled happiness that they got the chance to run into you.

You might be thinking that I'm talking about your pet, who is always glad to see you, but I'm not. I'm actually wondering if you know of someone who embodies this type of kindness and sheer happiness when they see you.

Wouldn't be great if we all knew someone who made us feel like we were somebody and that we mattered, and when they thought of us, it was always with kindness and good thoughts?

I don't mean to be negative, but I would be surprised if 98% of you could tell me about someone (who is not a relative or spouse) who treats you with unbridled true love and kindness. Isn't that interesting? We can all think of a few folks who are always nice or polite or even kind, but it's somewhat of a stretch to think someone who lights up when they see us, someone who makes us feel special.

Wouldn't it be great if I could find a friend like that for you? Wouldn't it be great if you were that person?

Really! You could be that person who shows a level of kindness not seen very much in today's world. And wouldn't it be great if people said things about you like, "She makes me feel important every time we meet," and, "He makes me feel valued"?

Why does this seem like such a farfetched idea? Is it silly to want someone to make you feel special in an honest and friendly way? I don't think so. I think most of us would love to have a friend like that or be treated that way by our current network of friends.

I have a small group of friends, and we've been together for over 25 years. Although we don't express our happiness about seeing each other so overtly, I can honestly say that we do try to be a light for each other in our dark days. That connection we have, we've all come to understand (as we've gotten older), is a real blessing. Not many friend groups can withstand all the highs and lows that life brings their way, so over time, they tend to drift apart unless someone in the group is the instigator to keep the coffee club together.

If you have a group of lifelong friends, I hope you will consider being more verbal in your appreciation for their friendship. It can only help strengthen the bond you already have, or it can be a soothing touch to help heal a broken or distant friendship. We never know what others are going through.

I know it is hard to overlook a slight or have to think about forgiving someone and maintaining the friendship. But if you want to grow past that aspect of your personality, consider being the person who makes others feel valued. What's awesome is you can start today!

When I was growing up, my parents encouraged my brothers and me to learn to make friends. My dad used to say, in all seriousness, "If your schoolbooks interfere with your education, toss them out." What he meant was although school is important, in life, you'll go much farther if you maintain a network of good friends and are well thought of by others.

I can remember how this played out well for me when I was running for office. As I was going door-to-door asking for votes, I went to the door of a small home in my district. When the lady opened the door, she was genuinely happy to see me. Come to find out, we went to high school together and had not seen each other in years. I can clearly remember when she told me she'd be happy to vote for me because I had always been nice and friendly in school. Although we did not run in the same circles, I was nice to everyone.

How remarkable that my being nice years earlier was remembered, appreciated, and rewarded.

When old school friends see you, what do they remember? How about work colleagues? When you run into them at the store, how do they introduce you to their family? Or do they quickly scoot down another aisle, so they won't have to interact?

I am not encouraging you to be fake. If you don't feel like being a person who is kind, encouraging, and thoughtful, let's not do it. If it is fake, that will cause you more harm than good, and you can just keep on being your grumpy self; we won't be surprised.

But if you want people to come to your funeral and say nice things and mean it (and not just come to make sure you're dead), you might want to consider making a few changes in your daily interactions with others.

How hard would it be to make others feel valued, to truly feel cared for and remembered? Wouldn't it be great if you were the one person that others remarked about how you were somebody who made everybody feel like (a) somebody?

I want to go through a few ways you can start this process. It's not hard. It's simply a matter of developing a new habit – one that is others-focused and not inward-focused.

I think the world would be a better place if a few more of us would start saying nice things to other people. It is so rare nowadays for someone to give a genuine compliment. Not because they don't think about it, but because it is just not in our nature to show that type of kindness (or what I like to call Southern Hospitality). Those of us who live below the Mason Dixon line are known for our genteelness and respectable ways. Now, if we can just add that kindness to our words, we'd all be better for it.

The other side of that cordial compliment is when a compliment is given that you learn to say thank you and accept it. There is nothing worse or shows such poor manners than to degrade a compliment given by someone to you. It takes the joy out of the day, and no one should have to convince you to accept the kind words given. So, get used to saying thank you and pay forward the gift of kind words to others.

Because wouldn't be great to be known as "somebody who makes everybody feel like (a) somebody." Those words are from one of my favorite internet sensations – the Kid President.

GO WHERE YOU'RE CELEBRATED—
NOT TOLERATED

Recently, I stepped down from a leadership position that I really enjoyed. I like to be called the chairman, but the reality is I do too much. I am not great at time management, so I had to make some changes to protect what little time I have to do the things I am required to do. And in my case, the next in line for leadership was a great choice to step in and sail the ship.

It's never easy stepping away, but there comes a time when you know you should. The key is to listen to that little voice or heed the tug in your heart that the organization might be better off without you at the helm. It's hard; I know.

I am someone who likes challenging myself to see how well I do (within reason, of course). However, once I see that I am up to the challenge, it rarely holds my interest. I get bored easily and tend to wander off, looking for something else to capture my attention. I'm pretty sure that I am like half the world in that way, and the other half of the world will stay until they are asked to leave.

What I find interesting as I work with others is how full their life is with things that are not required. I agree that it is good to give back and do your part when you are able, but I wonder if you are still hanging on to the projects and organizations that have lost your heart and soul interest.

Are you filling your time to keep busy so you don't have to do the things you should be doing? You know, like your taxes, polishing your shoes, cleaning out your car, attic, garage; the answer is probably yes.

Why is it that we fill our lives with things that at one time were of great value? I think it is because many are afraid of being forgotten.

My friend gave me some advice a long time ago that I have not forgotten. She said, "Go where you're celebrated – not tolerated."

Perceived obligations for so many of us hold us long past the due date. And just like the *best if used by* milk label, the date comes, then it's over. You might want to consider leaving.

And let me give you a few reasons why.

1. You've done your part. You've set a direction, cleaned up a mess, steadied the ship to sail to new harbors, and good for you! Now, go.

2. Others need your seat at the table so they can learn and contribute, and that will not happen if you're still sitting there. Don't make them pry your cold, clammy hands off the table and take you out to bury you. It's too bad you didn't go on your own accord.

3. The organization needs new blood and new ideas from the new people who would like your seat at the table. So, now it's time to go.

No matter how much they tell you they need you to stay, they really do want you to go. They just don't want to hurt your feelings, lose your financial support, etc.

Stepping down is never easy, and the thought of being dispensable hurts the pride, hurts the self-esteem, and hurts your heart since it was something you once loved (and maybe still do), but it is sometimes necessary for you to move in a new direction.

I hope you understand the concept of go where you're celebrated – not tolerated.

I'm not saying that tomorrow you cancel your membership in all your charitable or service organizations, but this year, why don't you consider stepping away from a few of the places that you spend large amounts of time? Nothing makes a heart grow fonder than when you reappear in a year or two (if you still have an interest), and then you can see the results of your years of hard work that built an organization to its prime.

It is always hard to know when to step away, so here are a few ideas for when you should. I worked in the political realm, and there is nothing worse than a politician who keeps the job but stops listening to their constituents and taking their concerns to heart; if that's the case, it's time to go. In business, many want to keep the job because it makes them feel important, even though they no longer contribute but hold a space; if that's the case, it's time to go. Or how about a coach who is no longer interested in learning new play or new ideas on training, focus, and health? If that's the case, it's time to go!

The one I hear the most is that family members are resentful because of the perceived duty of a parent to an outside organization trumped family and friends. If that's the case, it's time to go.

Nothing is as sad as to see people hanging on to power that was lost long ago.

I'll never forget a situation I saw unfold on a national scale where a lady built a recognized political organization, but as she got older, it began to decline. She refused to understand the needs of the audience and keep up with the times, and then she had a stroke and guilted her board into allowing her to stay. Now, the organization is in shambles, and those who finally moved her out are not able to pick up the pieces of what was once a marvelous organization – all because she would not let go. So, the organization she built, she killed. That's a very sad state of affairs.

I could go on and on about once-great organizations that are now nothing or are so damaged because leadership would not let go. The truth of go where you're celebrated – not tolerated did not win out. The flame died, the people left, and all that was good is now gone.

How about you? Are you hanging on in hopes of being remembered or thought of kindly? If you overstay your welcome, that is the last thing people will remember about you.

Let me talk to you directly and move this to your personal life. Do your friends celebrate you or tolerate you? Does the person you're dating or even married to celebrate you or tolerate you because they don't want to be alone? Do your work colleagues celebrate you or tolerate you because they have to at least until you retire?

It's hard to reconcile, but you know in your heart the answers to these questions, so now the question is, what you will do about it?

If you've listened to my show for a time, you know that I say to move on and find those who will care for you, to leave and find someone who will love you or be strong enough to live your life to its fullest even if that means doing it alone. I subscribe to the thought that if you keep doing the same thing and expect different results, then it's not going to happen no matter how hard you hope. That's why I believe that you and I should go where you're celebrated – not tolerated.

I looked up the word tolerate, and here is what I found:

- Endure something: to withstand the unpleasant effects of something.

Now compare that to celebrate, which means:

- Show happiness at something: to show happiness that something good or special has happened by doing such things as eating and drinking together or playing music.

Take some time to figure out who celebrates you, who shows happiness that you are you. It is important that you and go where you're celebrated – not tolerated.

LIFE IS AN ECHO

I saw a poster the other day that said, *Life is an echo. What you send out comes back.* What you sow, you reap. What you give, you get. What you see in others exists in you. Do not judge, so you will not be judged. Radiate and give love, and love comes back to you.

Life is an echo; I never thought about it that way. It seems to me that most of the time, when I do something, I assume it dissipates. I don't expect it to stay around to be repeatedly recalled back to me like an echo down a mountain path. A few times, when I was growing up, due to the location, I was at a place where an echo could be heard. It's an odd sensation to hear your voice resonate down a canyon.

It seems when we speak, most of us assume our words go away into the air never to be heard again. They seem to dissipate or fall on deaf ears.

We do good deeds, and someone says thank you, and then it's over. It is not often that we expect to *reap what we sow.* Life's disappointments seem to cloud out that option.

We give to our church, our school, and our community and receive a nice thank you note or a tax write-off, but most of us do not expect anything big in return, and I doubt many truly believe that the measure of what one gives they receive in return.

When it comes to the thought that *what I see in others exists in me,* I hope only the good is what exists in me and nothing else.

About the only thing on the poster that I knew for certain was if you give love to family, friends, and others, you have a good chance of feeling a sense of love returned.

The poster affected me because it seems true for today's standards. If everything I do is mirrored in a way that reflects who I am and what I do or what I believe in – yikes! That's an eye-opener I was not expecting.

How about you? If your life is an echo, what are you hearing? What are you sending out that comes back to you?

I spend a lot of time talking about, thinking about, and reflecting on words: why they matter, how they have meaning, etc. We need to be careful about what we say because if life is an echo and comes back to us, it might hurt us to hear what we said. I used this quote a while back: "Be sure you taste your words before you spit them out." And on a gentler note, "Kind words can be short and easy to speak, but their echoes are truly endless." Friends, what are you sending out that is coming back that reflects you – the real you?

So many people think they can say whatever they want because it's their right or they have freedom of speech and are entitled to their opinion. Although that is all true, as you well know, the world doesn't work that way anymore. If you say it, it will echo back, or someone will echo back at you with your words.

I see this in politics and business and the church, from our leaders and those who would like to be. For some reason, they don't think that what they say will be an echo back that will be repeated and remembered and posted on Facebook and Twitter or other social media sites. Why anyone would think that is beyond me when we have so many ways to capture the spoken word and replay it until one is ground into dust.

Friends, we have a responsibility to guard what we send out because it will come back to us and reflect how others see us. Like looking in a mirror, we should want our reflection to show our true heart, our true meaning, our true desire, or, better stated, our truth and not what others interpret our truth to be.

If life is an echo, let's think about what we sow in comparison to what we reap. I know that if you sow discord, you'll reap heartache, but if you sow kindness, you will reap joy.

Think about how this works in life. You and I know good-hearted people who have sown kindness in word and deed, and now at the end of their days, they are sought out and heralded for their wisdom and kindness. Compare that to those who finagled the company's books to only benefit themselves and a few of their cronies before the organization fell; no one is reaching out to them unless it is through their lawyer.

Do not think for one minute that you can sow lies, hate, stealing, or revenge without it coming back to you or your family. If you have found yourself in this predicament, make it right while you can because there will come a time when you can't, and the world will be told about your sowing and reaping.

The same is true with the idea of what you give, you get. What do you give to others? Are you generous with your time, your talent, and your money? I know that there are only so many hours in a day, so giving away too much of your day will not serve you well in any area, but what about what you *can* give? Are you willing, or are you holding back because you just don't want to? I fully understand that we can only give so much before the well runs dry, but please hear me. I believe you have a responsibility to refresh *yourself* and give back what you can because others might need what you can provide.

Have you ever found yourself not liking someone and yet you can't put your finger on why until someone else says, "Oh, you're just like so and so," and then it hits you that you both have the same quirky qualities. (Yours aren't that bad, of course.) But what a rude awakening it can be to see ourselves reflected back to us. If what you see in others exists in you, it should give you pause for reflection because if you don't like what you see, only you can make that change for the better.

I'm not going to spend time talking about not judging others since we all do it even though we say we don't, and we know deep in our hearts that we should not. I believe that if we saw everyone as our grandmother, grandfather, mother, father, sister, brother, cousin, uncle, aunt, or friend, our world would be a very different place. We could put the human back into humanity, and wouldn't that be good for all of us?

Finally, radiate and give love, and love comes back to you. Now, this is one we all know is true, but what are you going to do about it? Are you going to give of yourself for others? Are you going to empty yourself for others who you claim to love and care for, respect, and admire? I hope so. When that happens, love truly does come back to you. Love in its purest form comes back to you, and that is an echo I think we'd all love to hear.

Life is an echo; it all comes back—the good, the bad, the false, and the true. So, give the world the best you have, and the best will come back to you.

There is a story about a man and his son who were walking in the forest. Suddenly, the boy trips, and feeling a sharp pain, he screams, "Ahhhhh!" Surprised, he hears a voice coming from the mountain: "Ahhhhh!" Filled with curiosity, he screams, "Who are you?" but the only answer he receives is, "Who are you?"

This makes him angry, so he screams, "You are a coward!" And the voice answers, "You are a coward!"

He looks at his father and asks, "Dad, what is going on?"

"Son," the man replies, "Pay attention!"

Then he screams, "I admire you!" The voice answers, "I admire you!"

The father shouts, "You are wonderful!" And the voice answers, "You are wonderful!"

The boy is surprised but still can't understand what is going on. The father explains, "People call this 'ECHO,' but truly it is 'LIFE!' Life always gives you back what you give out! Life is a mirror that reflects your actions. If you want more love, give more love! If you want more kindness, give more kindness! If you want understanding and respect, give understanding and respect! If you want people to be patient and respectful to you, give patience and respect! This rule of nature applies to every aspect of our lives."

Life always gives you back what you give out. Your life is not a coincidence, but a mirror of your own doings. *(Author Unknown)*

DO WHAT LIES CLEARLY AT HAND

What do you do when you don't know what to do? That is a question that has come up a lot lately with some projects I am working on. Sometimes, despite my best intentions, I look down the path of life and wonder, what do I do next?

I am sure it is an issue that many face because in our world of plenty, we have many great choices. And sometimes, there are more ways than one to get to the finish line. But how do you know what road to take? And what measurements should one use to make sure they're doing the right thing and the best thing for their purpose?

What I have found is similar to my thought for today. Whenever I don't know what to do, I try to do what comes next.

What comes next in a moderately logical order helps move me to the next goal, the next job, or the next project.

Instead of stopping, because stopping doesn't get you anywhere but stuck, you have to take a leap of faith, a walk of courage, or a run to the finish line; you must push through.

Lately, I have been reading a little devotional book that was sent to me by a friend. In the book, I came across this quote from Sir William Osler: "Our main business is not to see what lies dimly at a distance, but to do what lies clearly at hand."

I think we can get discouraged; even though we can see a light at the end of the tunnel, the end seems so far away. Instead of becoming discouraged, let's turn our fear into courage and do what clearly lies at hand.

When you don't know what to do, you have a few choices: you can stop, you can redirect, or you can move in the direction that you feel led.

Stopping seems to be the most common of all the options. I cannot begin to tell you about all the people I meet when I am out speaking who come up to me to talk about the next steps for their life and when I ask, "What are you doing now to move you to where you'd like to go?"

They look at me and usually reply, "Well, I don't know what to do, so I'm just waiting."

"Waiting for what?" I ask.

"You know...waiting."

"Waiting for your knight in shining armor? Waiting to win the lottery? Waiting to get the call from who knows who? Really, what are you waiting for?"

Unfortunately, most don't know who or what they're waiting for. They're just waiting. They're waiting for someone to show the way, waiting for someone else to do the work, waiting for someone to make their life complete.

I understand that we feel safe when we wait for something to happen, a chance opening, a call to come, an opportunity to present itself, but when we stop for any great length of time, it might signal to our self that we have given up, we've grown weary, or we've accepted the idea of failure. When that happens, I find it fascinating that the short rest along the path now has become a stopping point—the end; it is finished.

At times in life, you do have to stop. If you're heading in the wrong direction, stop and get back on the right path. If you find yourself careening to the edge of the cliff, stop and hold on. If your life is dangerously close to ending, by all means, stop and breathe and get help to get back on track.

There is no shame in stopping unless it would cause great harm to you or others.

Instead of stopping, perhaps, you can redirect your walk to set you on another path for success, and if you can, then by all means, let's take the other path.

Please don't be discouraged if others question your choices in life. They don't know what you're going through. They don't know your calling. I doubt they know the reasons you have for your detour, but as long as you are continuing to move down the path for your success, I encourage you to keep going.

Many of us grew up hearing the poem *The Road Not Taken* by Robert Frost

"Two roads diverged in a yellow wood,
And sorry I could not travel both..."

Sometimes in life, you have to redirect or take the road less traveled to reach your calling, your destination, and your future.

One of the reasons the quote "Our main business is not to see what lies dimly at a distance, but to do what lies clearly at hand," caught my attention is that too many times, I see people of goodwill simply get stuck staring down a darkened track hoping to make sense of the darkness instead of turning around and looking at the light that lies clearly at hand.

For you to be able to do that, you must move in the direction that you feel led.

I like to believe that most of us have an internal compass that knows the way to true north. I know you probably hear that phrase true north a lot, but do you know its meaning? Here is what I found; true north refers to a point on the earth that remains stationary, for all practical purposes. By using the North Star as a reference, one can always tell the direction of true north and by measuring the angle of the star from the horizon, determine their latitude. The North Star is the last star in the handle of the Little Dipper.

Hence the metaphor: In life's journey, we are often uncertain where we stand, where we are going, and what the right path is for us. Knowing our true north enables us to follow the right path.

Or stated for my purpose today, move in the direction that you feel internally led.

I believe each of us, when we strip away all the expectations of others and stand alone in the light, will find and see and make a decision to follow (or not) our true direction. If you are healthy enough to understand that you have been put on this earth for a purpose, you should know instinctively that you have worth, you have value, and you have significance

As a person of faith, I believe that our Heavenly Father knew us before we were born, and if He knew us, then rest assured that He knows you now, and He knows where you are going.

You have choices: you can stop, you can redirect, or you can move in the direction that you feel led. Choose wisely; your future depends on it.

The Road Not Taken
by Robert Frost

Two roads diverged in a yellow wood,
And sorry I could not travel both
And be one traveler, long I stood
And looked down one as far as I could
To where it bent in the undergrowth;
Then took the other, as just as fair,
And having perhaps the better claim
Because it was grassy and wanted wear,
Though as for that the passing there
Had worn them really about the same,
And both that morning equally lay
In leaves no step had trodden black.
Oh, I kept the first for another day!
Yet knowing how way leads on to way
I doubted if I should ever come back.
I shall be telling this with a sigh
Somewhere ages and ages hence:
Two roads diverged in a wood, and I,
I took the one less traveled by,
And that has made all the difference.

Here are some other things about true north I came across. True north is a navigational term referring to the direction of the North Pole relative to the navigator's position. True north differs from magnetic north, which varies from place to place and over time due to local magnetic anomalies. A magnetic compass almost never shows true north.

The direction of true north is marked in the skies by the celestial North Pole. True north is the direction towards the actual geographical North Pole, the axis that the world revolves around.

True north also happens to be within about one degree of the position below the North Star, or Polaris. And you'll remember from science class that the "little dipper" where we find the North Star is called Ursa Minor. Also known as the Little Bear, it is a constellation in the northern sky. Like the Great Bear, the tail of the Little Bear may also be seen as the handle of a ladle, hence the name **Little Dipper**. It was one of the 48 constellations listed by the 2nd-century astronomer Ptolemy and remains one of the 88 modern constellations. Ursa Minor is notable as the location of the north celestial pole. However, this will change after some centuries due to the precession of the equinoxes, which is a gravity-induced, slow, and continuous change in the orientation of an astronomical body's rotational axis.

So, from any point in the northern hemisphere, if you look towards the North Star, you are looking true north.

And now, you know.

TODAY IS A NEW DAY

"Today is a new day. You will get out of it just what you put into it...If you have made mistakes, even serious mistakes, there is always another chance for you. And supposing you have tried and failed again and again, you may have a fresh start any moment you choose, for this thing that we call failure is not the falling down, but the staying down."

—Mary Pickford, actress

I like the thought for today. Maybe it's because I just got off the road speaking to a group, and in the course of my travels, I heard once again about how failing in the past is messing up the future. And I completely disagree!

We've all made mistakes in our past, but remember, that was the past. Since we're not living in the past, you've got to look to the future. Remember the quote, "You can't start the next chapter of your life if you keep rereading the last one."

Mary Pickford has it right. If you have made mistakes, even serious mistakes, there is always another chance for you.

I've heard the most amazing stories of human frailties that have wrecked lives, and yet (as I remind them), they are still here. Mistakes – even serious mistakes – can be pushed past if you're willing to do the work. I encourage you to buckle down and push hard because there is always another chance for you if you're willing to let go of pride, hurt, and anger and move forward.

The pride is usually self-pride. You can't believe that you did something so stupid to mess up your life. You can't believe you messed up so much and survived. But you did so now what are you going to do? Sit around and wallow in your self-pity? I hope not. It's awful to watch and worse to listen to.

Hurt is a hard one, especially when you occasionally see the person or people you hurt. No amount of sorry can move past some of the mistakes we've made. The hardest person to forgive is yourself, and once you've done that and then moved forward to ask forgiveness of others, you're done – even if they don't forgive you. If you've acknowledged your mistake and said you're sorry, you are done. Stop replaying, stop rehashing, stop reliving the error of your ways; it will drive you to depression or anger that will not be quelled.

They may want you to continue to hurt because it's a badge of honor for their sorry life, and frankly, they like to hurt, which is weird in my book. It gives them something to talk about at prayer meetings. But once honest forgiveness is asked, you're done, and they can deal with their anger their way. You walk away and send blessings and kind thoughts back to them.

Anger is a tough one. For the life of me, I don't understand why everyone is so angry. Most people don't know why they're angry, but they are. For many (who don't want to admit it), they are angry because they think someone else got a better deal, a bigger break, an opportunity that they should have gotten, etc. Well, I hate to break to them, but life doesn't work that way.

I have a great quote on my board: "Jealousy is all the fun you think they had." You've created in your head a scenario that is probably so far from the truth that even you can't admit it. So, cool down, friend. No one likes to hang around angry people. Besides, it's not good for your heart, your soul, or your mind.

I like Mary Pickford's next line: "And supposing you have tried and failed again and again, you may have a fresh start any moment you choose."

Imagine that you can have a fresh start any moment you choose. It doesn't matter where you have been; it only matters where you're going. I know the briars of your past want to cling to your present but pluck them off and toss them away.

When I was a kid, there were blackberry bushes all along the mountain path where we use to play, and the lure and desire of the big deep purple berries were more than the pain of gently picking up the prickly stem and bending under and reaching for the fruit. Nothing was harder than trying to figure out how I ended up in the middle of the briar patch and having to crawl out to avoid being scarred for life in search of blackberries.

The scratches and stains would last a while, but once I was home and showered, my fresh start appeared with only a few reminders of my time in briars, and it's the same for you.

You can have a fresh start because you are ultimately in control of your thoughts. When you think about it, the one thing you can control in this life is your thoughts. That is why it is so important that you (and I) focus on the positive – the good, the right – not the dark, the deep, or the angry.

You can have a fresh start any moment you choose. *You choose.* You decide for your life. Don't look to others to make you whole. Decide today to be different because even though you have tried and failed again and again, failing doesn't make you a failure. Staying down does.

Failure is not the falling down, but the staying down.

And staying down is a choice you make every day when you dwell on something you cannot change.

Do we wish we had done better, not made that mistake, or had taken a different path? Sure. But wishing and hoping and dwelling isn't going to change a thing (well, except for your state of mind), which is why I am talking to you today to encourage you to let it go and get going.

My message today is to get up and get going because time is precious, and every minute, every hour, every day, every month, and every year that you waste, you cannot get back.

And let me remind you that in those years of wasted time, your world will change, your kids will grow up, your loved ones will die, your job will change, your finances will be different, your body will break down, and your days will be different, so think long and hard about what you're doing today and if it is what you want to remember for your tomorrow.

Today is a new day. You will get out of it what you put into it.

Here in the South, we're finally seeing the signs of spring – a new beginning. The winter is past; the cold nights are only a memory. The sun shines brighter and earlier in the morning, and the birds awaken us with the call as the day beckons us to get started.

Today is a new day. You will get out of it exactly what you put into it. If you have made mistakes, there is always another chance for you. And even if you have tried and failed again and again, you can have a fresh start any moment you choose, for this thing that we call failure is not the falling down, but the staying down.

Today is a new day. So, wherever you are today, take a minute to think about this new day. It's an opportunity to make a meaningful contribution to those you love and to yourself.

DREAMS ARE FREE

I have had a lot of great opportunities, but one of the ones I'm privileged to be a part of is I am a TEDx speaker coach.

TED (Technology, Entertainment, and Design) is a nonprofit devoted to spreading ideas, usually in the form of short, powerful talks (18 minutes or less). TED began in 1984 as a conference where Technology, Entertainment, and Design converged, and today, their conferences cover almost all topics, from science to business to global issues, and are in more than 100 languages. There are also independently run TEDx events in many local communities.

The Mission of TED is to spread ideas from every discipline and culture to seek a deeper understanding of the world. They believe passionately in the power of ideas to change attitudes, lives, and, ultimately, the world. On TED.com, they are building a clearinghouse of free knowledge from the world's most inspired thinkers and a community of curious souls to engage with ideas and each other, both online and at TED and TEDx events around the world, all year long.

For a number of years, every Sunday, it was my practice to choose and watch five TED talks on subjects I knew little to nothing about. It was a great, free way for me to educate myself on topics that I never had thought about, and in the comfort of my living room.

Recently, we hosted TEDx Greenville here in my hometown, and I was the speaker coach for the presenters. I had such a grand time with these amazing folks. This year, we had a presenter who is an

179

artist, but she uses more than a brush or paint; she engages people into her art, and her TED talk was "Dream for Free."

In her presentation, she collects dreams from people in exchange for a lottery ticket. For every ticket that she distributes, she asks the recipient to write down his or her desires for what they would do if they won. For each presentation, she purchases 50 tickets and gives them to people she meets in public places such as city streets, restaurants, convenience stores, transportation centers, festivals, parks, and laundromats. She says on her website that she understands that the lottery is a complex social issue, but she is using these tickets to encourage people to dream big – bigger than they would if she were to give away dollar bills.

What I love about her site is that she posts actual handwritten dreams of those who have taken her up on her offer of a dream for free.

Let me share just a few with you.

- One person wrote they would finally get the dental care they needed

- Many offered to take care of their parents' home, car, or buy them a new stove

- Some would start a nonprofit

- Most would travel

- Open a business or music studio

- Most would pay off student loans, family debt, and debts of friends

- Some would save for their future

- Many would give to charities like diabetes, heart health, or open a free healthcare clinic for the uninsured, donate money to HIV/AIDs

- Some offered to adopt children so they could have a home

- Some simply wrote *help the poor*

And then there were those who dreamed big:

- Buy an island

- Go to Jamaica

- Hire a polka band

- Build a roller coaster between their favorite coffee shop, house, and their favorite bar...

Yes, dreams are for free!

What is your dream? I know that life gets in the way, and many of us put our dreams on hold until we have more money, the kids are grown, the job is finished, etc. But if you had the chance to take a few minutes and dream, what is it that you would hope for? What would you like to do? Where would you like to go?

I like to think in a hopeful way, and to do that, many times, I have to get out of my own way and let my imagination flow, to step back a minute, and just go with it as I dream...or daydream, in my case.

I have been blessed to have several dreams come true. I've had a travel bucket list for as long as I can remember, and in the past few years, I have been able to go to some of those "dream places."

I always wanted to go to Russia, and I was able to stand and behold St. Basil's Cathedral in Kremlin Square. It was a lifelong dream to walk into the church and admire the handiwork of years ago. Then, while in Turkey, in Istanbul (my favorite city in the world), I had the good fortune to visit the Hagia Sophia. I had read a book called *Jewels* once, and the author had a ring handed down for generations made from a few stones from the mosaic in the angels' billowing robes. It seems some great uncle had swiped some stones that he shouldn't have, but now, she is the owner of the ring that set the story in place. And lo and behold, if some stones aren't missing from the angels' clothes that I saw. I had the opportunity to visit the Sultan Ahmed, or Blue Mosque, and the Spice Market, which I had dreamed of all my life. And then to the other side, I've been to the Dome of the Rock in Jerusalem, to the Wailing Wall, and I visited the hospital where I was born (and adopted from) in Beirut, Lebanon. Dreams do come true in one way or another.

I am living proof that dreams do come true and not just for travel, but opportunity, and I believe the same thing can be true for you.

And the greatest gift of all is that if you put your mind to something, somehow, things seem to fall into place.

I have found the key is simply to dream and then to put feet to those dreams and set about to make something happen.

I love the thought that dreams are free – anytime, anywhere, anyhow. You can stop and breathe and let your mind break free of the current issues at hand; you can set forth a new path.

If I were able to offer you a ticket to dream today, without thinking too hard about it, what would you dream about? What do you dream to do? What do you dream to be or have or become?

It is fun to think about. We have the freedom to wish out loud and, perhaps, put plans in place or at least prayers in place to make something happen.

I know this is a lighter thought than my usual conversations. But when I listened to the TED talk and heard about the project and the effect it has on those who, for just a minute, stop and set aside the cares of the world and simply dream, I found it to be life changing. As I go through my days with clients who are working towards a goal or are digging out from issues that have been weighing them down, we dream together of getting through or what it will be like on the other side of the issue. Then, I see real dreams come true, and their lives change.

There is a lot of work out there about dreams and how they can help many achieve things in life, great and small. Medical science proves that daydreaming or dreaming is good for your mind and body because it allows you some space to simply be.

If I were to offer you the chance to scratch off a million-dollar ticket, what would you do with the money? What is the first thing that comes to mind? What you answer says a lot about you, in a good way. It says you're open to thinking on the bright side and allows you some space to breathe and think and hope and pray.

And please note, although I do not advocate gambling, I do advocate for you the option to dream...because dreams are free, and for many, they do come true.

TAKE A CHANCE

I've seen this poster a hundred times on school bulletin boards, coffee shop info boards, and at Whole Foods on the community board. But recently, for some unknown reason, it finally caught my attention. It's an 8.5 x 11 sheet of paper, and the bottom of the sheet is clipped so you can "pull a ticket," and the headline is *Take A Chance*. Each ticket says *Chance*.

It is interesting to see how many little slips of paper hang on the sheet waiting to be taken. I guess some folks don't see it as anything they'd be willing to do – you know, take a chance – so they leave the free life-changing ticket alone. Others probably think it is just for fun and not a real idea or opportunity because who can afford to take a chance nowadays? And then, there are a few brave folks who will tear off the ticket and stare at it a while then stuff it in their pocket or purse.

I don't know about you, but I am one of those souls who will tear off a ticket every chance I get, and I put it in my pocket to remind me to step out of my comfort zone and to take a chance. What can it hurt if I hope for the best and prepare for the worst, or I hope for the best, and it doesn't come to pass? Well, maybe in some strange way, I'll come out ahead anyway. At least, that is what I'll hope for.

If I believe that good will come if I do my part, then a little slip of paper is just what the doctor ordered for me to be reminded to move in the direction of my dreams. I'll take every ticket I can and stuff them into my pockets.

In my lifetime, I've taken a few big chances in business, and so far, so good. What I learned years ago is you never know the true state of your current situation until you walk into a new place and see what could be. The old saying is true; you don't know what you don't know. But I believe that you and I need to keep looking, keep moving, and keep pushing in the directions of our dreams.

Take a chance. Why does that phrase strike terror in the hearts of so many people?

Fear has killed more dreams than failure ever has or will, and yet, we stand on the sidelines hoping, praying, wishing that someone, somewhere, somehow would take a chance and choose us, but for many, they fight the urge to take a chance on themselves or others. It's odd; isn't it?

I like the Zig Ziglar quote, "FEAR has two meanings; forget everything and run OR face everything and rise...the choice is yours."

Friends, if you want others to take a chance on you, you might have to let your guard down just a little bit and take a chance on them.

Let me touch on three areas that I believe you and I need to take another look at so we can live up to our aspiration to take a chance.

Let's start with your job. If you are sitting around hoping for another opportunity, you might have to step out of your comfort zone and take a chance to seek a new position, a new location, or a new title. I doubt anyone is going to give you something unless you ask for it and make movement in the direction of your desire.

I work as an interview coach to help people put into words the type of job, opportunities, and salary they would like to have. It sounds simple enough, but in reality, it's hard to craft a message about your worth, especially if you were brought up not to speak boastfully about yourself. But as I tell my clients, if you don't toot your own horn, there is no music.

If you dream of a different job in a different place with different people, here is the truth: You've got to step up and start the change. Being realistic about what you can afford to do (within the bounds of taking care of you and your family), you need to take a chance.

If you're a great employee, they don't want to lose you. But until you ask for something different, no one can read your mind to offer you another position, opportunity, or chance. It's your job to be bold and ask, *What is the worst thing that can happen?* Be relieved from a job you hate? Well, I hope you don't hate your job, but more importantly, I hope you find the courage to take a chance on a job, position, or opportunity you desire.

Next, let's discuss family. Together, are you having fun? As a family, do you enjoy life? Do you enjoy the company of your friends and family – in-laws and outlaws? If not, you are the only one who can change that. Now, with the caveat of your family, you might need to fall back in love again, even with your teenagers. When it comes to family, the most important chance you took is when you both said, "I do." You committed to each other 'til death do you part.

Are you happy with your family life? When I ask that question to many of my clients, it seems to cause a faraway look, like they have to think about it. And then they come back into the present, and most say yes. Sure, there are a few things they would like to change, but overall, they feel blessed, lucky, happy, and loved, and that makes all the difference. For many, they took a chance and had a family; they took a chance and adopted a child. Many took a chance and invited an elderly parent to live with them. They took chances that in the moment seemed hard, but now, it seems like life, and that is the chance they are grateful for.

I would be remiss if I didn't say that when it comes to you, be careful about the chances you take. You have responsibilities that require you to be cautious, so you don't want to make mistakes today that you'll pay for tomorrow.

Take care of your health – mental, emotional, physical, and spiritual. Take care of your body, your home, and your possessions; these are things we don't take chances on.

When I encourage you to take a chance, take a calculated chance on your success, on your growth or personal development, and on opportunities presented to you that seem wise. I know it's hard to find quiet time to think about the direction of your life, your job, and your future. But at some point, you must sit down and map out where you're going because if you don't know where you're going, any road will take you there. And the roads that you're choosing might not lead to where you want to go. You can't afford to take a chance on that.

What I believe you can take a chance on is your ability to be whatever you want to be. Take a chance and believe that you are stronger than you feel, wiser than you think, more powerful than you know, and braver than you believe.

Only you can pull a ticket. Take a chance and step into the light. I am a fan of *Britain's Got Talent.* Night after night, people of all ages step out on stage into the spotlight and sing, and the reaction of the audience is priceless as they mentally size up the person as they walk on stage and then have their perceptions dashed when a child sings like an angel or an adult sings opera like they've never heard before. Within 90 seconds, lives are changed. Dreams are either realized or dashed, but they all have one thing in common: they took a chance. They took a chance on TV to make their debut. They took a chance to be heard, seen, and respected. No matter if they win or not, in the taking of the stage to take a chance, they changed their lives forever. Why? Because at some point in their mundane life, they read the sign that said *Take a Chance,* and in an instant, they pulled the ticket.

Today is the day you set aside your fear (false expectations appearing to be real) and take a chance on love, on life, on you, and the gifts and talents that you have been given. Pull the ticket and pin it to your vision board, put it in your wallet, or leave it on your desk and be reminded to be brave, to be bold, to be who you were born to be.

LIVE IN SUCH A WAY THAT IF ANYONE SHOULD SPEAK BADLY OF YOU, NO ONE WOULD BELIEVE IT

My friends send me email jokes and cartoons all the time. I had a few friends who I had to ask to put me on the weekly list and not the daily emails. (I have no idea what they do all day to allow them to surf the web and send their network 20–30 jokes and stories all day but good for them.)

A while back, I got this one, and I liked it: "Live in such a way that if anyone should speak badly of you, no one would believe it."

Wouldn't that be great if you and I were so well known to be good people that if anyone were to say a bad word about us, no one would believe them?

I think that is a goal worth striving for, to know that our reputation is so stellar that like water off a duck's back, no one would believe we'd do a bad thing that is being said about us.

When I was thinking about this line, a few other great quotes came to mind:

- "You can't build a reputation on what you're going to do."
  – Henry Ford

- "It takes a lifetime to build a good reputation, but you can lose it in a minute." – Will Rogers

- "Kind words can be short and easy to speak, but their echoes are truly endless." – Mother Teresa

- "The end result of kindness is that it draws people to you." – Anita Roddick

- "Be it resolved…trust yourself. Create the kind of self that you will be happy to live with all your life. Make the most of yourself by fanning the tiny, inner sparks of possibility into flames of achievement." – Golda Meir

- "Speak when you're angry and you will make the best speech you will ever regret." – Ambrose Bierce

- "Who you are speaks so loudly I can't hear what you say" – Ralph Waldo Emerson

I am sure we all do our best to live a good life. I don't know about you, but as I've gotten older, I have slowed down. Now, I take my time instead of rushing.

I've worked hard to learn to listen more and talk less. I've learned to give most people the benefit of the doubt. I've gotten softer in my approach to issues than I was when I was younger. Oh, the benefits of wisdom that come with age.

I have lived a good part of my life in the public eye, so I knew early on that I needed to live, as we say in church circles, above reproach, which means that I must be blameless and conduct my affairs in a right and proper manner. And for me, it was not only the living in the bright light of public office but also for the reputation of my family and friends. No doubt, I have made some great errors and mistakes that even I look back and think, *What was I thinking?* But lately I have begun to think about the legacy I am leaving.

How about you? Putting aside your mistakes and missteps, how do you think you are being thought of or remembered? Have you thought about how you'd like to be remembered? I'm sure that as the years tick by, we all probably begin to look back as well as forward in thinking about how we're leaving a lasting legacy.

I was such a talker when I was younger, and sometimes, people ascribed to me things I did not say. When I find out that has happened, I have become bold enough to pick up the phone and ask for clarification. I often end up having to listen to the sputtering of their comment that I supposedly said.

There was a time when I would let things slide and chalk it up to their dishonesty and not let it bother me because I knew it was untrue. That is, until a dear friend told me how disappointed she was in what I had supposedly said to others about a speech she had given, which for the record, I never said. At that moment, I picked up the phone and called the rumor-starter and told her who I was sitting with and asked for an explanation of the comment that she had made. She said she thought she heard me or maybe she misunderstood and was joking. I am proud to tell you that she has never misquoted me since. And my friend apologized for not being secure enough in our friendship to know I would not have said anything unkind about her to others.

Truthfully, my feelings were hurt because I thought my actions of living in such a way that if anyone should speak badly of me, no one would believe it would have spoken for themselves. Even though we strive to live a positive life and be good people, even good friends will fail you because for some – even those know better – it is so hard to trust.

My friend and I are fine today; our friendship is stronger than ever. We were rocked by that incident years ago, and it made clear the value to both of us that living life at peace and in harmony is the best way to live.

I learned two big lessons in that uncomfortable position that I would like to share with you. The first lesson is, sometimes, when a friendship is on the line (in my case, a dear friend) or you're simply being questioned, or your reputation is being bumped up against, you have the right and responsibility to speak up and take action against those who are doing damage to you.

You cannot allow others to harm you, your friends, and your family because someone talks too much or they want to be funny and hurtful in an odd sort of way or they simply want to be the center of attention. In today's world, you need to speak up and defend your honor, your name, your family, and your friends.

The second lesson I learned very quickly that day was if it is worth fighting for, fight hard. My friend didn't expect me to pick up the phone and make the call to the offending chatterbox. Had I been in the wrong, she would have accepted my apology, and we would have been fine. But the fact is I wasn't wrong, and I didn't say anything unkind. I'm pretty sure the offender never expected me to call her out for what she had said, but I was not about to be wounded because of someone else's selfish actions.

Yes, I know today's topic is a little unusual for an encouragement for your life segment. However, if you want to be an encouragement to others, sometimes, you've got to let them know that you stand up for them, you defend them, and you're not going to allow others to tear them down.

Yes, it does sound like junior high all over again, but because everyone is so sensitive nowadays, we need to come out swinging to protect those we love and care for.

And we need to keep working on our reputations, so if anyone should speak badly of us, no one would believe it.

So, how do we work on our reputation? Here are a few rules to remember:

1. Tell the truth

2. Keep your word

3. Pay your debts

4. Be loyal

5. Show compassion

6. Put your family first (even the ones you don't like)

7. Make right things that are broken

8. Give credit where credit is due

9. Always do the right thing (even when no one is watching)

10. Be good and kind to others (including animals)

I think it is important that we "Live in such a way that if anyone should speak badly of you, no one would believe it."

THE REASON MOST PEOPLE GIVE UP IS BECAUSE THEY TEND TO LOOK AT HOW FAR THEY STILL HAVE TO GO, INSTEAD OF HOW FAR THEY HAVE COME

Today, I want to encourage you to keep on keeping on. I saw a quote recently that said, "The reason most people give up is because they tend to look at how far they still have to go, instead of how far they have come."

Isn't that so true!?

For many of us, we become discouraged at what seems to be either lack of progress or how slow the journey has been or how long it seems we've been walking towards our goal – until we look back and see just how far we've come.

Today, if you find yourself discouraged, allow me to encourage you to keep on keeping on, and let's stop and reflect on how far you've come in a relatively short amount of time. Slow and steady wins the race and keeps you focused on your goals, your dreams, and your hopes.

Every day, I see people who did not think they could survive a breakup, and yet, here they are weeks, months, and years later not only surviving but, in many cases, thriving in their personal lives. It is similar when someone loses a job and finds another, and in hindsight, they realize how quickly they have landed on their feet and how much happier they are in their new space. Or when a loved one passes, and you're not sure you can go on. Before you know it, a week, a month, or a year go by, and here you are, still standing.

I want to focus on how well so many of you are doing against all the odds because you are the ones who look down the line and see just how far you've come.

Listen, I know it is easy to get discouraged and give up. Without a doubt, it is hard out there, but for so many, you've beaten the odds and are finally on the other side. No matter what has come your way, you've held your own, you've survived, and you're still standing. You may not understand how and that's okay as long as you're standing in the light of a new day.

Look around. You're still here, and you're doing well. Maybe for some, you're doing well enough. And I think that deserves a moment of recognition for your tenacity or, as I like to say, grit.

Angela Lee Duckworth is a former 7th-grade teacher who took time off and obtained a PhD in psychology. Dr. Duckworth studied passion and perseverance for long-term goals. She studied kids and adults at West Point, the National Spelling Bee contest, new teachers, salespeople, and many others in a determination of what was the best predictor of long-term success. She wondered, why did some kids with high IQs not perform as well as kids with lower IQs?

She quickly realized that IQ wasn't the only thing separating the successful students from those who struggled. Grit mattered more than any other predictor —socioeconomic level, IQ, or talent, in later success.

Dr. Duckworth has described grit as "sticking with your future day in, day out, not just for the week, not just for the month, but for years and working really hard to make that future a reality."

People who have grit understand the reason other people give up is because they tend to look at how far they still have to go, instead of how far they have come.

I am a great believer in celebrating the small things in life. I think if you are constantly waiting to celebrate great successes, you miss out on so many small victories that can help spur you on to more success.

I was recently speaking in Massachusetts at a young women's leadership conference, and as I talk with what I consider tomorrow's leaders, I often encourage them to build their self-talk in a positive way by building on small successes. You could wake up in the morning and do what I like to do: look in the mirror and say, "Deb Sofield, you're a rock star," or "Deb Sofield, you are so funny," or smart or kind or fill in the blank with a positive self-affirming statement about your self-worth. It makes for a much better day. Hey folks, if I had to wait until I did something BIG to celebrate, I'd never get to do anything because big things are hard to come by, whereas little successes happen daily if you'll just slow down, pay attention, and be grateful.

For those who are struggling to keep going due to the magnitude of the battle or issue or family problem at hand, I encourage you not to give up. You've got to stick with your future and work hard to make that future a reality.

Quick caveat, if you've listened to my show for any amount of time, you know I am adamant that if you are in a relationship that is harmful physically, mentally, or emotionally you need to seek help and walk away. If you are being harmed, there is no shame in walking away to save yourself or your family. It has nothing to do with grit and everything to do with common sense to protect yourself.

I don't know the magnitude of the battles you're fighting, but I do know that if you walk away, you're sure to lose. But if you fight on, you never know when you might just win.

Don't get trampled down by the issues at hand; you never know when things can change in the middle of the struggle as long as you keep on keeping on and doing your part honestly and fairly.

And when it comes to family, don't worry, the kids do grow up, siblings occasionally come to see the light, and parents many times come to understand that they're not so great at decision-making since the world has changed so much.

My message is not to give up – at least not yet. Let's give it a little more time. You've come a long way from when you started, and although the journey seemed long and hopeless, many of you today are closer than you've ever been and are more hopeful than you've been in years.

With all my encouragement for today, I realize that the reason most people give up is because they tend to look at how far they still have to go instead of how far they have come. But at some point, you've got to stop and take an assessment of your progress and be encouraged that you've come this far, and if you're not encouraged yet, hang on. You will be if you keep on keeping on and traveling the road to your future.

I am glad that today we can celebrate your success. The fact is that you're still standing against every storm, but most importantly, you're still standing because you realize that sticking with your future — day in, day out, not just for the week, not just for the month, but for years — and working hard to make that future a reality is the best way to live the life you've imagined and to do what you were born to do.

YOU ARE THE MESSAGE

Recently, I was having dinner with a friend, and she and I were talking about one's life being the message they send to the world. It got me to thinking about the title of an old political book I read years ago by Roger Ailes called *You Are the Message.*

For those considering a life in public office, the book was a good reminder that every deed, every word, and every action reflects who we are and how others would see us.

You are the message. What does that mean, exactly? It means that when you communicate with someone, it's not just the words you choose to send to the other person that make up the message. You're also sending signals about what kind of person you are.

You are the message comes down to the fact that unless you identify yourself as a walking, talking message, you miss that critical point. The words themselves are meaningless unless the rest of you is in synchronization. The total *you* affects how others think of and respond to you.

This book was one of the first books I read when I was younger that brought into the light the idea that how you live your life, the words you use, and the body language you display is the message you send to the world. For a kid of fourteen, that was a big deal because I did not hear that type of message from my peer group or my teachers; the only ones who reminded me of my responsibility to others were my parents.

What I find interesting as a coach and trainer both in the political and corporate world is, often, I watch my clients from the sidelines. I observe how they "show up in the world" in which they hope to master. If you are the message, then you and I need to seriously think about the message we are giving to others.

I started my radio show last year with a lot of rules for public speaking because that is my love, and I see how success in that field can change a life, a career, and a direction for those who master the skills. But over time, it became clear to me that although many appreciated the information, what they really wanted was a reminder that they are amazing, they have done good things in your life, and for that, they should be celebrated.

I also realized that until others knew, believed, or were cajoled into understanding that they are fearfully and wonderfully made, that they are unique in the world, and that there is no one like them, they have a hard time believing that they are put here for a reason. And until we understand why, we will never fully comprehend the concept that we are the message.

Think about it. What messages are you sending to your family, your friends, your colleagues, or those you interact with on a daily, weekly, monthly basis?

For some, you're not sending a good message because your message is not defined. Your message is diluted, and your message has become dull.

I worry when a message is not defined because it's easy to become sloppy in your work, undisciplined in your habits, and unprepared for your future. But the worst part is that your message is confusing to others because we judge you by your actions, which speak louder than any words you'll use.

You're being watched and graded and judged; it is what it is. I know it is not fair, but what are you going to do about it? I encourage you to think about what message you are sending to the world.

To get on a right path for success, you have to commit to doing the hard work (and yes, it is always hard work until you get into a groove) because when you are not committed to your calling, you'll be sloppy in your work and all over the board with ideas that don't work, and jobs that don't pan out, and you'll miss opportunities because you've not defined your hope for your outcome. That's a recipe for failure!

When your message is not defined, it is easy to be undisciplined in your habits because you have not set parameters to meet and exceed expectations in your life. It is hard to count on someone who is undisciplined because we never know if you're going to show up and deliver. People who are undisciplined in their habits rarely do a good job twice. Oh, maybe you'll get by one time, but you'll not be consistent enough to maintain a following or measure up to standards set by those who need you or your services.

And when you haven't defined your calling, you could be limiting your future. There was a time when teaching public speaking got tiresome for me because I felt I was beating my head against a wall when company after company told me that computers were the way of the future and no one needed to learn public speaking skills. Had I given up or changed my direction, I probably would not be doing my life's work today. I was definitive in my goals to define my future.

For others, your message is diluted because you do too much. Friend, stop all your multitasking and do one job well and then another and another; otherwise, the old line is true in your life that you are the jack of all trades and master of none. Your message is diluted because you're leaving pieces everywhere and nothing makes up the whole, and that cannot be working out well for you. You might need to stop and get help in writing up a plan and stick to it day in and day out until you succeed.

I learned early on that I needed to stick with what I do best and what pays the bills even when my fleeting interest was elsewhere. And when I am financially secure, then I can go and try other things to see if my passion meets my paycheck. I cannot allow my message to be diluted, or I will lose my path forward.

But my greatest concern is that for many, their message is dull because they have lost their passion for life.

I see people every day who, by not having a plan in place or a map to follow or a reason to be, become absent in their lives. Over time, you do the same thing every day and every night. It's like you're running in place. You're going through the motions, but no life is being lived; the lights are on, but no one is home.

Come on, your message should not be dull! Your life should not be limited! You can go and do and be whatever you want, so why are you living a lifeless life? And why are you not doing something about it? Dear friend, step up and get going. I know you've hit a hard patch in your life, but it will pass. Look at all the time you've lost waiting for who knows what. I know that you are or have been struggling with loss but believe it or not, time will heal the wounds, and memories will grow more beautiful. I understand that physical pain is more than you can bear some days, but that should not keep you from doing the things you've dreamed of. I worry when I see good people who've grown dull because of the things that life has thrown their way; instead of throwing it back, they've allowed it to crush their spirit. What message is that sending to the world, to your loved ones, and to yourself?

You are the message. Every deed, every word, and every action reflects who you are and how others will see you.

Let's be amazing.

LISTEN AND SILENT ARE SPELLED
WITH THE SAME LETTERS

I find great joy every Sunday morning in listening to the *New York Times* crossword puzzle editor and NPR's puzzle master Will Shortz. Will is an American puzzle creator and editor, and I think it is fascinating that he is the only person known to hold a college degree in enigmatology, which is the study of puzzles. Who knew you could go to college for that?

I play along when he presents the on-air quiz to one lucky contestant and then gives a challenge for those of us listening at home. Sometimes, I can figure out the puzzle, and sometimes I have no clue what the puzzle answer will be, and that's when I'm glad that the NPR host helps the hapless player who is connected to the show by phone. A few weeks ago, on the show, Will did a series of anagrams.

An anagram is when you rearrange letters to make different words, using the same letters. So, the definition of the word anagram *(n.): a word, phrase, or sentence formed from another by rearranging its letters: "Angel" is an anagram of "glean."*

When I was thinking about my show this week and what I wanted to work on, the word that kept coming to mind was listen, and then it hit me that listen and silent are an anagram; they have the same letters, but create different words, and what is interesting is that these two words (in my opinion) have the same value when it comes to their true meaning.

Alfred Brendel has a famous poster that says, "Listen and Silent are spelled with the same letters – coincidence? I don't think so."

I find it interesting that those two words are so closely aligned, and when I came across this quote from Rachel Naomi Remen, it hit home for me. She says this:

> *"The most basic and powerful way to connect to another person is to listen. Just listen. Perhaps the most important thing we ever give each other is our attention... A loving silence often has far more power to heal and to connect than the most well-intentioned words."*

The power of listening is probably one of the most underrated skills we learn as kids. Everyone wants to talk and be heard, but it seems to me that so few know how to be silent and listen.

I love the quote that says, "Most people do not listen with the intent to understand. They listen with the intent to reply."

Trust me, I'm talking to myself today as well as to you because I think listening is a skill that we can all brush up on at any age in life, and then, we can give the gift of loving silence to others.

It seems so simple to stop and listen, but we know that it is not something most of us do well, so when you start listening and slow down on your constant chatter to your spouse, friends, and family, they are not going to know what to do. In fact, they might look at you like something is wrong and even question your motives. You must be ready to explain that you are working on your listening skills and you want to understand all the information that they are giving. It will take a few times for your spouse or friends to become comfortable with your new actions, but don't worry; over time, they will come to appreciate the fact you're trying to be a better listener, friend, and confidant.

We all know that listening is important; that's a given (even though we don't do it or don't do it well), but let me give you three reasons why I think we all need to get to work on this wonderful and simple gift we can give to others.

- People need to know that their words matter

- People need to know that you listen, and you hear them

- People need to be assured that you're listening without judgment

Let me take them in that order.

People need to know that their words matter.

Every time I pick up a magazine, it seems the topic these days is about building stronger relationships in life, work, or family. When you and I are silent and allow someone to have their say, and we listen to them until they are done talking, it gives them a sense of completion.

Your gift of silence and allowing them to speak will, for the most part, settle a place in their soul because it is obvious to them that their words matter. So, in turn, they matter, and isn't that what everyone is searching for? Reassurance that they matter.

When someone speaks to you on a personal level, they need to feel that you care for them and that you care enough to value their words, which, in turn, for many equals you valuing their feelings, their emotions, and their life.

Sometimes, people just want to be heard, and they struggle to get the right words out to express their truth. You know how frustrating it is when you want to say something and the words don't come, or you can't think of the right word to use, but if you'll just slow down and allow the brain to catch up with the mouth, the right words will come and what needs to be said will be. Friends, remember, most people simply want to know that they matter, and they express that need by the words they use. And then they wait for us to either accept or reject them by our use of words. We can, in a word, dismiss their feelings, belittle their emotion, or devalue their worth if we're not careful to understand that what they need from us is to know that their words matter.

People need to know that you listen, and you hear them.

I speak a lot on the value of your words because I see from my work that it is important for people to know that they are heard above the noise of life. You give a great gift when you are silent and allow others to speak and be heard. And I say that because I hear a lot of people talking, yet no one is listening, and what we need to do is combine the two so that we speak and are heard. And if you were to ask me, I believe this issue of people not listening is what causes some of the greatest anger that we see and hear nowadays in the media, at work, and in our own families.

It is important that we stop and pay attention to others when they speak, and when they know that you're listening and that you hear every word they say, you give them a sense of self-worth. By doing that one simple action, you're giving that person a voice and showing them that you listen and hear them, and that simple act will have a long-lasting impact on them.

It is not a far stretch to think that others just want to be heard. Really, don't we all? My guest a week ago said that his phrase of the week was *seek to understand.* I have thought about that since he mentioned it, because that simple action could change everything, and, in its simplicity, it proves value and provides a sense of worth and place when we seek to understand. By doing so, it becomes apparent that we are listening and that we hear what is being said.

Perhaps, the hardest part of listening is to do so without judgment.

Marc Chernoff says, "Most people don't need your advice, they need your time and positive reinforcements. What they want to know is often already somewhere inside of them. They just need time to think, be and breathe, and continue to explore the undirected journeys that will eventually help them find their direction."

We're a nation addicted to advice; we like to give it and get it. Turn on your TV most afternoons and someone is doling out advice on life, love, happiness, weight loss, kids, in-laws, and pets. And although that makes for entertaining TV, it doesn't work in real life. I wonder if we stopped to see the needs of our friends and family and co-workers, could we stop and just listen (without judgment) and allow them to find their way forward with us quietly or even silently encouraging them onward?

There is nothing more damaging than to rush to judgment when all someone needed or wanted or hoped for was a little space of silence to find their voice, to hear it clearly, as they work out their plan for their life at that moment.

If we did our part of listening without judgment and allow others to "talk it out," I think we'd be the blessing that so many need today because, in the comfort of friends and the safety of companionship, the respect we give others will let those we love to know that their words matter, that we are listening, and we hear them without judgment.

FAN THE FLAME

Because I am a speaker, I have the opportunity to travel around the world, teaching public speaking, presentation, and media skills to elected officials or those who would like to be. When I was speaking in the Middle East a while back, I was training some dynamic up-and-coming young women who were seeking a seat on their local council, and one day at lunch, I noticed that one of the ladies was reading a book of poetry by Rumi, a Persian poet and philosopher.

It struck me as unusual that someone would be carrying around a book of ancient poetry, and, so, being a good visitor, friend, and teacher, I asked about her book and what she was learning. The reply was simple: "Well, Ms. Deb, for me to grow beyond myself, I need to know what others say and think and then decide for myself if their words are good for my soul." *Hmmm,* I thought, *that's pretty profound for a young lady who is looking to make her mark in the world.*

And then she went on to extol the words of the ancient sage and encouraged me to learn about him and to discover the wisdom of the ages. So, I have, and in my study, I have come across quite a few reflective sayings that I have grown to appreciate. One is my topic for today, and it is from Rumi, who said, "Set your life on fire, seek those who fan your flames."

There is so much in that simple phrase. I could talk for days about the truth that lies within.

But, in our time together, let's talk about you and those you associate with who should be fanning your flame for success.

As a coach, I see a lot of people who, at one point in their lives, set their hopes and dreams on fire and were supported by friends and family and co-workers to succeed. They worked very hard to make good things happen, and it was a joy to see how their success has opened doors for them to be who they were born to be and do what they were born to do. And on the other side of the coin, I see those who were on fire but did not have the support to help them push through to the end, and their flame burned out, and all that was left was a puff of smoke of what could have been an amazing life.

You know life is funny like that. You start off with such hopes and dreams, like the ones I hear from all the kids who are graduating this year. The world is their oyster, they have the world on a string, they see themselves as presidents of corporations and masters of industry, and I hope and pray that they continue to burn bright once they land their first job and begin their path to success. My hope for the kids of today is that they set their life on fire and do their heart's desire.

Now, those of us who are a little older and wiser and who remember those days of enthusiasm for life and love and opportunity, let's commit to fanning the flames of this generation, so they can achieve their dreams. Do not be the person to throw cold water on their parade. Be kind enough to let them find their way. Be strong enough to fan their flame for success. And be committed to helping them along their journey.

Many of us are doing our life's work because someone loved us enough to fan the flame once we set our lives on fire. And that's the key, because, remember, you are the only person who can set your life on fire. You have the final say on what you're going to do to change your world. You are the only one who can step into the light and shine when you let your life, hopes, and dreams catch on fire and burn bright until you reach your final destination, whatever that may be.

I am mystified when I see amazing people who set their life on fire and then partner with those who quench it. I see it all the time, and it makes me exasperated; I must admit. Whether it's someone who demands you give up your dream for theirs or someone whose heart's desire is to go into ministry, military, or missions and everyone says no, or whether someone finds great joy in working a job that does not pay well but fills their life with joy and their friends belittle their position because it is not impressive enough. No matter what it is, it is heartbreaking when I see a life on fire be drenched with cold water to douse the flame never to light again because you've partnered with those who quenched your fire.

And you know what is so sad is, when that happens, I meet empty people living hollow lives because the joy is gone; their spark has gone out. I spoke about that a few weeks ago, about people whose lives have become dull because they are just going through the motions of life with no real life being lived. The lights are on, but no one is home.

Ah, friend, that is not a way to live. You've got to figure out what it will take to strike a match to relight your fire, even if you have to do it alone. And, trust me, there are worse things than being alone, like being alone with someone. It is heartbreaking, and I see it all the time. Someone demanded that they had to marry, they had to take the job, they had to move to another place. Together but alone will kill your flame faster than any polar bear plunge ever will. Not only will you not be on fire, but they also won't help you fan your flame for success.

I'm not sure what has put your fire out, but I do know that you are the only one who can relight it. And then you need to surround yourself with friends who will fan your flames. If you stay with your loser group of friends who have no interest in helping you grow and be and become, then you've set yourself up for failure because they will never fan your flame. And good luck with relighting a flame that is constantly blown out by others.

Don't blame others when your fire is out or only flickering with no real warmth of success. Well, I guess you can blame others, but you and I know that this is a cop-out. If your fire is barely burning, only you can pour on the gas to light it up; you can't expect others to know how to help you get going when you've allowed your flame to die out. Friend, that is your responsibility, so stop blaming others. I am so worn out with all the stories of bad marriages, unkind parents, loser friends, and bad business partners, or anyone else you blame for putting out your flame. They didn't put your flame out; they just didn't fan it for your success. Be honest; you let it die out because sometimes it's easier to be average.

I know for many, at one time, friends and family did help fan the flame, but now they don't, and no one really knows why, and that's okay. It could be that their lives have taken different turns, and fanning your flame isn't a priority and, although that is disappointing, you really can't blame them since it's not their responsibility to set you on fire. You're responsible for your flame, your life, your light, and, while you've been waiting around for someone else to light your fire or fan your flame, it burned out. So, now, you have to make some choices.

My hope today is that you choose once again to set your life on fire because you have so much to offer others with your wisdom, your knowledge, and your insight and expertise. You have so much to give back that would be of much help to others if you would just recall the warmth of the flame you let die out. You have so much to teach others about living a life on fire as you fan their flame for success.

Imagine, if you reset your life on fire, you might be the guiding light to others who have lost their way. Your life on fire might be all that is needed to encourage others to do what they were born to do. Your life on fire might be the light at the end of the tunnel some people need to see to gain strength for their journey.

Your life on fire could change everything for you and others. And if you're strong enough to fan the flame for others, you might change their world, and who knows, when they catch on fire, what good they can do for others all because you lit the flame.

"YOU DON'T NEED MORE TIME; YOU JUST NEED TO DECIDE."

—Seth Godin

I don't know about you, but I always need more time, a few more hours in my day. I know we all have the same 24 hours, but, for some reason, I lose a few and end up running late or behind schedule much more than I like. And that's a problem since I have no patience for those who are chronically late. It's my pet peeve, and yet, I do it also.

I saw this statement online the other day from Seth Godin, and, in my opinion, Seth has been a great voice in the business world for common sense ideas and strategies for success. Well, Seth Godin says this, "You don't need more time; you just need to decide."

Don't you hate it when the obvious is stated? Because he's right. You know you don't need more time; you just need to decide.

The problem for so many of us is that we hate to make a decision, and we do that because we think that another opportunity might somehow, very possibly, maybe one day come up that might be better. So, we think, *Why close a door when something else might happen?* And although that sounds good, rarely does it work out that way. If it does (by some amazing feat), well, that's a long time coming, and you know it.

I would venture a guess that little to nothing else big comes along while you are waiting, and then you've missed the opportunity that was right there before you – in your grasp, in your sight, in your hands waiting to be dealt with. The quote is right; most of us just need to make a decision today and deal with the options later if they come at all.

As much as I'd like to focus on the issue of time today, I'm going to set that aside and talk about the idea of deciding, and why that is important for your success in your personal and professional life.

Years ago, I coined the phrase that "leadership is about making a decision and sticking with it." The reason I came up with that is that it has happened too many times that I am at a conference and they don't start on time because we are standing around waiting for another speaker to show up, the coffee to be delivered, or the handouts to be printed, which ultimately blows the schedule off course because the leadership of the event was not strong enough to decide to start on time.

Admittedly, there is nothing that chips me off more than people who will not decide to make something happen; I hear the excuses all the time.

They say, "I need more time to think about it." Really? Some of you have been thinking about it for years, and you still haven't decided. Or I often hear that people can't get to it right now because they are so busy doing other "important things" that keep piling up in front of the hard decision they need to make, so they don't make the time to get it done. Or my all-time favorite excuse is that they need to pray about it more. Let's be honest; some of you keep praying because you're not getting the answer you want, so let me remind you, dear friend, that if it's out of His will, it's not going to change, no matter how much time you take praying for something that is not right for you. Friend, you don't need more time, you just need to decide to trust that all things work together for good.

Another problem with not making a decision and waiting around is you never know what you've lost in the interim. At a conference, if you're not careful, the audience will leave or wander off to other events that run better and are on time. And that is unfair to the speakers who have worked hard to create an amazing presentation that now needs to be cut short to make up for the organization's disorganization that has pushed back the schedule and has everything running late.

For a job that could provide a great opportunity while you're still thinking about it, taking more time than necessary to fully vet your opportunity (because you didn't put much forethought into your future plans and where you wanted to go) means that now you're pushed to the wall to make a decision fast. And while you're hoping for a better offer, more money, or a different title, someone else will fill the space, take your job, and move into what would have been your new corner office because they made a decision to move when the opportunity presented itself.

In your personal life, some of you are running out of time with making life-changing decisions for your health. You keep gaining weight, and you're becoming depressed about your size or how bad you feel physically, emotionally, or mentally. Or maybe, you're not taking your medicine because you're being lazy about being disciplined to take it on a regular basis or not eating vegetables and drinking enough water because *5 Guys Burgers and Fries* is a whole lot better tasting than foods that are good for your body.

And for some, you need to make a decision today to honor your spouse or your kids. Time will not wait for you to say the words they need to hear – "I love you." "I'm sorry." "I'll make this right." "We'll do this together." "I value your opinion." "You mean the world to me." "You make me proud to be your father or mother." Trust me, kids need to hear your words of affirmation more than they let on, and I can pretty much guarantee your life will improve if you would say kind and loving words to your spouse. Come on, make the decision to speak up because you don't need more time to do the right thing, say the right thing, and be the right kind of person. You just need to decide to do it.

I love the power of the words *you just need to decide*. Some of you need to decide on some issues that you've put on the back burner, hoping by some miracle that it will solve itself. Come on, you know that is not going to happen. You have to decide and then stick with it if it is what is right for you or your family.

You need to pull out that issue that is weighing heavily upon you and make a list of the pros and cons. Some listening today need to slow down, sit down, and get down to work on answering the question of "What will we gain?" or "What will we lose if we go in this direction?" And I strongly encourage you to find a way to involve those who your decision will affect. I know you're the parent, boss, leader, but by bringing the team along, they will stand firm with you when the winds of adversity blow.

We all think we need more time, and sometimes we do, but make sure you ask yourself, *why?* Why do you need more time when you're pretty sure you know what the outcome will be? Why are you prolonging the pain if you know how to end the suffering? Why are you not making plans now to get things done that have been waiting for you to make a decision?

Besides the fear of failure, which nine times out of ten is not true or fatal; besides the personal issue of indecision, which at this age is ridiculous that you can't make a decision; besides the work it will take, let's think about why you are not making the decisions that you need to be making.

There is no good reason. You just need to decide. Stop being lazy. No one is going to do this for you. You need to step up and get going because time is wasting.

My final reason for you needing to get going is because you will never be this age again. You won't have the strength tomorrow you have today. Life happens, and when you pick up the pieces, you are going to wish that you had started earlier, back when you had the time, the strength, and the energy.

Friend, you don't need more time – you just need to decide. And I think this weekend would be a great time to do just that. Come on, let's get started!

BE A WEED

If you listen to my radio show, you know that little things in life make me wonder. Big things make me wonder too, like how many stars are in the universe, and what are we going to do about the trash in our oceans and overfishing by some countries? But sometimes, my mind seeks to know how little things work, like how is it that a dandelion can push its way up through asphalt, the road that my car drives on, and yet, this determined little weed can push through and sprout and grow and break the roadway seeking the light?

As I was walking around my neighborhood, I noticed a bump in the new asphalt, and a day later, the bump started to form a crack. Soon, I saw the beginnings of a small flower pushing through, breaking the asphalt – a dandelion, no less.

My curiosity got the best of me, and I went online to figure out how this is possible. And, of course, the World Wide Web gave me the answer I could not figure out on my own. Since asphalt is porous, it doesn't take much for a seed to fall into the cracks. A little dust, a little water, and soon the seed starts to form in the crack and begins to grow, reaching for the light. The main idea is not that the weed breaks through concrete or asphalt; the asphalt breaks around the weed!

Plant or weed roots will grow anywhere there is water. The edges of a concrete slab or asphalt drive are particularly attractive, as all the runoff water from the slab's surface collects there. The roots will continue to grow into any gaps beneath, exerting enough force to lift it.

Imagine lifting a piece of paper from its center; the unsupported ends will fold down. It can do this because paper is flexible. The same happens when the root lifts the asphalt, but because asphalt is brittle, the pressure will eventually cause it to shatter, creating a crack, thus the answers to my question.

I think we should learn this lesson from a weed. If you really want something to happen in your life, you need to make a way, or you need to find a place where you can grow. It may be in the cracks of your life, but friend, all you need is a foothold to plant your roots deep enough to sustain the elements.

The reality is that the little seed would not germinate if it didn't have water or dirt or sunlight to help it grow, which is why I constantly preach that you need to surround yourself with those who fan your flame, not those who blow it out. You need to look around and see who is planted deep enough to help you anchor in the hard times, but, most importantly, you need to find the strength to push through the hard times, so you can bloom against all the odds. The simple fact is this: If a weed can make it, friend, you can too.

We all need a little sunlight in our lives, and if you're not finding a place in the sun to grow and stretch and bloom where you're planted, then you need to move. No one is going to move you; no one is going to check the temperature, the weather, and the pollen count. Unfortunately, it doesn't work that way. You have to figure out how to break through, but the good news is, if you dig deep, you'll find a way. And the better news is that sometimes in the cracks of life, you'll find a sliver of dirt to replant your life to grow into the person you always knew you could be.

In the brokenness of the highway of life, you can bloom where you fall. If a little weed can break through and disrupt a highway, by pushing against the odds to the surface looking for light, food, and nourishment, I have no doubt, with the power of your mind, the strength of your character, the force of your self-determination, you can survive.

When I was at my former house, I had some plants in the back of my two-story home that were growing a little sideways. One time my yard guy was there, and I asked, "What is up with these plants which aren't growing so well?" He replied that they were stretching around to see the sun. They were never meant for the shade, and that is why they're not tall and seemed to be growing sideways. They were simply looking for the light. Wow! If that is not a metaphor for people, I don't know what is! You know, some are bent, some are a little sideways, but when they are exposed to direct sunlight, they straighten up and grow tall.

I contrast that to some indoor plants I recently had to separate, in hopes of growing them larger. My favorite peace lily seemed to be growing full, but with no flower, so last week, I hauled it out to the yard, pulled it out of its container, and gently cut it in two, where it had very strong roots. The shock of the cut and heat of the outdoors started my plants to wither, until I was able to fill the new pot with soil and then soak down leaves and roots. With its new freedom of space in the new pot, it quickly recovered. It was fascinating to see that, within a day, the plants (now I have two) both have perked up and are already starting to grow new leaves.

I find it interesting that what it needed was space and a little room to grow, to spread its roots, to rebuild a stronger, more robust plant that I'm hoping will soon have a few lilies in the leaves.

Isn't that just like life? I meet people who need to cut some old roots, to spread their leaves, and rebuild their base, and, maybe, to be replanted in a new pot with some space and new soil in which to grow and bloom.

I'm not saying that everyone needs to break out of the old container. But for some of us, it would do us some good to think seriously about removing the old negative leaves or worn-out soil or broken pots to allow ourselves the freedom to grow towards the sun and put down roots that go deep, looking for life-sustaining water. Because, if we don't, we won't blossom, and we may even rot and be good for nothing but the recycling bin.

I know that today's message is a little out of the ordinary, but I have been enamored with the little weed on my street and the old plants on my porch and new plants in my house. As I watch them grow, two against all the odds and the other two in a wonderfully welcoming place, they are all on their way to blooming where they're planted.

People tell me all the time that they don't have much in this world, and it seems like everything is hard for them. The soil is hard, the sunlight is hard to get to, and the rains don't come as much as they need or as often as they'd like, and yet, I know that with a touch of dirt, water, and sunlight, they can beat the odds and bloom, no matter who they are, what life has thrown their way, where they are in their journey, or when they were planted.

I encourage you to hang on. The days are warm and welcoming, and it doesn't get dark until later, so you have some time to rest and grow and bloom in your own way.

And for those who seem to have it all, be prepared when life decides to cut you in two to make some room for more growth or simply to add another plant to the household. Even when you're broken, be assured that you can sustain the cut, if you'll reach towards the light and dig deep to plant your new roots. Be encouraged that the sun will rise tomorrow, the warmth will dry your tears, the light will make it easier to see your path forward, and in your own new way, you, too, can bloom where you are planted.

For today, be like a weed. Go ahead and push against the asphalt, find your break in the road, unfurl your leaves, and open your petals to show your true colors. And then, bloom.

THE PAST IS A PLACE OF REFERENCE, NOT A PLACE OF RESIDENCE

I had a client tell me about a family situation that happened while she was in high school, in which, due to unforeseen circumstances and the economy, her family had to declare bankruptcy, and in the blink of an eye, their lives had changed. Although that would be traumatic for any young person, this young lady's parents held the family together, vowing to rebuild and continue to provide to the best of their ability for their kids. Instead of allowing that experience to define this amazing young woman's future, she simply used it as a place of reference in her life, and not as her residence. She picked up the pieces of her new life and put them back together again the best way she could, and from there, she graduated high school and college and went into the workforce, and a few weeks ago, that young lady was crowned in the Miss America system.

I was her interview coach, and I have watched amazing young women, like her, pursue their dream of becoming Miss America, and after my client was called to the *top 16...top 10...top 5...*the judges saw what many of us have seen in her life—a determination not to let her past define her future. This kid is going to continue to pursue the life she's worked for and imagined. This is not a young lady who was born with a silver spoon or had parents who could pay for all her gowns and shoes and interview outfits. No, this is someone who mapped out the costs, laid out a plan, and diligently pursued every aspect of what she could control and was rewarded for it. She was considered by some to be a dark horse in the pageant because she came with what she had: raw talent, great looks, and an intelligent mind, with speaking skills to match.

I want to use the idea that your past is simply a place of reference and not a place of residence in your life, if you'll make it so.

You and I know so many people who say they can't go on because of what happened in their past; it seems to be the excuse they cling to when life isn't what they say they want. You hear these people tell you all the things they can't do because of some issue in their past or present that "keeps me down." These are folks who tell you over and over that it is always someone else's fault.

You know what I have always marveled at? Many successful people I know of came from nothing, and I mean nothing. Some were orphans, others were abandoned at a young age, others didn't have shoes or a bed or a home or didn't have anyone to check up on them, and yet, at some point in their life, they figured out how to beat the odds. Oh, they remember their past, but they don't let it define them, and they certainly don't live there now.

I contrast that to others I know who were born with a platinum spoon in their mouth, who now "work" at the family business because no one in the real world would ever hire their lazy, self-absorbed, half-witted, not wanting to work self; for them, their past is a place of residence that they are unwilling to leave.

I'm sure you've seen both within your network or some version of these two types of people but let me encourage you to remind them that living in the past is not great for their future. We've all made mistakes, but that should not define who we are today, and, if it does, we need to close that door and throw away the key.

We've heard the stories of famous people who at some point in their lives were told to pack it up and go home because they would never make it, and while I am sure the cemetery is filled with almost famous people today, the world is filled with those who would not give up, no matter what they were told by others, and we re-tell their stories of success, to remind our generation and the next that opportunity is what you make of it.

You have choices; everyone does. You may not have a lot of choices, but today you made at least 100, from getting out of bed to what you ate for breakfast to what you're doing right now. And, by tonight, you'll make 100 more choices. Oh, you've got choices, it's just a matter of what you'll do with what you've got.

I have a friend (nicest guy ever) who I have watched for many years. He is not great at business. For a time, it looked like he was doing okay because he was using other people's money, but the reality is, he's a failure, and when you ask why he hasn't been as successful as others in his family, he always says stuff like, "Well, I learned from my dad, and my dad didn't teach me, and my dad this and my dad that." It is so ridiculous because 1. His father has died 2. His father was successful in business 3. He's lazy. He simply doesn't see it because he keeps busy with busywork and never gets real paying work done. And we all watch as he uses all his resources to pay others to do his work because he likes to be the boss, so he's always broke. He has gone through hundreds of thousands of dollars since he's not good at business. And now, the money has run out, and he is really in a bind. He's too old to make the money back and too tired to work the hours needed to be successful. He is so full of self-pride that he can't see he is not successful. He refuses to listen to advice and the wise counsel of others. He wanted to be his own boss because he hates being told what to do and thinks he's smarter than everyone else, and, the worst part is that he has thrown away a major part of his life by not living up to his ability, his calling, and his family legacy. He lives in the past and makes that his current residence and not his reference to learn from and go and do and be successful. All who know him say the same thing: "It's a shame he is such a failure, when he could have had it all."

How about you? Are you making excuses for why you're a failure? Yes, I said the word failure because, as hard as it is to say, I don't know any other way to describe what you're not doing with your life.

You were made for more than this. A lot of you live in America, where anything is possible if you'll apply yourself to the pursuit of success in whatever field that may be. Even if your past haunts you, your future doesn't have to be that way. Even if you come from nothing, you can create your life to be anything you want. Even if no one believes in you, remember, you were created by a loving God who knows the plans He has for you.

You have a responsibility to get going. No one is going to do it for you. Hear me, NO ONE is going to help you be outrageously successful but you. Think hard, work hard, plan wisely, and move past any issue from your past that is holding you back.

Remember my favorite lines:

- Don't let yesterday take up too much of today.

- Don't look back, you're not going that way.

- You can't start the next chapter if you keep rereading the last one.

- You can't reach for anything new if your hands are still full of yesterday's junk.

- Accept your past without regrets, handle your present with confidence, and face your future without fear.

- You can't climb the ladder if you're still clinging to the bottom rung.

Trust yourself; believe the old tried and true saying of the inspirational speaker of yesteryear, Napoleon Hill, author of *Think and Grow Rich,* a classic for those of us in the inspirational business. He was famous for saying, "Whatever the mind can conceive and believe, it can achieve."

Friends, you've got to believe, take it on faith, that if you work hard and move forward daily, one day you will look back and see just how far you've come. A few weeks ago, I did a show taking the theme that the reason most people give up is because they tend to look at how far they still have to go, instead of how far they have come.

Don't be that person that gives up. That's not who you are, and that is certainly not who you were born to be. If you use your past as a starting point for your future, you'll be okay.

Please don't give up. Please don't be discouraged by what you don't have at this moment. And please consider that you can find your path forward and walk boldly towards your reward, but you have to keep moving, keep working, and keep on keeping on because your past is simply a place of reference, and not your place of residence. You deserve better than that.

DON'T GIVE UP...UNLESS YOU SHOULD

If you're like me, you heard the phrase often repeated by your parents, that we should, "never, never, never, give up," quoting the great Winston Churchill. Well, although that sounds nice and good, the reality is that sometimes you need to give up and find something else, do something else, or be something else, especially when the direction you're going in is getting you nowhere. And the damage you are doing will last a lifetime if you don't stop.

Not to be disrespectful to my elders, let me rephrase that quote to say, "Don't give up...unless you should." Why? Because, sometimes, the path you're on is the wrong one, and the only thing to do is to walk it back and start over. If Robert Frost was right, when the "two roads diverged in the yellow wood," and he took the one less traveled by and that has made all the difference, then why are you on the main road going in the wrong direction?

I know, I spend week after week encouraging you to go and do and be all you can be, live your best life ever and, friends, I believe that to my very core, that you can be amazed at life or you can have an amazing life. That choice is yours. But I am well aware that sometimes in life, you need to give up and go in another direction, so you will find the success, the satisfaction, and security that you need to find for you and your family.

Friend, if you are on the wrong path, if you have made mistakes great or small that are doing damage, or if you are about to do something thoughtless because you know you're headed in the wrong direction, give up now! There is no shame in changing your mind, reviewing your options, or simply saying that enough is enough and walking away. You have choices in life; make the right one.

The wrong path is always the wrong path, and it doesn't change. The only thing that changes is you, and that's not good.

It is hard to convince people that sometimes the best thing to do is to go against the conventional wisdom of *don't give up* because it is not right for you, or it is not right for you at this time, and that is when you need to forge a new path that will provide other options.

I was on a campaign with a friend, and one night we decided to go out and put up his 4' by 8' campaign signs. We were humming along with our auger, digging great holes, and putting our signs into the ground with the greatest of ease until we found the most perfect spot at a fork in the road. We jumped out and pulled our equipment to the curb and start to drill. We drilled until we hit rock. At that point, I was thinking we that needed to go on down the road and find another great spot, but my candidate was thinking that we needed to lean harder on the auger and drill through the rock. I can remember saying to him that it wasn't going to work, to which he replied that I needed to be tougher and keep working because, as he liked to say, "We got this, Deb." Well, I couldn't see the wisdom of trying to crush rock for a campaign sign and my friend didn't see the wisdom of backing off until we broke the auger drill and had to call it quits for the night.

As we were driving back to the campaign headquarters, it was quiet in the truck, and the reason we had to give up working early in the evening was because he lived by the phrase that you don't give up, and I live by the phrase that you don't give up...unless you should.

If you're like me, you grew up hearing the phrase, "Winners never quit, and quitters never win." That's what they told us on the basketball court, but in business and life, sometimes quitting is the best thing you can do, especially if it interferes with your life, your goals, your family, and friends.

By nature, I am not a quitter. It is not in me to quit. As I have gotten older and have pushed through things that I should have left well enough alone, I have suffered the physical consequences. I am not as young as I used to be, and pushing myself from conference to conference because I love what I do and I love helping people has taken its toll on me. But, if in the end I lose my voice and I lose my health, then I lose me. And what do I have left? Not much, and that's when I think that I need to learn to give some of it up, so I can keep the rest of it.

As a society, we push that no one should ever give up, and sometimes, that should be the case. However, sometimes, that advice is simply the wrong advice. Sometimes, people are heading in the wrong direction, and the longer that they refuse to give up, the farther they're traveling down the wrong path.

I was reading an article by Marquita Herald, and she was talking about those who will tell you to never, ever give up on a goal, no matter what, because you never know what tomorrow will bring. The more you've shared your goal with the world, the louder that cry will be because, after all, you shared it in the first place, so others could cheer you on and keep you from quitting. The problem is that, despite what all the success stories proclaim, there is always a chance that, regardless of your good intentions and how hard you work, you could pursue a path for your entire life without ever reaching the dream you desire. Or worse yet, you could spend your entire life pursuing the wrong dream for your life.

You may say, "Well, Deb, if they're headed in the wrong direction, of course they know to give up and turn around." Friend, I wish that were true, but due to the pressures of others, the pressure you put on yourself, the pressure of family responsibilities, and social networks that often scrutinize every move, it makes it hard to give up sometimes.

It is much easier to go with the flow and keep your head down, so no one notices you, but is that a way to live? I don't think so.

Sometimes, your best bet is to quit and save yourself.

When I say that, you know what I'm talking about. You're married and having an affair you need to quit. You claim to be honest, and you steal time, money, and supplies from your boss, and you need to quit. You criticize others for not living up to your standard, and, yet, in your spare time, you're watching things online and going to places you'd never step foot in, and you need to quit. You're going in the wrong direction.

If these are your private habits, then you need to quit now because one day it will all come crashing down, and then your reputation, your family, your job will suffer since you didn't do the right thing and quit the things you know you should have. As odd as it sounds, I am not here to judge you. I'm simply asking that you stop doing the wrong things in your life. Open the newspaper any day and read about people who we all thought were one way, and then we found out (after they were arrested) that they were someone else.

When your life or your habits have landed you in such a terrible state of affairs, it is time to give up and start over. And that's the other part of this message. Just because you gave up on some things doesn't mean you can't start over on new things. You can develop new healthy habits; you can create a new plan or path for the next part of your life. You can do whatever you put your mind to as long as it is good for you and your family. It takes courage to admit that you're ready to start over, that you're ready for a do-over, or a retake, but that courage will come when you make the decision, as difficult as it may be, to do the right thing.

I don't believe that you need to make a habit out of quitting and starting over; if that's the case, we have other issues to deal with, but for some, you need to make the decision to forge a new path.

Let me remind you, don't give up...unless you should.

A PLACE CALLED SUCCESS

"The road to success is not straight. There is a curve called Failure, a loop called Confusion, speed bumps called Friends, red lights called Enemies and caution lights called Family. You will have flat tires called Jobs, but if you have a spare called Determination, an engine called Perseverance, and a driver called Willpower you will make it to a place called Success."

I came across this quote awhile back and have wanted to use it for some time, but the time never seemed right, until now. When you think about your ability to draw upon your determination, your perseverance, and your willpower, all of these or any one of these three personality traits will be the key to your success.

I know I talk a lot about finding success in your life, and the reason I do so is that I don't see or hear that in today's news or from anyone on TV or most radio stations, be it talk, music, or a religious station. The idea of being inspiring isn't so popular nowadays, and only talking about inspiration without putting a plan of action in place, well, is just talking, and we all know how far that gets you. And if you don't know, the answer is nowhere.

There was a time when the chatter of inspiration was all the rage, but with anything that is not based on self-determination, perseverance, or willpower, success will be hard to find. But never fear, there is a way through, and that way is by doing the one thing most of us avoid, and that is work – yes, hard work.

I was having lunch with a friend the other day, and in the course of our conversation, he told me about how he did all these good deeds for others and spent hours helping many worthy non-profit groups, and in the end, no one offered him a job and he barely got a "thank you" for his hours of service. So, now, what should he do? I suggested that first, he stop giving away all of his time without pay, and second, and I hated to say it, he's got to go back to work.

Why? Because the road to success is not straight; there is a curve called Failure, a loop called Confusion, speed bumps called Friends, red lights called Enemies, caution lights called Family and you will have flat tires called Jobs, so you have to find within yourself the belief that you can continue to move forward, no matter how tired, broken, or lonely you are.

Most of us understood growing up that success was something you found along the way while doing your work. What we didn't count on was the curve called Failure. Our parents may have warned us that we might fail, but for most of us, that conversation never took place because they wanted more for us than they had, and they were taught not to talk about failure, but to be positive and not burden their kids with the hardships of life. Bless the Baby Boomers who tried to see the glass half full. I, for one, appreciate that.

Growing up, I never had to deal with the idea of a loop called Confusion. I guess being the youngest and having all brothers who lived life in black and white left little room for misunderstandings at my house. I knew at a young age that going in circles was not a great way to live my life, so I was taught to make a decision and stick with it (unless it was the wrong decision, then make a change and stick with that), unlike many of my peers who would spin on small issues that made them go in circles. Whether it was a boyfriend or a school or a family issue, they would get all worked up and, in my opinion, be unreasonable in their emotions, allowing their current emotional state to be their guide, which, as you can well imagine, didn't serve them well.

The problem with a loop called Confusion is that it is hard to know how to exit the loop and set your course. If you're on the loop of Confusion now, let me encourage you to 1. Slow down so you can exit, 2. Take the exit, 3. Pull over and stop and think about the direction you want to go, and 4. Set your GPS towards your new location. Don't circle in confusion anymore; you're wasting your time and energy.

In today's quote, we are told that in life, you will have speed bumps called Friends. Even in the best of times, good friends will go missing, which is odd, since I expect them to go packing when things get hard, but not so much when things are good. When friends don't encourage you or are not fully happy for your success or do not reach out occasionally to make sure you're okay, you have choices. You can find new friends who will have your back, or you can reach out to your friends to reengage. You make the choice to think of them as Speed Bumps or a Freeway; think long and hard about those who slow you down to a stop in your life or those friends who encourage you to speed up and keep going.

What most of us learned at a young age was that, no matter how hard you tried, you would occasionally come across someone who would end up being an enemy. When you're a kid, the enemy is the other sports team or rival high school or even the school bully, but as we progress in life, many have come to learn that some people are hell-bent on being an enemy, and there is nothing you can do about it but avoid them at all costs. I've been in politics a long time, and I have a few folks who are not my friends. I have watched them do whatever they could do to cause me harm, and they did. Sometimes, I could block their hateful actions, and sometimes, I could not because they would do it under the guise of inclusion or whatever the politically correct term was in vogue at the time. Yes, they caused great harm, and yes, they knew what they were doing, but sadly, they didn't care. So, I live by the words of the great Winston Churchill, who said, "You have enemies? Good. That means you've stood up for something, sometime in your life." So, for the record, stay away from hateful people. Let them be someone else's enemy.

Now, I need to tread lightly as I talk about caution lights called Family. Ah, family the people who are supposed to have your back, the tribe you're a part of, the people you look like, and yet, sometimes, they can be the worst people you'll ever associate with. If I had a nickel for every story I have heard about how family members will steal, lie, and cheat other family members over money, property, or the family dishes, silver, and jewelry or how family members will say the meanest things and act like they're doing it for your good. For the record, it's not good, so don't listen to them; they're psycho. They say you can choose your friends, but you can't choose your family. While that is true, you don't have to be bound to your tribe if they are not positive or healthy or loving. No law says you have to put up with meanness; you can love from a distance. You can send good wishes from another state. Friend, you need to protect yourself, so even with family, use caution.

Let's talk about your job. Is it a Flat Tire? Are you dying on the vine? Is it drudgery? Are you bored? Only you can make that change. There is nothing worse than having to go to work and not liking what you do. Should you start looking, networking, and talking to those in the fields where your interests lie? If you feel like your job is a Flat Tire, I'd think about making a change or taking a chance. I got the best email the other day from Lindsay, a great young lady I coached in church basketball. She said,

Hi Deb. I wanted to personally invite you to the ribbon cutting ceremony of my new business, on Main St. I have been listening to your podcasts every Tuesday and you have truly inspired me to live my best life ever. I had been contemplating making a move back to the art world, but I didn't know exactly what that was going to look like. I knew that I would be successful at anything I did that I was passionate about, but I was at the point where I needed to take action on it and not just talk about it. And then one day there was a perfect opportunity available to me, and I took it! I am so excited that every day I get to surround myself with art, talk about art, and be my own boss! If it wasn't for listening to your show, I might not have been in the right place to jump on this opportunity. Come by the gallery so I can give you a tour and personally thank you for helping me with my journey.

Wow! You've got to know how that makes me feel, not only because I am so proud of Lindsay but also because she fully understands the thought for today, that the road to success is not straight. There will be failure, confusion, speed bumps, red lights, and caution lights. But she had the courage to change her flat tire because she had a spare called Determination, an engine called Perseverance, a driver called Willpower, and there is no doubt she will make it to a place called Success, and, friends, you can too. That's my hope and prayer for you.

ENCOURAGEMENT IN THESE HARD TIMES

Awhile back, when I decided to change the core concept for my show from *Speak Without Fear* to *Encouragement for Your Life,* I felt it was more in line with my heart's desire to be an encouragement to others.

Don't get me wrong, I am still a 100% believer that your ability to speak and be heard is your best avenue to climb the ladder for personal and professional success, and I will always encourage you to develop your speaking ability because it truly is the one thing you can do to change your life.

As I look around the world today, I am concerned about our world, our children, and our leadership. I see firsthand what happens when a nation is divided against itself. And I'm troubled that the division is for personal gain and not for any other purpose because it is the true embodiment of a phrase, we all know: "United we stand, divided we fall."

I think it is important in these hard times that you and I find a bit of encouragement or sanity, and in our own way, in our own world, with the gifts we have been given, we recreate moments of peace and encouragement for ourselves and that we share goodwill and peace with others.

And that can be as simple as delivering a meal or a phone call to check on someone or a kind deed for others. I'm not advocating that you pay off someone's mortgage (although that would be nice), but I am suggesting that you think about what you can you do to show kindness and be an encouragement to others? What can you do to spread the message to those who need a kind act or deed? This world is so full of bad news that I find many are falling into a depression of their inward soul and seem to have no respite from worry, distrust, and fear.

To be encouraging in these hard times matters; if you don't step up and do it, who will? I'm concerned that no one will. No one knows who you know that needs the help you can provide. It falls on you to step it up and give a bit of yourself.

It is hard to find a fleeting thought of encouragement as you watch what is going on in the world today, whether it is war in the Middle East, battle lines being drawn in Ukraine, planes missing or being shot down, or the vitriolic rise of hostilities directed at those who are of different faiths. All along, we saw the undercurrent of violence bubbling, but it seemed somewhat contained, not anymore, as our world seems to literally be on fire.

And in the midst of it all, as I look around, I don't see and hear many options to encourage good people to keep on keeping on. Not to the exclusion of what is going on in the world, but alongside it, so that in the midst of the pain, we find peace.

Today, I'm asking that you step it up and make it your job to encourage yourself and others.

Anatole France said, "Nine-tenths of education is encouragement."

I completely agree. Family, friends, and co-workers watch to see how encouraging you and I will be during good times and bad, and if we set the standard, others will feel safe to follow our lead.

I'm a firm believer that it is one thing for me to encourage you and gently cajole you into encouraging others, but it only works if we have a plan in place, and it is a workable model. Nothing much changes by only saying words; we've got to do the work to change ourselves to see the bright side, to walk into the light, and leave our baggage behind, so we can encourage others to be their best.

You may be saying to yourself, "Well, Deb, how do I go about encouraging others?" Let me give you a few ideas.

I travel a good bit, and I have gotten into the habit of mailing postcards to some of my friends who are older and don't get out much. It's a small thing but remember what it feels like to receive an unexpected card or note in the snail mailbox? It makes you feel good, and it costs me almost nothing to brighten a friend's day.

Also, when I am made aware, I pick up food for friends who are sick. It's nothing earth-shattering, but there is no greater love than a friend who shows up with food, not only in the hour of need but also, sometimes, in the hour of sheer tiredness.

Or how about the one event that my generation does not know what to do about – a funeral or a viewing? I know we're all tired and busy, but you can do your part by showing respect or, at the very least, sending a card or make a donation. There is nothing sadder than to know that a life is gone and so few people made the time to show up for the celebration for a life well lived. I recently went to a viewing for a former teacher of mine, and I knew his daughter. Out of our class, I was only one of a handful who dropped by to give my regards. I can't think of anything worse than coming from out of town to take care of family business, and not one friend who lives in town shows up to say they care.

I could go on and on, but friends, you know what to do; it's only a matter of doing it. And for the record, these are more than just good manners. These are rules of a truly good person who will go above and beyond to show respect. I know respect is not a word you hear much nowadays, and isn't that too bad because, at its core meaning, respect provides a sense of worth or excellence of a person. By showing respect, you can demonstrate encouragement. And respect is quite simple. You can show respect to the elderly by holding open the door, to your peers by congratulating them on a job well done, to your spouse who completes you, or to your kids who bring joy to your otherwise dull life. Yes, you can show respect! And by doing so, you'll be an encourager.

As much as I am asking you to be encouraging to others, I wonder who encourages you? Can you think of that one person or group that you have that encourages you to be your best, to do your best, and cheers wildly for your success?

Well, I trust family and friends fill that spot, but if they don't, let's find a way to be reminded about some of the good things that we've done. One way is to write down on a piece of paper the times when you were successful or the times when, against all the odds, you won. I know you have those successes in your life; you've just forgotten about them due to the daily grind of life. In order to put ourselves in the best possible light for success, we need to be reminded of the good things that have brought us a measure of success, and in turn, it will fill your encouragement bucket.

There is no doubt that when you think back on a few successes in your life, your brain works to reconfigure how to get back to that place of success. It was that bit of space that allowed you to breathe, to be, to put order in place for your accomplishments, and when you feel successful, it is easier for you to find the extra measure of grace or mercy or love to give encouragement to others.

Your mind is a wonderful file cabinet where you've stored away bits of paper that have your lifetime of daily successes written on them. Almost every counselor I've spoken with has agreed that one success, whether large or small, is a benchmark for many to be able to find their way back to success.

Today, I am going to intertwine the words of encouragement and success because I believe both are needed to find a safe place to stand and stand tall.

Another reason that I think it is important to write it down is that you need a tangible object to recreate in your mind the feeling of accomplishment. Just knowing that the award is on the wall, the medal is in the drawer, and the certificate is on the bookshelf is a visual reminder that you've had success before. It doesn't matter if it is in your work life, your social life, or your family life, the fact stands that you've been successful once; you can be again.

Once you stand firm on the foundation of your success, it should give you what you need to be an encouragement to others, to be able to cheer them on, to be able to let them know you've walked a mile in their shoes and you're still standing.

For today, set aside the cares of the world and family and job and life, as great as they are, and step it up to be an encouragement to others. The old saying is true: No one cares how much you know until they know how much you care. And with that in mind, let's show care and concern for others by being an encourager.

TRY APPROVING OF YOURSELF

The other night, I half-heartedly watched a thread of a conversation unfold on Facebook, and it reminded me of an odd habit that I am seeing in so many people these days, which is being unusually mean and harsh about themselves in a public setting for the sheer purpose to draw attention to themselves and have others heap undue praise on them to help settle them down. They post sad comments and then eagerly wait for their "friends" to reply to the post, proving that they have value and that the sad sack isn't that bad, that mean, that angry, that ugly, that chunky, etc. You know the drill.

I think it is a weird self-esteem issue born out of sheer loneliness to publicly draw such attention by saying mean and negative and derogatory comments to garner the attention of others. And I'll credit Facebook with making this a phenomenon that I see more and more, and it's not good! It's not healthy, and ultimately, the damage is greater than the moment of increased self-esteem.

Without a doubt, some people feel sad or lonely since we're such a single society. What I mean by that is social media has created a cadre of marginal friends who fill the void of true friends and family, but only for a time. Eventually, they go away and leave the attention-seeking wanderer to be even more outrageous with their comments to elicit a desperate response.

I don't want to waste time today talking about those who play games to keep themselves in the center of attention, but I want us to be aware that there are all types of personalities out there. We must be on guard to help those who truly need, appreciate, and want our assistance. And let's agree that tough love will not allow us to spend a minute more on those who, when you offer kind words of encouragement to help them, the more they like to shock you with their seemly low value of themselves. Frankly, there are not enough hours in the day to straighten out those who play this game for control or who are always fishing for compliments. Those are the odd habits of emotionally draining people. You know people like this, and although it is hard, we need to step away, so their issues don't affect us.

Let's recognize this behavior and walk away. Although we can care for them, we do not need to be lassoed into their rodeo. This slice of society is a sad, self-centered emotional wreck of a person that, without professional help, you and I can't change.

There is an opportunity for you to help those who are looking for a true friend or colleague to help them see the light from the darkness that they find themselves in. I love the quote from Louise Hay that says, "You've been criticizing yourself for years and it hasn't worked. Try approving of yourself and see what happens."

Today, I would like to speak to those who truly struggle with finding the good in themselves. You know who you are; you're the ones who don't talk about your issues but sit silently, and you don't engage when you could be a part of the team. You're the ones who prefer to be alone instead of being with the group, and you are the good folks who quietly go about your business, keeping your hurt wrapped tightly around yourself. You silently criticize yourself because you've not been taught to value your worth, or no one has shown you kindness in a long time. You simply don't fit in well, so you sit on the sidelines. I see you enough to know that you'll come if called, but occasionally, you need a friend to notice you and then reach out and quietly and confidently help you. You are, without a doubt, a loyal friend for life if you'll allow others to reach you. Please know that a lot of good people would like to help you get going again.

Because you have become lost in your own pain of divorce or death or broken relations or job loss or health issues, you've become a little confused, and that's understandable. But today, I am asking you to try approving of yourself and see what happens.

The quote for today is real for so many: "You've been criticizing yourself for years and it hasn't worked. Try approving of yourself and see what happens." This simple quote gently asks for you to decide your future.

Imagine what would happen if you, just for today, decided to speak words of affirmation to yourself to remind you that you're okay, that you feel good, you look nice today, and you did well on a certain project. And, friend, once you learn to approve of yourself, wouldn't that make for a better day, a happier and more present and fulfilled you, knowing that you are enough?

I am a fan of Dear Abby, and each New Year's Day, she runs the poem called "Just for Today" that she has borrowed and adapted from the *Al-Anon* poem and slightly changed the words. I have edited it even more to fit with my thought for today as you decide your future.

JUST FOR TODAY, I will live through this day only. I will not brood about yesterday or obsess about tomorrow. I will not set far-reaching goals or try to overcome all of my problems at once.

JUST FOR TODAY, I will be happy. I will not dwell on thoughts that depress me. If my mind fills with clouds, I will chase them away and fill it with sunshine.

JUST FOR TODAY, I will accept what is. I will face reality. I will correct those things I can correct and accept those I cannot.

JUST FOR TODAY, I will improve my mind.

JUST FOR TODAY, I will make a conscious effort to be agreeable. I will be kind and courteous, and I will not speak ill of others. I will improve my appearance, speak softly, and not interrupt when someone else is talking.

JUST FOR TODAY, I will refrain from improving anybody but myself.

JUST FOR TODAY, I will do something positive to improve my health.

JUST FOR TODAY, I will gather the courage to do what is right and take responsibility for my own actions.

When you take responsibility for your own actions, you have to commit to approving of yourself and see what happens.

You have to think long and hard about how you will do things differently because you can't go back to your old ways. That is a sure recipe for disaster.

So, starting today, let's make a list of what we can do to keep us in the right mindset for success.

The hardest thing you need to do is to commit to discipline, to do what you say you will do every day, and then do it every day, whether it be getting up and making your bed, picking up the house, exercising, meditating for a few minutes, eating a healthy breakfast, dressing your best, or maintaining your personal hygiene. Remember, when you look good, you feel good, and when you feel good, it sets a place of peace in your soul that you can feel and others can see.

I don't like the idea of working on myself any more than the next person, but if I don't and you don't, nothing will change, and the quote for today will not apply because you'll go back to criticizing yourself. And this time, you'll be right and that would be heartbreaking. So, friend, commit to approving of yourself. You've done your part; you've committed to finishing the hard work. Now, commit to seeing with new vision your amazing future.

"You've been criticizing yourself for years and it hasn't worked. Try approving of yourself and see what happens."

LET YOUR LIGHT SHINE

Have you ever met anyone who seemed to light up a room? Just by their presence, they bring a new dimension to the group. Sometimes, these folks are loud in personality and style, and sometimes, they are on the quiet side, but what they all bring is a feeling of joy in the truest sense of the word. They radiate an aura of calm and peace and tranquility, and frankly, they are great people to be around.

You may be saying, "Well, Deb, bring them on because we all could use a friend like that!" I agree, and so my thought for today is, *how about you be that person*. Who is to say that you can't set aside your sadness and worry and fear and anger and be the light that you're supposed to be? Yes, I'm talking to YOU.

I'm done with hearing excuses about how hard it is to get going in life with work and family and every other excuse you have for not doing your part. Hey, guess what? It's time you grow up. This is your life, and this is the life you've been dealt, so you have a responsibility to fill the space, no matter how big or small or even if you don't feel like it. And if you don't like your current life, well, then start to make the change. No one is stopping you but you, so stop blaming everyone else for your sad-sack life.

Let me tell you that some days I don't feel all that encouraging. I've got a lot going on, and I'm busy, and I'm tired. Being a sole proprietor, I do it all, but guess what? Really, in the scheme of life, I've come to learn that no one cares what my troubles are. Of course, they care on a surface level because that's polite. But really, in the course of the world spinning in orbit, I'm like everyone else, and I have a responsibility to do to my part, to let my light shine, whether I feel like it or not.

Why do I feel this responsibility, and why am I pushing you today? When all is said and done, you're blessed whether you can see it, admit it, or own up to it. It doesn't matter what you think. You're here, and by the act of being present in your current situation, you have a responsibility to do your part.

Do you know what our part is? (I'm in this with you.) It's to let our light shine. Our part is to be our best, to care for others, to carry our weight, and to stop slacking off in hopes that someone else will do our job. I know that there are days or weeks, or maybe months, when you can't give much to others, due to life getting in the way, but you can do something. I've never met anyone who could not, at the very least, give something, whether it is time, a listening ear, fixing a simple problem, making a meal, or giving someone fresh vegetables or flowers from their garden.

The problem is pride. Most of us think we have to do BIG things for others so everyone can see our generosity and largesse, but that's not the case; most of the people in your circle have all they need. They might not have all they want, but they have enough to get by. So, why do you think you need to blow it out of the water? The answer is typically self-pride; you want to be hailed, recognized, and loved. I don't blame you, but that's not what we're talking about today. You can do that when you inherit a million dollars or win the lottery, but for today, do your part and let your light shine by your words, your actions, your time, and your love.

You know that money doesn't make it easier. Trust me, there is always someone with more money than you, but what they don't have is your spirit, your heart, your kindness, and your light that can shine in the darkest hours. There is not enough money in the world to buy that or take it away.

I meet a lot of people who have given up on living their best life ever because it is easy to be average, and they think it is okay to be good enough.

If there is one phrase that makes me want to scream; it is the phrase "good enough." What happened to being great? What happened to being better tomorrow than you were today? What happened to pushing yourself to be your best and to setting an example for your family, friends, and co-workers to be the best they can be? Why do you settle for average? Besides the fact that it's easy, why do you settle for less than your best? Have you thought about it? Why do you give so little when your time on this earth is so short? Really, why do you shortchange those you claim to love and care for by being less than your best?

Is it because you were told years ago by people who really don't know you that you're not good enough, and you believed them? Friend, they're wrong! Have you bought into this world's false advertising that everyone is physically beautiful, smart, and rich? Those people on the magazine covers are only there for a year or so, and then they fade away. Why? Because they are not real. When did you accept the words of others who don't want you to succeed because they live in a world of scarcity and not plenty? These people don't have room for one more; they are selfish and take everything they can. That's not you. Those are not your people (and if they are, run away). Why are you settling for less than your best? And why are you listening to people who don't have your best at heart? Why are you spending time with negative, selfish, unkind people who are takers and not givers?

Why? Are you comfortable there? You can't be. It's not your tribe, and over time, they will dull your light until they blow it out.

I know the world is full of takers, people who will take everything you've got and ask for more, but remember, those are damaged people who want everything for themselves and will not share or give to others, unless it is on their terms, and their terms are not reasonable by any stretch of the imagination.

If someone is a taker and does not give back to you or to others who have helped them, walk away. You don't have to keep giving because, friend, it will never be enough, and they will prey on your kindness and goodwill until you are spent. Then, they will walk away and look for someone else to steal from. And, yes, I believe that those who are takers are stealing, and it is wrong.

I don't care how damaged they are that they use it for an excuse. I hear it all the time: their parent died, they got a divorce, they lost their job, or no one loved them, so they have a bad self-image. I know I sound harsh, but I hear it all the time all across America, and I'm over it. These takers will never change because somewhere along life's path, they took a detour and let their light burn out, so they don't have to share any more with others.

If you know someone like this, run away from them. They can find their own tribe and steal from each other, but starting today, they are done stealing from you. You've got to walk away and don't look back, as appealing as they are, because you want to help them to look at their past, watch their present situation, and notice it is the same thing over and over and it never changes. So, it is time to free yourself. You've done all you can for them. Do no more because they are dimming your light.

I am all about being your biggest, brightest rock-star light, but I'm surprised that, for most people, being a night-light is about all the light they can muster to shine. Just a faint light, so they don't bump into things at night or stub their toe going to the bathroom. It's nothing too great, barely enough to get by. Why? Because average is good enough for many of you. Your marriage is average, your family is average, your job is average, and you're just comfortable living in an average world. Whew! How you can do that is beyond me, when the light you could be shining could change someone's life.

So, friend, you've got to think about this. Think about what it would take to let your light shine, your inward spirit, soul, and being allowing you to shine brightly. And the reason that this matters is because you have a responsibility. Like it or not, you have a responsibility to shine brightly for others to see their way through the darkness.

Ray Davis said, "Your greatness is revealed not by the lights that shine upon you, but by the light that shines within you."

And I love the quote from Maya Angelou, who said, "Nothing can dim the light which shines from within."

I agree. The light that shines within you is a lasting light to show the way not only for you but also for others. So, that little light of mine, I'm going to let it shine. I won't put it under a bushel, and neither should you. Shine on, friend! Shine on.

CHOOSE HOPE

Like everyone else, I was very sad to hear about Robin Williams's death. I wanted to bring someone on the show to talk about depression and fear and other maladies that cause people to lose hope, but I struggled because I don't want to prolong the pain of his passing. (I grew up watching him on *Mork and Mindy*; I thought he was so funny). I don't want to focus on sadness. We have enough of that going on in the world. What I really want to say would be a rant about getting help, seeing your life for what it is, and making the hard decision to fight to live another day. But that would add little value to the conversation, so I'll hold my tongue and focus on what I believe could be your saving grace in our time together, and that is finding hope in your life.

For many years, I was not a fan of the word hope. There was a time in one of my talks that I spoke about the minute value of the word hope that has everyone waiting for something to happen, but it won't because we're waiting, and waiting doesn't get the job done. I don't give that talk anymore for a lot of reasons, but one is that as I look around today, I see for many that hope might be the one word they cling to, and I have no right to dispel their trust in a word that gives them the strength to go one more day.

I think hope has two sides. You can hope all day the dishes will get washed, but they won't unless you do it. You can hope to lose weight but eating a dozen donuts will not help with your weight loss plan. You can hope to meet the person of your dreams but sitting at home in front of the TV every night isn't a very good plan for success, and friends, you can hope all you want for everything you want, but without action, you're only hoping and waiting and wasting time.

Since hope is an idea, although that's great, without action, it gets nothing done. Unless you're hoping because you have little to nothing else to hang on to, and, if so, then go ahead and hope. And that is the other side of this simple word.

Hope that things will get better because they probably will. Hope that you'll understand the meaning of the current situation because, in time, it will be made clear. Hope that your kids will be okay and your parents will find peace. Hope that your life will have meaning to those you love and to those who watch you live your life. If hope is all you have today, tie a knot and hang on. As I have gotten older and my type-A personality is softening, I've become more generous towards the word hope. I see that for many, it is all they have in the interim while hoping for something to happen. I've always liked the quote that hope is the little voice you hear that whispers *maybe* when it seems the entire world is shouting *no!*

It is odd how the one word that made no sense to me when I was younger and pushing the envelope of life now is as clear as day to me as I watch and wonder how some can make it through the night. I've heard it said that if you keep hope alive, it will keep you alive.

We toss words around like they have no meaning until they do, and then the meaning is what we cling to when we feel like we have nothing else. If hope is all you have, then stand firm in the storm.

I doubt we'll ever know the reasons why people take their life; why people abandon their families; and why some just walk away from jobs, friends, church, the community without explanation. I have often wondered, *Did they not know that others did care or would have offered more attention if they had known the depth of sadness and despair?*

It's at that time when I think hope might be the best answer to keep one's head and heart in line to do the right thing even when it's hard. Hope changes everything if you'll hang on.

If you're struggling today, I want you to slow down. You might even need to stop and make a list of the good things that have happened to you. I know you think it is a waste of time, but you're wrong. It is a good thing to write down and remind yourself of your hopes and dreams and opportunities in life in real-time. And the reality is if you don't write it down, you'll forget.

As I was cleaning up my office the other day, I came across a notebook where I had started to keep a list of good things that had happened to me, not because I was depressed, but because I wanted to keep a record, a tangible list of successes and answered prayers. Sometimes, I forget that I made requests and they were answered, surprising even me of obviously so little faith.

I can remember the big things I prayed for that were answered, but as I read through the other items on my list, I was renewed and refreshed at the blessings I had received that to others would have been small and insignificant; to me, they were everything from a new car and a new home to adding some new friends in my life.

I have things written in my book of opportunities I was hoping would come my way, of speaking jobs I had hoped for and was chosen, of conferences I wanted to speak at and was chosen, and of writing a book that would be published. I remember the first time I was asked to speak at some top campaign schools in the country. I was thrilled and thought, *That is cool! I hope I'm not a one-hit-wonder,* and then, I was asked back a second time, and that was amazing for me. Then, I was asked back *again,* and I've been back for many years. Speaking at Harvard and Yale were on my list because those opportunities mean something to me.

Hope is a funny thing. You've got to be willing to put yourself out there and test the waters to see if you can swim, or maybe you should stay close to the shore. There is no magic formula to know if something will work unless you do the work. And when you do the work and are successful, or even if you're not, it's okay. You're still here trying, working, pushing, hoping, and who knows, maybe the timing isn't right, but it will be one day, and then it will all make sense.

Not everything in my notebook has come true or at least not yet. There are still mountains to climb, so to speak, but they're written down in ink not to be removed, but to be accomplished in time, hopefully in my lifetime.

I must say that as I've gotten older, I have become a very hopeful person, not only for me but also for so many of my clients. Their success is my success, and I work hard for them to be successful. But there is the other side of life that many times we don't see or recognize, and that is those who seem to be hopeless.

Have you ever met someone who seemed hopeless? Not someone who plays games for attention, but someone who has an emptiness in their soul due to the death of a loved one or the loss of something? It is a very sad acknowledgment of the empty place. If you know someone like that, be aware, be kind, be gentle and, remember that for some, you just being there is all they need. Make sure they know you're there by an email or a card or call. Don't let them wonder if anyone cares, let them know. I read a quote from Desmond Tutu, who said, "Hope is being able to see that there is light despite all of the darkness."

A friend of mine lost a parent a while back and told me that, over a lunch they had with a close friend, the friend decided to give some of what they thought would be tough love, and told them to chin up, go forward, stop crying, pull yourself together, and let go of your sadness. Instead of tough love, it came across as harshness, and to this day, that friendship is damaged due to the unkind words that were spoken. I know it is a fine line, so let's err on the side of kindness and hopefulness.

I think it is interesting when people tell me that, if they just had more money, they'd be happy; if they just had the career of their dreams, they'd be happy; if people recognized them for their great talent, they'd be happy. It seems like it would make sense, but then we look at Hollywood with all its bells and whistles, bright lights and bigger-than-life dreams and opportunities, we could list all the celebrities and athletes, the well-known and unknown people we've lost who had all those things, because when all is said and done, it didn't matter what they had on the outside. It was what was on the inside that mattered, and the same is true with you and me and those we love.

Hope is a funny thing. It takes action on your part. If you can't move right now physically, emotionally, mentally, or spiritually, hold on! Hold on tightly and give in to the little word that offers you a respite on the road of life, and that is the word hope.

Once you choose hope, anything is possible.

YOU'VE GOT THE POWER

When I was younger, I often heard the phrase, "You've got the power." I think it was a commercial I heard on the radio, but I remember that it was also told to me to encourage me to move forward in whatever I was doing because, in the end, you and I have the power to do amazing things in our lives and for others.

Power – *Bing Dictionary* defines power as:

- Capacity to do something: the ability, strength
- Strength: physical force
- Control and influence over other people and their actions

Power. We often think of others having power over us or over those we love, and, yet, giving power away is something many people accept of others, on purpose or unknowingly. Some choose not to and simply walk away. They don't give others the power to direct their life. Smart people take control of their lives

We choose power in every aspect of our lives, so I want to focus on where you give your power away and how you can get it back and use it for good.

I saw a quote the other day, along the lines of almost every successful person begins with two beliefs: *The future can be better than the present*, and *I have the power to make it so*.

I like that thought. At any time, you have the power to make it so, to change how today and how tomorrow will be. Don't let your past drag you down, especially if you gave your power away and it didn't turn out so well. I'm not going to dwell on your past, as I am about looking forward to your future starting today.

I have used the quote before, but it is worth repeating, that at any given moment, you have the power to say, "This is not how the story is going to end."

Let's think about that, at any given moment, you have the power to say, "*This is not how the story is going to end*." And you can make that pronouncement with confidence when you realize that you have the power to change, to turn around, to recreate, or begin again.

Some of you may end up doing this alone, and as hard as it seems, it will be okay. You will be surprised by the freedom and energy you will have when you stand up for yourself and create a safe place for your mind and body, heart, and soul.

Some of you may be able to bring others along with you as you stand firm in your new direction, because you took the power to rewrite your story, and they will be willing to be a part of that. Remember, alone or together, you have the power to make the changes you feel, believe, or simply dream of, if you will trust yourself. I've heard it said that knowledge is power, but enthusiasm pulls the switch.

Some of you may have allowed others to take away your power to choose your friendships, or a job, or an opportunity because it didn't suit the other person. And you being agreeable let some great things pass you by. Stop and consider what could be next if you independently allowed yourself to be open to the possibilities. You need to take your power back and live your life and use *your* power for good

I want to talk about you. You've heard the line that *you are either as beautiful or as ugly as you believe you are;* you define your beauty; that's not a power anyone can have over you.

So, I'm asking you to look in the mirror. Do you like what you see? Not to get into a discussion of a little needed weight loss or maybe a new hairstyle, but the soul looking back at you in that reflection, is that you? I hope so, and I hope you don't have to look so deeply to see what we all see because it is there on the surface, your kindness, your goodness, your love for others.

And by the way, if it's not the real you looking back, no pretense, no drama, no false made-up image to cover your sad self-esteem, get to work on yourself. We need you in a good place to bless others because you've settled this in your heart. You know your beauty inside and out is a true reflection of your heart and soul.

That's what power does for you; it gives you the breathing room to make decisions for yourself.

If someone has questioned the beauty of your soul, think long and hard about maintaining that friendship. Do not to let anyone cloud your beauty; it's not for them to do, and if that is the type of person they are, you need new friends. By the way, if you are the one who has said such a hurtful comment, go and apologize and make it right. There is no need to be cruel in such a broken world.

I heard an old saying. It said, "I'd rather have four quarters than a hundred pennies." Yes, I choose a close network of positive people and not hundreds of fake friends. Why? Because I have the power to choose what is best for me and how I want to live my life. There was a time when fifty pennies were fine but not now. I'm in a different place with different hopes and dreams and an open-door search for opportunities. Fifty pennies don't fit on the bus going in the directions of my dreams. You and I must choose wisely because our future depends on it.

I often speak in my introduction to the radio show that you are fearfully and wonderfully made, and because of that promise, friend, you have much to give and plenty left over to give to others. You're okay; in fact, you're better than okay. I like to think of you as amazing because you define your beauty.

And because you define your beauty and own your power and have come to understand that you are in control of your life and your actions and reactions, reach out and help those who, for some reason, cannot see the light.

Author Leo Buscaglia said, "Too often we underestimate the power of a touch, a smile, a kind word, a listening ear, an honest compliment or the smallest act of caring, all of which have the potential to turn a life around."

Imagine that, you can turn a life around by just following your natural inclination to flash a smile, say a kind word to the check-out clerk, listen when your parents call to tell you about their week, tell your kids you're proud of them, or your spouse who needs to hear your acceptance.

Don't you agree that if you have the power to make someone happy, you should do it? The world needs more of that!

As I look around, I see a world in need. I look for those who are strong enough and who have the power to lift others up. When I see that, I make it my job to encourage them because I have the power to do so, and so do you. Encouragement should be our superpower.

If you have given your power away, today is the day that you take it back and use it for good.

You don't have to do what the others do; you don't have to go where the others go, and you certainly should not have to portray yourself as someone who is not to be accepted by others.

You have the power to be your amazing self. Now, go and get your work done, and I'm asking that along the way, you look up from your work and invite someone else to find their power. Help them find their:

Capacity to do something: using their ability and strength

- Whether by physical force or force of personality
- Using their power to control and influence other people and their actions for good (*Bing Dictionary*)

I've always liked the admonition from the *Book of Proverbs*:

"Do not withhold good from those to whom it is due, when it is in your power to act."

You have the power. Go and use it for good.

"IT NEVER HURTS TO KEEP LOOKING FOR SUNSHINE."

—*Eeyore*

It has been a week. I can't remember when, in the course of a weekend, I have seen so much sadness and pain and frustration and disappointment. I'm not sure if it's the moon in its phases or life is just hard with all that is expected of us. There is a lot going on, including, kids back in school, football teams winning and losing, financial issues that seem to plague even the most stable of families, kids gone bad, and parents at wit's end.

Life is hard, I know you know that, and although we don't dwell on that fact, it is what it is. So, now, what are we going to do?

I am concerned about the sadness and disappointment that I see in so many of my friends and acquaintances, and it's everything from emotional to mental to physical, and the pain is real.

As I speak around the country, and as I meet people at my book signings, I have repeatedly wondered what the underlying cause of such pain is, and I keep coming back to three ideas.

These include, sadness stemming from grief or loss, disappointment about life and one's expectations, or true physical pain caused by injury.

I want to talk about your outlook on life and the pain that you are putting yourself through to justify your sadness and disappointment, which is rooted (I believe) in expectations. Physical pain is different, so it is not part of my discussion today.

The quote at the top is from the *Winnie-the-Pooh* story, as said by the ever-sad Eeyore. Although not my favorite character, he does have some good one-liners, and today's message is perhaps his best line. In the midst of it all, I want to encourage you to remember that no matter what you're going through, it never hurts to keep looking for sunshine.

I am sure there are many reasons that one could find to be sad today, but what I see is a constant low hum of emotional emptiness that simmers until someone breaks. If you find yourself sad for more than a few weeks, I encourage you to seek medical help. Your doctor can help you, but you have to do your part and go see them.

If you know you don't have a medical issue, then you really need to set aside some time to figure out what has happened that has thrown you for such a loop that you're staring into the darkness with no desire to turn on the light. Friend, if that is you, you need to walk the issue back and figure out when this started, what happened, and how you're going to find help to move forward to heal your heart and find peace, so you can get back on track now!

If you have suffered the loss of a friend or family member (or even a pet), sadness is understandable for a time but anything longer is not. So, let's reset the clock for what is acceptable for recovery and then start to make small steps to find yourself again. Remember, your job is to look for the sunshine, not continue to block it out.

For those of you who know what has happened, but you're unwilling to deal with it because it's your exquisite pain, it's what you cling to, it's your badge of sadness so you let it fester to make you and everyone around you miserable, so you're the center of the universe of miserableness, that is ridiculous. You need to grow up and get on with life and stop being such a loser. The fact is, if you want, you can heal your heart at any time. Nothing is holding you back but your pride, and *that* is sad. You know that you are not meant to be sad; it is not who you are. It might be who you have become, but it is not you, and you have to do the hard work of finding your joy in life again even though sadness or grief or loss has happened.

And you know that those who have passed on don't want your tears, they want you to go on and do the things you had planned. They want you to enjoy the life that you built together; they want you to find joy and happiness and peace. They are at peace. You need to find your peace and settle the hurt and sadness in your heart. You need to do this work for you and others who care about you. Some of you are leaving your best years empty because you are choosing to be sad. It's easier than the hard work of looking for the sunshine but let me remind you that the warmth of sunshine and the light that it gives will, if you let it, relight your soul and spirit, and that is what those who have gone on want for you.

I'm always surprised that so many people are disappointed in life. You didn't start out that way, but here is where you're ending up, and it's not good. For many, disappointment is a self-imposed limiting belief that something *out of your control* has made your life miserable. Friend, it is foolish to think you can control the universe to meet your demands and expectations, that is not what life is about. And when you let the disappointments of life set you back for days, months, or years, you are wasting the gift of life that God has ordained for you.

He has the whole world in His hands. He knows your name, and He knows your broken heart, but you must pull yourself together and get on with the living of life while you're still on this earth; that is the least you can do to honor the one who created you.

No doubt, life can throw you a hardball that will blow you back from the base, but you have to make a choice. The easy one is to walk away from the game and whine about your circumstances. (And just so you know, we're over your sad-sack Eeyore moaning and groaning.) The hard choice is to step into the box and swing for the lights with all that is within you, with all that you could be, with all your strength and might.

You're not a loser; you're not even the losing type, that's not who you are. No, you're better than that, or you used to be, but if you are not careful, you're going to lose your edge, and then you'll be in a worse spot than you are in today. Keep looking for the sunshine. You need to get that fire in the belly to get you back into the game, and I don't care if you're sick, tired, or broke, tell me someone who isn't. All I care about is your success for a lifetime.

And let me say one more thing to remind you to stop wasting your energy and joy in life because your kids aren't doing what you had hoped for (kids nowadays are crazy, and your best bet is to cover them in prayer) or your spouse has walked out (I know that has got to hurt, emotionally, financially, and even physically the loss of a once-loving partner) or your heart is broken (whether in one piece or a thousand, the pain is real, no denying that) or you didn't get what you thought you deserved or you didn't receive the reward, the recognition, the respect that was owed. Yes, all these hurts are real, but you are stronger, wiser, more knowledgeable now than you were before. Why are you wasting the gift of a second chance when you can change, redirect, rediscover, or discover your purpose in life?

Before you say, "Well, Deb, you just don't understand," stop. I'm not going to let you off that easy. Let's face it, no one (on this earth) will ever understand the depth of your sadness or disappointment, let's settle that one now. Now that you know that, what are you going to do about tomorrow or the next day and the day after that?

It never hurts to keep looking for sunshine.

I know I'm being hard on you. I am well aware my message is hard especially if you're hurting. I don't want to add to your troubles, but I want you to remember that all you have is 1,140 minutes today and tomorrow and, I assume, the next day. What I need you to understand is that the time for you to get past your sadness and disappointment is now, and every day you lose is a day you'll not get back to change your life, and that would be sad and disappointing.

Keep looking for the sunshine.

ONE SMALL CRACK DOES NOT MEAN THAT YOU ARE BROKEN; IT MEANS THAT YOU WERE PUT TO THE TEST, AND YOU DIDN'T FALL APART

Today, I want to shout out a cheer to some of you for sticking with it and getting the hard work done or accomplishing a goal that you set. You're basking in the glow of a good job well done. My theme today is a quote from Linda Poindexter, who said, "One small crack does not mean that you are broken; it means that you were put to the test, and you didn't fall apart."

That is impressive! You and I know a lot of folks who, when put to the test, tripped and didn't get back up again, or they decided that if it can't be perfect, they'll just stop. Or, worse yet, some don't even try. That doesn't make any sense when, in reality, *trying* is what we're after.

We've become a harsh society where expectations sometimes are so out of whack with reality that we lose the joy of small accomplishments. You'll see this with your kids sometimes. Perhaps, they are on the track team or the swim team, and they didn't quite make the cut and, instead of realizing that their time was two seconds better than last week, they moan and groan and threaten to quit. Instead of understanding two seconds this week will be four seconds next and only getting better with practice to one day win, we let them focus on this week's failure and not the progress of the season. If that's happening, you need to be the adult and let them know that progress is the best path forward, and you'll cheer them on until they reach their goal.

In the grand scheme of life, we'd all do well to lighten up on each other, and instead of always pointing out mistakes, we should complement each other for jobs large and small done well, and not only for others but also for yourself.

How about you? Are you being realistic in your goals, and are you recognizing your accomplishments? I hope so! And if you might have fallen down this week, no worries. Pick yourself back up, and let's try again. You might have cracked, but you're not broken, and that in itself is a positive. Let's be real about what we can and can't do; let's do our best and then rest in our success.

It takes a strong person to be mindful of small successes. Some people easily overlook their progress because, on the outside, it doesn't seem so big. But if it matters to you, then it matters to those of us who love you, as we cheer you on to your best self.

I'm not sure what tests you are going through these days, but I encourage you to find your true north, your center and hold it together, even when it feels like it is slipping from your grasp.

And please don't think that your past is a predictor of your future; in many cases, it is not, because you've walked that path and found it wasn't for you, so don't worry about what could happen again and focus on what will happen, as you set your course and chart your direction for success.

This comes full circle when you know in the depth of your heart, soul, and mind that you didn't fall apart. And here you are today, stronger, better, wiser. Find joy in your success today. Celebrate your "not falling apart."

I have a number of dear friends who have gone through the pain of divorce and yet have maintained the steady, calm, loving rhythm of running a household full of kids without outwardly giving in to the anger, hurt, and frustration of the divorce. Of course, it was not easy, but they survived that one small crack and quickly realized that they are not broken. Goodness knows, they were put to the test and didn't fall apart. And one day their children will rise up and call them blessed, no doubt in my mind. So, find the reassurance of success, even in a cracked world.

I am always concerned when people want to tell me the same story over and over again about a past failure. It feels like they are focusing on the crack instead of being thankful, grateful, or relieved that they didn't break.

I read an article by Lori Deschene, who said, "You've got to stop telling the story of your fracture. It may seem like another way to understand what happened, or maybe it feels helpful to hear someone say you didn't do anything wrong, and you don't deserve to hurt. In all reality, this just keeps you stuck right where you are: living your life around a memory and giving it power to control you. No amount of reassurance will change what happened. You can't find happiness by holding on to a painful story, trying to place it in a new, brighter light. You can only find happiness when you let it go and make room for something better. You don't need another person's permission to let go and feel okay."

Why? Because you were put to the test, and you didn't fall apart.

Since you know what it is like to crack and not break, how can you be an encouragement to someone else? Are you in a place where you can say a kind word or do a good deed to someone who is struggling emotionally, financially, or physically?

If you were to add up all your friends who are hurting, you'd run out of fingers and toes, so what can you do? What if you do it sooner rather than later?

Simply sending a note, making a call, or showing up to help would mean the world to a person who needs you.

And, by the way, even if no one was there for you, will you be there for someone else? I love the Anne Frank quote, "How wonderful it is that nobody need wait a single moment before starting to improve the world."

And the theologian and philosopher Albert Schweitzer said, "I don't know what your destiny will be, but one thing I do know: the only ones among you who will be really happy are those who have sought and found how to serve."

Whether it is helping the elderly neighbor by putting her newspaper closer to her front door, being a rock-star neighbor and mowing someone's yard who couldn't get it done this week due to unforeseen circumstances, or paying it forward at a drive-through, do it to show that there is still a little humanity in the world.

You know what I think is impressive? When I meet people who I know have gone through some hard times, but they don't dwell on it. In fact, they never mention it, but they tell me about the things they do for others that mean more to the person who was provided for. And, remember, it doesn't have to be the big things (although that is always nice) but the consistent, small things many of you do.

If you've ever delivered for Meals on Wheels or worked at your local soup kitchen or food bank, you will have a completely new view on life and be utterly grateful for your station in life at this time. Most of us have no idea how many get by with so little, and yet, they live next door to our parents or to us. Neighborhoods change, and people come and go, but the needs grow with age, and if you and I can be of help in any small way, we'll have done our part in this spinning orbit.

You are a survivor!

At times, I admit that I can be a little hard on you for making sadness and discouragement such a big part of your life, so instead of me hammering you today for not living up to your full potential, I'm going to put my megaphone down and say, "Well done. Good job! Keep up the good work. I'm proud of you."

And I'm especially proud of those of you who have been put to the test, but you didn't fall apart.

Steve Maraboli is famous for saying, "This life is for loving, sharing, learning, smiling, caring, forgiving, laughing, hugging, helping, dancing, wondering, healing, and even more loving. I choose to live life this way!" And I hope you do, too, friend.

PEOPLE AREN'T ALWAYS GOING TO BE THERE FOR YOU. THAT'S WHY YOU LEARN TO HANDLE THINGS ON YOUR OWN.

You know what I think one of the hardest things in life is? It's when you have to do things on your own. I tend to work alone, it's the nature of my business, but sometimes, I like to work with others; I like to hear what they think, or I like to see the process of working together to accomplish a goal come to fulfillment. I also like the comradery that happens when you put good people together to make stuff.

If you can find your tribe and make good things happen for yourself or others, more power to you. You are blessed, but for most of us, unfortunately, people aren't always going to be there for us. That's why you need to learn to handle things on your own. I saw that phrase a while back, and it was a good reminder that, sometimes, instead of waiting for someone to help me, I need to pick up the tools and get to work, and friend, you do, too.

Some of you are waiting for others to help you get going on projects, on dreams, on memories. Still they haven't come through, so you're still waiting. How long will you wait, and why are you giving your power to someone else when you could go ahead and get the job, project, dream fulfilled with your own effort?

Some of you may need to reevaluate the relationship with the friend that is not doing their part, and if it is something you really want to do, go ahead, and get started. Hopefully, you'll meet some new friends on that new road to give you the encouragement you need to do what you wanted to do, see what you wanted to see, or at least make your plans to accomplish your dreams. And the good news is that when you start, your tribe will follow.

One of my pet peeves in life is when someone says they're going to do something, and they don't. It's really hard for me to give them a second chance. I move at a fast pace, and if someone can't or won't come through as promised, I'll find someone who will, or I'll do it myself. And I won't put myself in a position a second time to have to lean on them, since they didn't come through when they promised. Maybe that sounds harsh, but for me, it's better than becoming angry or hurt or frustrated because others didn't come through.

I can still love those people, but I won't put myself in a position to cause further harm to the already fractured relationship.

The fact is people aren't always going to be there for you. That's why you learn to handle things on your own. And that's my theme for today.

I encourage you to find the strength to do the things that need to get done or some things you've been dreaming about or simply make a plan to do the thing you've always wanted. But you've got to get started now, and not someday, because there is no someday; that's a false idea.

What needs to get done in your life? Really, what needs to be started or finished? Is there a project that has been lying around since last Christmas? Do you need to take the time to update your resume, your will, or your insurance? Do you need to clean out your closet, car, attic, office, house, or kids' toys? What is the project that hangs over you that has caused you to stop, when with a little effort, you can pick it back up again and finish the job and be done and feel that sense of accomplishment?

When you talk to professional organizers, they will tell you that within hours of completing a long-standing project that has been hanging around, a heaviness will lift from the client's shoulders; they say it is almost visible to see the change. I think that is cool. Just the fact that you did what you committed to doing will change your outlook for the better. Your mind set a deadline, and now, your spirit is waiting for completion.

Those of you who know me know I am all about cleaning stuff up and out from the attic, garage, closet, or office. Why? Because when you're not weighed down with stuff (or junk, or dirt, or mess), you will create space for something new, better, brighter, cleaner but it will not happen until you get to work. Many of you will be doing the work by yourself. But that's okay because it is about progress and moving you to a better place, so you move in the direction of your dreams.

A while back, a friend came by the house, and as he was looking around, he asked me where all "my stuff" was. I told him, "Everything you see is all I have. I don't have stuff lying around because that causes clutter, and my working brain cannot deal with that. I know that might be strange, but sometimes, I can't get big things done until I have cleared out all the little things."

I have to be careful that I don't spend all my time on little things and not get to the real work that needs to get done. Over the years, I have realized that I needed to learn how to handle things on my own because people aren't always going to be there for me, and the same is true for you.

Now that you have made your Saturday list to get going and get things done and you're working down the list to success, let's move to what have you been dreaming about. They say when your mind wanders to the place of your desire, that is where your heart will go. So, if you think about painting the bedroom or buying a new car or going on vacation, start planning, saving, and researching now because there is a great chance that others will not be there for you, so you need to figure out what you want and then move in the direction of your dreams and desires, even if you have to do it alone.

When I ask you what your dream is, what would you say? A while back, I did a show called "Dreams Are for Free." An artist I know gives out lottery tickets if you write down on her form what your dreams are. What was interesting is many people didn't write down big audacious things, but real-life things like pay for college, buy a house, or go on a vacation without worrying about the cost.

I don't want to sound negative today, but since most of you will be doing your hopes and dreams by yourself, I want to stress that you need to stop waiting for others to make you happy when you need to be strong enough to make the decisions that would bring you joy. I hope that friends and family will come alongside you to enjoy the ride, but if not, stop sitting around waiting. And, goodness, don't sit around moaning and groaning; that will get you nowhere. So, get going on your own!

When I travel overseas, I will take an extra day or two to sightsee with a guide or by myself, and I can tell you that for that six-hour trip with strangers, we're all friends just sightseeing together, helping each other with photos, or walking together up to a castle. These aren't my friends for life; they're my tour bus stranger friends, but I choose to go instead of sitting in my hotel room, missing the sights and sounds and history of a place. And you can do the same thing, no matter where you are. Don't let life pass you by because your people aren't there for you at this time.

When you accept that you need to learn to handle things on your own, you will grow strong and learn to have faith in your ability, and without a doubt, you'll experience a sense of freedom of space and time and place. And, who knows, you just might fulfill your lifelong dream to see the Grand Canyon or go to a Broadway show in New York City or have your photo taken at the Eiffel Tower in Paris better to go alone than not at all.

So, whether it's finishing your list of projects around the house or office or if you're going to make your long-standing dream come true, I'm proud of you for getting going in your amazing life. And for those of you who aren't quite ready, then let's make a plan so that you can work the plan for your future.

There are a lot of ways to start. I encourage you to make a vision board, put up photos of what you want to do, see, or become; it is easier to plan when you can see the intended outcome. Without a plan in place, you're just talking about a pipedream, so this is why you have your vision board. And if you're not comfortable with sharing your dream right now, put your board on the inside of your clothes closet, so every day when you open that door, you'll be reminded of where you're going one day then go online and set an alert for airfare or ticket discounts or whatever you need to get the job done, and keep a list of pricing, so you get a sense of the true cost. And then start setting aside a little bit of money weekly to accomplish your dream. Even if you have to start small, over time, with your work and vision, it very well may come true, and wouldn't that be great?

IF YOU CAN LOOK UP,
YOU CAN GET UP!

I heard this phrase a while back, and it keeps nagging me. While I am sure it is true, I also know how hard it is to get up when you're feeling down. But isn't that what we need to be looking for, the light to find our way, the path to go where we need to go, or the unlocking of the door to our future? Even when it is hard, *yes* is the simple answer, and *how* is another story.

I'm not sure what you are going through today, but I'm sure some of you are going through some of the hardest times in your life. I know comments from an unseen radio host and author may not lighten your load, but I want you to trust me when I say that, no matter what happens in your life today or tomorrow, or if you're still unraveling yesterday, you'll get through it. You will find a flickering light to guide your way, or you will step out from the briars of life onto a path that will finally make sense. If you simply focus on the job or task at hand, you will find a way to unlock the door and open it for your success; you'll make it. The key is that you have to keep moving, working, walking, talking, praying, reaching, stretching toward the answer because, amid all your pain and hurt and tears and sorrow, I know that if you can look up, you can get up!

And it's in the getting up that you will find your strength to get going and start moving to begin the climb to your desired outcome.

The struggle is in finding the strength or willpower to keep going when you're flat on your back, when your energy is spent, when you've grown weary. It will not be easy, no one said it would be but here is what I know: when you finally reach your destination, there you will find rest. Why? Because it is there that you will be looking up to see just how far you've come and notice where you're going is just a few more steps ahead. Don't get discouraged. As hard as it is, you will make it, slowly but surely.

You see, friend, if you were to say to me, "But, Deb, I can't look up," it would be then that I'd know you probably can't get up.

If you can't look up and around and see where you've been, see where you are, and see where you're going, you're probably looking at the floor and not the ceiling. It is there that I'm going to ask you to stop and roll over and reframe your senses to find your space to get up.

The work is in the getting up and not letting your responsibilities, your job, or your relationships keep you from where you need to go, which is up and moving in a healthy and right direction.

Did you know that once you get up, you'll look up? It's just the way nature made you. Think about your kids as babies. They were enthralled with all that went on around them. They looked up into your eyes and marveled at the sights and sounds and colors and noise; kids rarely look down at the ground. No, they want to explore the world, and the world to them while laying on their back in the crib is all that is going on above them. Yes, you were made to look up; it's in your nature. If you can look up, you can get up. Never let anyone tell you otherwise.

I believe we're all born with a glimmer of hope, a candle that we nurture into a flame of lasting light. You've got it; you just need to trim the wick, so your light will burn bright and last a lifetime.

Last weekend, my friends took me out for a quick shopping trip to spend time together and celebrate my birthday. As we were walking down the sidewalk, my friend and I smelled the most wonderful scents, and as we looked around to see where the scent was coming from, we saw nothing that would make sense until we turned the corner and walked into the Yankee Candle shop. That is where we found the wonderful smells that we noticed while on the sidewalk. As we were looking at all the candles, I found one that smelled great. As I was checking out, the nice cashier asked if I wanted her to trim the wick. "Why?" I asked. "It's no big deal, is it?" "Oh, yes," she said. "When you trim the wick, the candle burns brighter and better and will not produce the black smoke and the soot that turns your candle jar black. Keeping the wick properly trimmed saves money by making your candle last longer."

Interesting! We need to cut the wick down to make it last longer. That is a great thought for life. See, so many of us want it all, even if it costs more in the end by burning us down to nothing. How much more sense would it make if we considered the option to trim the excess of our lives so we can have more, more light, more candle, more money.

My overall thought is that if you can look up, you can get up, but I want to add that I am well aware that the one thing needed is the strength to get up. I like the dictionary.com definition of strength: *noun; the quality or state of being strong; bodily or muscular power; vigor, mental power, force, or vigor, moral power, firmness, or courage, power by reason of influence, authority, resources, numbers.*

When getting up is the goal, it is good to know that it takes more than physical prowess. It takes mental strength, moral strength, and courage, all the personality traits that you already have. You may not have used them lately, but you have them now; you just need to dust them off and start working for your success.

When thinking about looking up, I was curious to find out how many muscles it takes to go from lying down to standing up straight and, although no one source could really say, a collective assessment seems to be that it takes about 200 muscles and in all layers of the body (the skeletal, the smooth, and the cardiac). It takes about 70 back muscles to pull the bone in one direction, and the others move it back again, to give us what we need for the strength to stand up. Time didn't allow me to investigate the whole answer, but I am sure it is a marvelous, miraculous design by our creator to give us life. It is our job to make our lives matter, and that will only happen when you look up and get up and get going.

Ah, friend, no matter what is happening in your life today, I hope you'll take the time to stop and contemplate the idea that, if you can look up (and you can), you can get up, and you must.

Your world is not broken, maybe cracked, but not so broken that you can't get up on your own strength to move in the direction of your dreams. You've done it before when you were knocked down; no doubt you can do it again, and this time, as you are pulling yourself up, think about how you got to this place and how you're going to get out so you can look up, get up, and not put yourself in this position again.

I started out by admitting that I know what some of you are going through is hell on Earth, and many of you, through no fault of your own, are having to carry a load you never dreamed you'd have to carry. I know that some days looking up is more than you have the strength to do, but please know that what you're going through will change in time, and if you can just muster the strength to look up, I know you can get up and get going in your life.

YOU CAN'T FIX YOURSELF BY BREAKING SOMEONE ELSE

You often hear the phrase that *life is precious, and we need to be careful with our words, our actions, and our attitude*, and I wholeheartedly agree with that statement and believe it to be true.

We all need to follow the wisdom of those words, but what I find so disappointing in watching others is the bizarre attitude of some people who think that by tearing everyone else down, they are building themselves up. Sorry, Charlie, it doesn't work that way because you can't fix yourself by breaking someone else. It's not possible; in fact, it's more dangerous than you'll ever know if you go down that road.

I am not speaking to the good folks who are reading this today, but many of you are the friends, acquaintances, partners, or family members who are so bitter, angry, nasty, and hateful that they waste their lifetime tearing down those around them in hopes of lifting their own status in life. I say to those who are so damaged, "You don't get far in life by standing on the broken bones of others, and frankly, you look foolish being *the* king of *that* hill."

If you are in a relationship where your friend, partner, family member, or significant other spend time tearing at the fabric of your life, you need to walk away. If you believe that life is precious, you need to learn to value your short life on this earth and value yourself enough to block the negativity of those who heap anger on you and others. They are damaged, and you can't fix them, nor should you try, when they have stooped so low to find their self-worth in tearing you down.

Let me give you three reasons why having this negative attitude around you will do a lifetime of damage.

1. If you allow someone to verbally pick at you, over time, you will, believe it or not, begin to believe that what they say is the truth.

Today, you know they're a nut, and you think it won't bother you. But over time, you will begin to question yourself when some issues arise, and you can't figure out what direction to go when questions are asked, and you don't know an answer or when conversations are started, and you have little to nothing to add. Their nagging, snarky comments that they snidely said to tear you down (to build themselves up) will start to seep into your subconscious, and over time, you'll begin to believe the negative talk because that is all you hear.

You have to guard your heart, your mind, and soul against the hurtful words that others use against you because they are not true and are meant to tear you and others down to build the other person up in your eyes and in theirs, which is a slippery slope since in the end everyone is damaged.

It's at that point that I hurt for you and everyone I see this happen to, whether in business or speaking or politics. Since you never started out with the current thought of your now-perceived limited ability, you've been lied to so much that now you believe it. The constant tearing down has now become the norm, so you don't hear it as anything unusual, but friend, this tearing down will kill your spirit slowly until one day you are an empty shell of the vibrant, loving, kind person you used to be.

I see this most with married couples where one of them thought they could love or push or force the other enough to grow them to maturity, but that didn't work, and over time, they've grown hollow in their lives. Due to perceived social norms of their fancy neighborhoods, they live as lonely people, certainly not what they had planned when they started out, but here they are years later wondering if being single would be as painful as being together.

This happens slowly, and then over time, it's hard to remember when this verbal abuse didn't occur. Yes, I call it verbal abuse because no one should have to listen to another be so unkind as to cause wounds that do not heal over time, being constantly kept raw and hurting.

Like it or not, I am well known for saying walk away if at all possible, and save yourself, and if for some unknown reason, you choose to stay, then have the courage to force the conversation back to an equal setting where no words of unkindness are tolerated or allowed.

You've got to be strong in your resolve. Since it has become a habit, your opponent can change for a day or two, but not much more, and if you draw a line in the sand and allow them to cross it more than once, you've given in and lost the battle.

Ideally, you should never allow your kids, your friends, your spouse, your boss, or anyone else verbally pick at you because the old saying is true: "There's always a little truth behind every 'just kidding,' a little curiosity behind every, 'just wondering,' a little knowledge behind every, 'I don't know,' and a little emotion behind every 'I don't care.'"

Today is the day that you understand the truth that no one can fix themselves by breaking someone else. It's not true today, nor has it ever been true; it's a lie that does a lifetime of damage.

2. Another reason why "you can't fix yourself by breaking someone else" is so damaging is that when you allow others to talk that way towards you, you've allowed their venom to affect those you care about.

Whether it is your kids or spouse or family or friends, if you accept the disrespect that they are showing, you have now involved others and friend, and that is not right.

I don't like to see it when someone rips into you, and I really hate to see it when they turn from you and smart-off to your spouse or kids or co-workers who have no dog in the fight, all because you didn't shut them down when they crossed the line in being disrespectful towards you the first, second, or third time. When you allowed them to buy into the false notion that they can fix themselves by breaking you and everyone around you, you did them a disservice, and now, you have to do the extra hard work to protect those around you who they verbally tear down.

Since you allowed this rude, unkind, uncaring attitude to affect those you love, don't you dare run away from your responsibility, do something about it, and the best thing you can do is to confront and demand a change of conversation or attitude or actions. (And, remember, always take someone with you to be a witness; don't do this alone.)

No one likes to be called out, and they will back it up and say you misunderstood them, and they were just joking or how could you think they would be that way. But, remember, zebras don't change their stripes, and leopards don't change their spots; their actions speak for themselves. Keep calm and stand firm, then walk away.

I love the quote, "How beautiful is it to stay silent when someone expects you to be enraged," and I love the line, "When tempted to fight fire with fire, remember that the fire department usually uses water."

3. When someone chooses to treat others with such disdain, you need to understand that they have lost a part of their heart.

Hurting people hurt people, and I've heard it said that manipulative people do not understand the concept of boundaries; they are relentless in their pursuit of what they want, and they have no regard for who gets hurt along the way.

Knowing this, you need to be on your guard to keep yourself and those you love safely away from them because when someone thinks that by breaking others down, they can lift themselves up, that is the most self-delusional, backward thinking that cannot be repaired without a higher power to show them their ways and change their lives.

You might ask me, "Well, how will I know who these people are or who they become over time?" Believe it or not, it is simple; always listen to your heart because even though it's on your left side, your heart is always right, and you'll just know it.

Remember, a healthy relationship doesn't drag you down, it inspires you to be better, and anyone who does not do that for you should not have a place in your life, and I don't care if they are family or friends or co-workers.

Hard words, I know, and I don't mean to be so hard, but I need for you to understand that you have to protect yourself these days, and if you agree with me that life is precious, the time to start is now.

REMEMBER, PEOPLE ARE LOOKING UP TO YOU, DON'T LET THEM DOWN

There is a small church near where I live, and on the outdoor board that shows the church service times and the pastor's name and other information, I saw that they had put up this phrase: *Remember, people are looking up to you, don't let them down.*

I like that thought because it is so true. I know I speak about this a lot, but, friends, hear me, you never know who is watching you, and you never know who is following your steps, as they live their lives. You matter. Your words matter. Your actions matter. How you live your life matters. Never forget and never think that you can just get by because someone is always looking up to you, so don't let them down.

My guest last week, who I see at all the political events I speak at nationwide, never knew that I was watching him. The first time I met him, I noticed he was different, and I wanted to see how he was able to make crazy things even out. I wanted to learn a few tips for my toolbox, and lately, as I am on my journey to be a better me, I have taken to heart the words of my message that no matter where I am, someone is probably watching me.

Part of this gives me no comfort since I make a lot of mistakes and then have to go and make corrections, but it is a good reminder that you and I work our whole life to build a reputation, and if we're not careful, we can lose it in an instant (many times unfairly). But our frenemies and the media don't care as they grind us to dust. We're just another story for today's headline and something else will take our headline tomorrow. And to think that we'll spend many years, and for some the rest of their lives, building back our reputation to prove to the naysayers that we were honest all along.

It was Will Rogers who said, "It takes a lifetime to build a good reputation, but you can lose it in a minute."

I have noticed in my own life that people look up to folks like you and me for a variety of reasons, and probably one of the most important is that we have self-respect. I love the definition found in dictionary.com: self-respect is a noun that means - *proper esteem or regard for the dignity of one's character.* I like that line, the dignity of one's character, meaning that we care for ourselves and our belongings and our family and friends. We try to keep our weight in check, our homes in order. Our work is accurate, and our attitude is sunny side up, even on hard days. I know it's not easy, but really, what choice do you have, especially if you're a person who cares about the dignity of your character?

We all know the old line that says *character is who you are when no one is watching.* Charles Hadden Spurgeon, a famous preacher of yesteryear, said, "A good character is the best tombstone. Those who loved you, and were helped by you, will remember you when forget-me-nots have withered. Carve your name on hearts, not on marble."

Someone who understands the concept of self-respect will, by their life and actions, carve a place into people's hearts because they fundamentally understand that people are looking up to them, and that is reason enough to do right, or as a preacher I grew up listening to would say, "Do right until the stars fall."

Another reason people look up to us is that we have and show respect for others. It's not hard to be respectful, but it sure seems that way today. I don't know if some people just think they need to bully their way to the top, but it doesn't endear them to anyone if that is the way they do business. And, really, no one looks up to someone like that, in fact, they do the opposite; they look down on someone who cannot show basic courtesy and respect.

Not to be negative, but one of my pet peeves is what I call a prideful sense of stupidness, like when I hear people say, "Well, they should just like me for who I am," or "Why should I change? It's not my problem that people don't like me." As a matter of fact, it is. Some people have the attitude that everyone else is wrong or stupid or dumb if they don't think they're as special as they do.

It's an odd sense of arrogance when some people think that being disruptive is okay or being unkind is acceptable or being generally mean-spirited or snarky or back-biting or bitter or ugly is allowed in today's world. What it is, is a complete lack of disrespect, that in very simple terms, pits those with manners against those who choose not to learn or respect manners. The truth is that anyone can learn to have manners, anyone can learn to do right, anyone can be honest, anyone can be kind; they simply have to make up their mind to do so, even when they don't feel like it. Because even in those times, people are watching or looking up to them to see what they will do. Friend, don't let the ones who are watching you down.

If your current issue of self-esteem is so confused that you think it is okay to be ugly in your attitude or manners or dress, by being disrespectful to others, I encourage you as a friend, to please reconsider, because you weren't born mean, hateful, and ugly. No one is born that way; it is just a reflection of something that has happened to you that you need to be healed from or released from, so you can learn to live your best life ever.

Another reason that people are looking up to you is that you are genuine. You are who you are, you don't put on airs, acting like you're better (or in some cases, worse) than you are. The fact is, when you are young, it takes a while to figure out who you are. When you're young, you try out a few different personalities to see which one fits your style or your mindset. The problem comes when you get to be older, and hopefully wiser, and you need to have this figured out, so you really are the genuine person you have created yourself to be, meaning that what I see is who you are in good times and bad.

We respect people who are genuine, who say what they mean and mean what they say, and that is a comfort for those who are looking up to you to know that, no matter what, your word is your bond. Goodness, don't you wish everyone felt that way? I don't know about you, but I am tired of people who say one thing and then do another. It's a sad day when you have to put everything in writing because an honest handshake is not how people do business. These are the people who hope no one is watching, but they are mistaken; if not today, one day, all their lies and deceit will be found out, and then they will have let everyone down.

Hear me, if you're not properly doing business, fix your ways now. The longer you live in a lie, the harder it is to come clean. You will not win in the end, no matter how smart you think you are. Why? Because you've lost your self-respect, and now you've lost the respect of others, and you're not genuine; we can all see that. But you know what the worst part is? It is that you have *chosen* to let people down, and that is a bad way to live.

Quickly, I want to touch on two other character traits on why it is important to remember that people are looking up to you, and you cannot let them down. Number one, a person of goodwill understands that having compassion coupled with discernment is the life that leaves a legacy. Remember the quote, "Carved on hearts..."

Compassion - *a feeling of distress and pity for the suffering or misfortune of another, often including the desire to alleviate it.* Why? Because you understand that others are looking up to you and watching, in hopes of learning how to live their best life ever. Understanding that life is hard, they are looking to you. Yes, they are looking to you to feel their distress, pain, and suffering and, through it all, to show them the way to success or freedom or free them from pain whether it is personal, emotional, or mental. You, by your life that they are watching, help them find a calm sense of being. Ah, friend, that is compassion at its best, and who wouldn't want to offer that drink of cool water at the end of a hard day? You would be soulless if you didn't care, and that would break my heart to know that you walked on by, and you let them down.

I'll end with the concept of discernment. I like to think of discernment as a way of knowing when you don't know; it's a gut feeling, a thought, a memory, an idea that you feel deeply, and just know what is right. But if you've lost your soul because you've lost your self-respect and the respect others, if you're not genuine and you lack compassion, you'll have no discernment. In fact, you probably don't even know what I'm talking about, and my thought for today is falling on your deaf ears. My prayer is that today you stop, hear, listen, and take action before it's too late.

You matter. Your words matter. Your actions matter. How you live your life matters. Never forget, and never think that you can just get by, because someone is always looking up to you, so don't you dare let them down.

"YOU CAN DWELL ON IT FOR THE REST OF YOUR LIFE. THAT'S DEATH. OR YOU CAN LET IT GO AND MOVE ON. THAT'S LIFE."

—*Brigitte Nicole*

One of the great joys of doing my radio show is all the nice people who call or email me and tell me how a certain show was meaningful to them, from how much they liked a certain guest to some asking questions about who to turn to for help. Since I am not a licensed counselor or an HR person, I like to suggest some good people I know who may be able to help those who reach out to me seeking answers.

I cannot help everyone, but I certainly will try to send them to those who might be able to help.

Occasionally, I will get a call from someone who, just by listening every week to my dose of encouragement, has allowed a dormant spark of a long-lost passion to flicker alive, and when that spark catches on and begins to create a little light, that's what pushes a few good folks to ask how to get started or restart on something they had always wanted to do but pushed aside for whatever reason.

A week ago, I met someone who said they'd always felt that they wanted to speak at conferences because they had gone through a lot in their life, and they wanted to let others know how they got through it. They wanted to be an encouragement to others. I get that one a lot. The problem with that request is that it is hard to find your tribe, those who will let you speak from the platform and then pay you for the information.

Not to be discouraging, but most speakers have been on the circuit for years speaking on topics they are experts on, and that is how a livelihood is made in this very competitive business. Yes, some can do well for a time with their topic and topics of interest come and go. Currently, there are a number of fine folks talking about storytelling, but in time, that will most likely dwindle down to the handful of speakers who can sustain the business.

Again, please know that if you have a passion and can craft a message that can change lives, you might be on to something. I encourage you to find those who are likeminded to your topic and see if they would be willing to have you speak to their group.

Probably the number one request I get from folks who call me is the desire to speak to the faith community because it seems pretty easy since most Sunday sermons are three points and a poem, and they know the texts, the congregation, and the words to all the songs. And since we are taught not to judge, many think that is a great way to get started.

I had a call this week from a very nice person. She has been listening to my show for over a year and finally got the courage to call me and ask to know how to start speaking.

When I answered the phone, she introduced herself and told me that she wanted to speak at women's conferences; then she began to tell me all the reasons why she hasn't been able to pursue her dream of speaking. She is married with kids in school and a husband who is ill but is doing odd jobs to help keep the family stable. She has to work, but doesn't like her job, and she can't quit because they need the money. She went on to tell me that she is not a good writer and didn't finish school, so she feels bad about that and doesn't feel good about her command of the English language. It was then when I had to stop her; frankly, I just couldn't listen anymore.

I have a very low tolerance for people who want to dwell on all the reasons why they can't follow their dreams, live their passion, or do what they feel they were born to do.

Instead of discussing all the reasons she gave me about her life being out of balance, I asked her to give me a few topics on which she would like to speak.

I got the usual marriage, mortgage, and munchkins line. You know, the "Let me tell you how to have a great marriage, how to make your finances work, and how to love your kids."

Well, that was a typical start, so I asked again, can you think about a few topics on which you would like to speak, and that people need to hear?

Once again, she started with how bad her life is, her husband and her kids and in-laws, and I had to stop her again and give her this quote that I had seen.

"You can dwell on it for the rest of your life. That's death. Or you can let it go and move on. That's life."

You see, I wanted her to let go of all of her excuses and move forward with her dreams and desires and see life, the life she wants to see and be in and have. I wanted her to move forward to pursue her dream of being a speaker in the faith community at conferences all over America, but she wants to dwell on all the reasons why it won't work. And I feel sure that, within all the hours of excuse-making, she refuses to make the small changes to clean up her life (and, I'm guessing, her house and yard and garage and closets and car and kitchen, also) because talking about it is so much easier than doing the work. I see it every day.

And I was brokenhearted that talking is all it seemed she was willing to do, but I decided to offer her a way out. I suggested that she write a paragraph a day, just a paragraph of what she would say, should she be given the opportunity to speak to a group.

I'm not looking for *War and Peace*, not even a *Readers Digest* short story. A start doesn't have to be anything major. I told her to start with a few lines every day about a topic that she feels would benefit others. And when she finishes writing her paragraph, she should send it to a trusted friend to keep her accountable to keep writing every day. I suggested just a paragraph on a small notepad, so she isn't overwhelmed, and I said I'd check back with her in a few weeks.

I feel like Paul Harvey, here to tell you *the rest of the story...*

I wish I had good news, but I don't. You see, she had chosen to talk about all the reasons why it still won't work, and she will (like my theme today) "dwell on it for the rest of her life. That's death."

I could not convince her to *let it go and move on. That would be life.* The life she "tells" me she wants for herself and her family.

When I think about the simple homework that I gave to her, I am reminded of a wonderful local TEDx speaker we had in my hometown about a year ago. He writes what he calls mini-sagas, stories he writes every day, and they are exactly 50 words, no more, no less.

He will tell you that the design and planning it takes to produce a mini-saga has made him more efficient, observant, and more disciplined in his everyday life. He was excellent, and his concept is intriguing to me, not only as a discipline but also as a creative outlet within a strict guideline that undoubtedly leads to success in other areas of life.

You might want to consider writing a mini-saga of only 50 words and see how well you'd do. Within time, I'm sure you'll improve your skill and word choice, word color, and creative verbal design. It would be a good step in the right direction to get your creative juices flowing for your success.

Brigitte Nicole's quote, "You can dwell on it for the rest of your life. That's death. Or you can let it go and move on. That's life," is very real for many listening today. You've spent a lifetime talking about your dreams. What would it take for you to get going on them, to live the life you've imagined?

Let me encourage you to let the past go. I know I have said this before, but if you don't make peace with your past, it will keep showing up in your present. Let past hurts, past failures, past falling downs go and move on. You can't change it now. If you've done your part and asked for forgiveness, or even if they didn't give you that chance to accept your request for healing, it's okay because it's over.

It's done. For some, it's forgotten; for others, it never meant a thing to them, so stop cheating on your future with your past, it's over. It's time to let it go and move on, that's life.

Now, breathe and clear your mind, soul, and heart, and move in the direction of your dreams. I'll be here every week to cheer you on.

A LITTLE BIT OF KINDNESS

"Three things in human life are important: the first is to be kind; the second is to be kind; and the third is to be kind."

– Henry James

"Be kind, for everyone you meet is fighting a harder battle."

– Plato

It doesn't take much to show a little bit of kindness, and if there ever was a time that your city, your community, your family, and your friends need that smidgen of love, it is now. We all need a little bit of kindness. It doesn't take much, but it does take some work in advance to make sure you're doing this right.

I've got to tell you, as the holidays are fast approaching, I can already feel the tension of what is supposed to be the best time of the year, the happiest time of the year, the season of love and joy, and tension is building because of the unknown. So, what would it take to make the unknown known, so you can relax and enjoy yourself? For many, it is a simple process as far as I can tell. You need to know where you're going, how you're going to get there, and how you're going to pay for it without causing undue hardship on you or your family.

Let's think about this. We haven't even gotten to Thanksgiving, and already the Christmas music is on the radio. Poor Thanksgiving! It's one of my favorite holidays, but it gets no love because it doesn't make any money for the market. What's with all that goodwill and thanksgiving for all our blessings? Goodness, we've got to hurry to Black Friday and let the official start of the Christmas season take place!

I don't want to focus on the money that this time of year seems to gobble up, but I will remind you of the Dave Ramsey quote, "We buy things we don't need with money we don't have to impress people we don't like." Don't do it this year; save yourself. You can do an act of kindness that money could never buy and do well by doing good.

Before we get to Christmas, I'd like you to stop and think about slowing down and not letting the season push you. I'd like to see you take control of the season and do what is best for you and your loved ones.

I'd like to press upon you to stop and enjoy the holiday known as Thanksgiving and be thankful for little things like the blessings of abundant food, clean water, warm homes, relatives who are still with us, and memories of those who have passed on.

When I think about our world's need for a little bit of kindness, I am reminded about why we celebrate Thanksgiving, as you all well know.

Thanksgiving became an official Federal holiday in 1863 when, during the Civil War, President Abraham Lincoln proclaimed a national day of "Thanksgiving and Praise to our beneficent Father who dwelleth in the Heavens" to be celebrated on the last Thursday in November. (Wikipedia)

With the arrival of the pilgrims at New Plymouth, they composed the "Mayflower Compact," which honored God, noting that Thanksgiving begins with acknowledging that God is faithful and earnestly giving Him thanks in advance for His abundant blessings.

Philippians 4:6 says, "In everything, by prayer and petition, with thanksgiving, present your requests to God."

When you think about it, the true meaning of Thanksgiving should focus on relationships, whether it is your relationship with your heavenly Father and putting your spiritual life in order or your relationship with your earthly family. For many, it would be a great thing to stop and take inventory of your relationships, family, and life as well. I like to think about this as a timeline. Think about the place in the timeline of life where your kids are. Next, take that one step further and notice on that timeline where your parents are. Last, place yourself and your spouse or life partner on that timeline and see where you are and think about where you're headed.

I want you to imagine the timeline to remind yourself how short life is, how briefly we are here to make a difference, to leave a legacy.

This week, I had a friend on the show to talk about living your best life ever by understanding what she calls the Five Essentials for Success. One of those concepts is the issue of happiness and unhappiness and what to do about it. I see so much dissatisfaction with life and work and family and friends, so I asked her to come and talk about how someone can find their way through the darkness to the light to live the life they imagined.

For the weeks leading up to Thanksgiving, I want to stop and focus on my theme of "A Little Bit of Kindness."

I'm sure you've heard the phrase that "A little bit of kindness goes a long way," and it does. In fact, it was scientifically proven that being kind makes you happier!

Dr. Wayne Dyer has reported that whenever someone engages in acts of kindness, no matter if big or small, the serotonin levels increase in both the giver and receiver of an act of kindness. In addition, they noted that anyone who witnesses an act of kindness also has an increase in serotonin levels. The giver, receiver, and those who witness the act of kindness all experience a boost in happiness!

I love the quote from Robert Furey, "Those who make compassion an essential part of their lives find the joy of life. Kindness deepens the spirit and produces rewards that cannot be completely explained in words. It is an experience more powerful than words. To become acquainted with kindness one must be prepared to learn new things and feel new feelings. Kindness is more than a philosophy of the mind. It is a philosophy of the spirit."

I like the thought that kindness is a philosophy of the spirit. You know, my favorite quote is from Mark Twain. He said, "Kindness is a language which the deaf can hear and the blind can see."

Kindness is simple, but it seems that we have lost the spirit of kindness in our busy world of just getting by.

Growing up, I often heard the phrase, "Don't sweat the small stuff." Although that's a trendy catchphrase in our hectic, fast-paced world, it can be good advice. But there's more to that quote. What's not being said is as important as what is being said. Don't sweat the small stuff, but don't forget the small stuff, either. More often than we realize, a small act can make the difference, provide a bit of hope, and may change a life.

Singer-songwriter, Glenn Campbell, had a hit song called "Try a Little Kindness." I always liked the words.

If you see your brother standing by the road...With a heavy load from the seeds he's sowed...And if you see your sister falling by the way...Just stop and stay you're going the wrong way... Don't walk around the down and out...Lend a helping hand instead of doubt...And the kindness that you show every day...Will help someone along their way...

The chorus went like this...

You got to try a little kindness
Yes, show a little kindness
Just shine your light for everyone to see
And if you try a little kindness
Then you'll overlook the blindness
Of narrow-minded people on the narrow-minded streets

As we come into this season of Thanksgiving, what small act of kindness can you do to make a difference? I hope you'll spend some time this weekend before the crush of wrapping paper, Christmas trees, and crazy family members coming to eat you out of house and home, to think about your blessings, your gifts, and your kind acts of goodness that define who you are, not only this holiday season but also every day of the year.

"FIRST IT'S IMPOSSIBLE, THEN DIFFICULT, THEN DONE."

—Hudson Taylor

Have you ever looked at a task and thought, *Wow, that's impossible!* Then you stop, or you start to find other ways to get the job done, and you realize that it's not impossible; it's just difficult. As you keep working, it isn't as bad as you thought. Now, it's still hard, but before you know it, the job that was out of range, too hard to do, couldn't figure it out, is now completed. Finished. Done.

Recently, I was having some quiet time. I was reading in a devotional book I really love about prayer and came across the quote from the missionary, Hudson Taylor. He said, "First it's impossible, then difficult, then done."

That thought stuck with me because it is true and has shown itself to be true in my own life. As I reflect, I can tell you about 100 times that I thought a job, a project, an issue was simply impossible, but then circumstances changed, and the impossible became possible. Still, it was difficult, no doubt, but then it was done.

I want to provide a bit of hope. No matter what you're going through right now (that seems impossible), if you'll work thought it, even the difficult parts that don't make sense, the hard parts that you can't seem to find answers to, the lonely hours that try your soul, if you just push through the difficulties, you will find yourself on the other side. You will be able to look back and marvel at how you got to the point of completion. When you flash back and remember that at one point you thought it was hopeless, you'll be grateful that you pushed through.

I don't know the issues that are weighing heavy on your soul today, whether it's your marriage, which for some is hanging by a thread due to one of you having an affair and the other finding out, or in your anger, you've crossed the line from frustration to abuse. Maybe, it feels like there is no forgiveness ever coming for what you've done, and the cold and silent treatment is creating a hollow, empty, lonely life. For some, it is simply a lack of love or desire. The flame is gone, and you're not sure if it's ever coming back or if you even want it to. You now wonder if faking another happy day is even worth it for you, for them, for the kids, the in-laws and out-laws. It seems impossible.

Well, that may be how it seems to you right now, but in time (if you want), you'll find a way. You will make hard decisions to do the right thing, to ask forgiveness and a chance to start over, to try again, to rekindle what you know and who you know is the right one for you and your family. It may go slowly, on shaky ground; lost trust does that. You can't expect more, but trust regained will prove that it is not impossible; it's just difficult, and over time it will be done. Eventually, you'll sigh with relief when you remember what you might have lost if you hadn't done the impossible and the difficult, which have led you to this day.

Or you're worried about your kids who have not turned out as you had hoped for, prayed for, and cried for. You're angry and embarrassed and simply at a loss of what to do. Your kids started out so great, and now, you hardly recognize them. They're not the sweet kids you remember, the ones you poured your life into so they would be productive, impressive, well-mannered young adults. Now, your kids are disrespectful, angry, and aloof. They still expect you to feed them, house them, and take care of them as they treat you with knowing disdain. It happened so slowly but sort of suddenly, and now, the only thing you can do is believe that you trained up those kids in the way they should go, and pray that they will find their way back to the path and not depart from it. Ah, friend, I know right now it seems impossible.

Let me encourage you to tread lightly when it comes to your kids, but don't give up on them. The world is a hard place for young people nowadays. Many of the kids I work with are so talented and smart, but they look around and see what "everyone else has" and they want it. They want to fit in; they want others to respect them, and they want to be adults in their kid's body. They find solace in drinking and relief in drugs. Escaping the duties of responsibility, for many, is their goal. Days turn into months and months into years, and one day, they will grow up and realize (although they will never tell you) that they wasted so much time in their drama in their heads with their friends. Someday, they will want to settle down and get on about the business of school and life and love. When they were young, life seemed impossible, then they realized that it was just difficult, and soon, they will be able to breathe a sigh of relief that they are done with those days; they are ready to fly right and do good, forgetting that they put all those grey hairs on your head.

Some of you may be worried about your job and finances. Once again, there is more month than money, and there is pressure to give more and more when you've got less and less. You're working more hours, but you are still struggling to stay financially afloat. You're working harder than your physical body can handle, but you don't dare say a word because you need the paycheck to take care of your family. For some, there is the pressure of not having a job right now and spending hours looking for work to meet your needs just to get by. There is the frustration of how you ever got to this place to begin with. This is not how it is supposed to be. With your skillset, your degree, your ability to work hard and be a great employee, how is it that there is not a place for you? Friend, I hear it every day, and it's heartbreaking and seemingly impossible to catch a break. There is no doubt that it is difficult, maybe impossible.

It's hard to enjoy *peace on earth and goodwill to men* when you have to sell your things at the pawnshop or on craigslist to buy for the kids, the family, the friends, and everyone else at the office.

The financial piece is a little harder. "Impossible," you may say; it is certainly difficult, and unless you get your financial house in order, it will not be done anytime soon. You know that you need to save more and spend less, but you must commit to doing it, to be disciplined enough to protect your future. Remember this simple fact: you are in control, so you need to take control of your future. Even if it means night school or a little more training for a short time to put you in a better financial position because it is not impossible; it may be difficult, but you can get it done. You're smart, you're able, and, with a hopeful attitude, you're unstoppable.

At some point, all your struggles and tears and pain and hurt and anger and frustration will be done. Finished. Over. And you will come through on the other side, victorious.

All the thrashing around to work and rework problems to find the answers will pay off after the anger and tears subside, and then, you will see clearly a path forward; that is, only if you don't give up. You must keep thinking, working, and praying for the answers to come. Impossible at first, difficult, to say the least, but then (out of the clear blue), you will be done.

I wouldn't be honest if I didn't tell you that it's not going to be easy, but it will be done, and let me remind you that how you deal with the ending will tell you and everyone around you a lot about your character in how you handle the aftermath.

I'm well known for saying that when it comes to politics, "How you lose determines if you'll ever come back." I'm not saying that you're headed for a loss, mind you, but I do want to remind you that your actions throughout the process of dealing with the impossible, the difficult, will be a determining factor in your final outcome.

So, friends, be steady in the storms of life, be hopeful as you seek your future, be kind as you deal with others, and be grateful for the lessons learned that you can teach others when you tell them that at first it seems impossible, then it will be difficult, but then it will be done.

DON'T WORRY ABOUT TOMORROW

"Therefore, do not worry about tomorrow, for tomorrow will worry about itself. Each day has enough trouble of its own."

Matthew 6:34

As I prepare for the holidays, I am constantly reminded of a verse I grew up with. It goes like this: "Do not worry about tomorrow, for tomorrow will worry about itself. Each day has enough trouble of its own." Although that does not appear to be the most comforting verse I've ever read, it is more true than not, and with that knowledge in hand, I can rest assured that what will happen will happen. If it is to be so, I can't do anything about it, so I might as well get about the business of life and getting things done that I promised myself and others that I'd do.

Oddly, I like this verse because it is a great reminder that each day has enough trouble of its own, so don't add to it by worrying or making yourself sick with fear. You've been warned, so you know what is coming; you even know what is potentially coming tomorrow.

As much as I want to control tomorrow, so I don't mess anything up or miss anything, it does me no good to worry and fret and become anxious for tomorrow because, ultimately, I have no idea of what tomorrow will bring.

I can prepare for tomorrow and get myself ready but worrying will not solve any problem I have coming my way. It's been said that "All worry does is steal joy from today."

I love the quote from Dale Carnegie: "Remember, today is the tomorrow you worried about yesterday."

I also like the quote: "Worry is a total waste of time. It doesn't change anything. All it does is steal your joy and keep you very busy doing nothing."

And the truth is that most of the things you're worried about right now will not come true and, most likely, will never happen, so you're either setting yourself up for disappointment or failure (or both), and that is a lousy way to live your amazing life.

Or, like Mary Hemingway said, "Worry a little bit every day and in a lifetime, you will lose a couple of years. If something is wrong, fix it if you can. But train yourself not to worry. Worry never fixes anything."

I came across the quote from Corrie ten Boom that says, "Worry does not empty tomorrow of its sorrow; it empties today of its strength."

And, friend, you really can't afford that, not in this life. I find that a lot of people are worriers; they worry about everything, things they can control and things they cannot. I'm not sure of the reason they waste so much time in fear (and that is what worry is, fear), but it seems to me that we have a national pastime, and it's to worry.

I'll tell you what I think worry does for many people; it gives them something to do. It makes you think you're taking action, but in reality, you're not. You're just wasting mental energy worrying about things you have no control over. You have decided that, instead of doing the things you need to, you will waste valuable time doing nothing. Wow! That must be fulfilling. I'm joking.

Listen, worry is nothing but wasting time, and maybe you have time to waste, maybe all your chores are done, maybe your shopping is all finished, and the house is decorated, and all the cooking is finished, house cleaned, shoes polished, files ready for the new year, attic spotless and garage and closets organized and cleaned out ready to give the extra to Goodwill. Wow, good for you. I'm impressed. If everything is done, then you've probably got time to waste sitting around worrying, but you know what? People who have all their stuff together are not the type to sit around worrying. Why? They realize that worrying won't stop the bad stuff from happening; it only stops them from enjoying the good in life today.

And smart people don't waste their seconds, minutes, and hours for days, months, and years doing nothing. Mark my words. You will never see an outrageously successful person be a worrier. Never!

Why is that? Because successful people know that "Things which matter most should never be at the mercy of things which matter least." Goethe

One thing I always find fascinating is when you see people who worry and fret and moan and groan, and then, when some unexpected incident happens, they forget all about the worries they woke with that morning. In an instant, they are now focused on the issue at hand.

Nothing puts life into perspective like a car accident or a fall or a house fire. Suddenly, all the worrying about the little things in life falls away when real issues are jolted into the forefront of our thinking.

I do not wish that any such misfortune enters your life; I simply want to remind you of how quickly you forget the issues that seem to weigh heavy on your mind when real, life-changing issues occur.

May I remind you that you'd do well not to worry. Let me go one step further and say, stop worrying about tomorrow and the next day and the next. Instead of worrying, let's stop and consider some options to help you focus instead of flitter.

Think in straight lines about what is due next. If you had to put a plan on paper (and I encourage you to write it out), what is due next to help you get things in order?

Don't make it harder than it is. Really, what is due next? Do you need some tools or more time or others' advice or help? If so, ask. What I find fascinating is that so many people are afraid to ask for help when the person who could help wouldn't mind a bit if you ask appropriately, then take the actions prescribed and thank them for their help and advice.

So, back to the task at hand; What is due next? Once you start your list, you will be amazed at how quickly things fall into place, but the key is you have to stop worrying and start working. Worry does not take the place of work. Once again, let's start with your written list of what is due.

I can tell you that when I have a list and stick to it, I am usually amazed by how quickly the items on my list are accomplished and how good I feel when that list is checked off, and I'm on to the next big thing. Working my list takes away my worrying about if I'm going to get it done. Once I put a simple plan in place (trust me, all my plans are simple), I don't have the energy to make anything harder than it is or harder than it should be.

The reason I want you to take a few minutes today to write out your list is because "There is no someday." My friend Stewart gave me a T-shirt that said, *Monday, Tuesday, Wednesday, Thursday, Friday, Saturday, Sunday – see, there is no Someday.*

I love that shirt because it speaks to the heart of the matter, which is that today is the day you have to make something happen.

So, friend, since there is no *someday,* you need to stop worrying about what *coulda, shoulda,* or *woulda* happened, and get going today. Stop allowing the false fear of worry stop you or even slow you down. We all have 1,440 minutes today to get things done, but it will only begin when you stop wasting your time and get to work.

Life is uncertain, and we live in the knowledge that *everything changes,* so let me remind you of one of life's truths. *Don't worry about tomorrow, for tomorrow will worry about itself. Each day has enough trouble of its own.* Don't add to it. Rest assured that you will have the strength to get through whatever life sends your way. You have to stop worrying, wondering, and doubting. Have faith that things will work out, maybe not how you planned, but just how they're meant to be.

Worrying will not change the world, it only changes you, so stop worrying. Work hard, take chances, and keep the faith.

"OUR DAYS ARE HAPPIER WHEN WE GIVE PEOPLE A BIT OF OUR HEART RATHER THAN A PIECE OF OUR MIND."

—*Unknown*

Recently, I overheard a heated argument in which one of the players was verbally harsh to the other and gave them what we'd call a standing down, told them off, gave them a piece of their mind. It was so sad to see the immediate crush of the other person's spirit. It was shocking and unsettling and simply heartbreaking.

I am not around people who yell. I didn't grow up with anyone who yelled in our family; it wasn't allowed, and when I witness the outburst of anger that is carried by one's raising of their voice, it rattled my insides, upset my psyche, and made me jittery. I had nothing to do with the fight, but I still had a powerful response.

I don't like yelling. I don't like to be around people who think that it's acceptable to yell, and I'm sorry to say that I have been witness to more than my share of watching people come unglued. And when I see this kind of behavior, I am reminded of the old saying that I grew up with.

"Our days are happier when we give people a bit of our heart rather than a piece of our mind."

I came across an interesting truism about yelling:

One day, an elder put this question to his friends:
"Why do people yell when they argue?"

One of them said, "We are yelling because we are losing our temper."
The elder said, "But why scream when the other person is right next to you?"

Another one answered, "We yell to make sure that we hear each other."
The elder said, "Couldn't we talk more slowly, with a quieter voice?"

Then everyone was silent...
The elder answered his question this way: "Do you know why we yell at each other when we are angry? The truth is that when two people argue, their hearts distance greatly. To cover this distance, they have to shout, to be able to hear each other. The more angry, the bigger the distance, they need to speak much louder.

"On the other hand, what happens when two beings are in love? They do not scream at all. They speak slowly, gently. Why? Because their hearts are very close. The distance between them is very small. Sometimes, their hearts are so close that they don't even have to speak, only whisper. And when love is even more intense, there is no need to even whisper, it takes only a look and their hearts know. This is what happens when two beings love each other; their hearts are close."

That "look of love" part is the part of the story I like, the idea that you can simply look at someone, and they know without a shadow of a doubt that they are loved and accepted for who they are.

Do you remember those days? Yeah, I know, that was a long time ago, before the kids, the house, the business, the loss, the joy, the pain; those were the good old days.

I like that parable because it is true, and it fits in well with my theme for today that "Our days are happier when we give people a bit of our heart rather than a piece of our mind."

In fact, not only will your days be happier but also the hardships of life will be a lot easier to deal with if you can get this truth right. And if hard decisions need to be made this holiday season for you or your family, your marriage, your future, could I ask you to consider this option? Would you consider giving a small piece of your heart to spare some small part of the other's heart to lessen the blow of the emptiness that will be coming?

I have heard about more heartbreak this past week than I have heard in months, and I am saddened by what has happened to good, kind people that are dealing with the pain of the loss of their marriage, and others this season who are experiencing the loss of their children, not by death, but by their anger. The kids have abandoned their parents.

I don't know what it is about these days that bring the greatest stress to people. Without a doubt, Hollywood and Madison Avenue have added to the cost of living, and financially, it is hard. The dealings with family you only see a few times a year is uncomfortable because you're seeing the aging of parents and the needs of their situation. Kids are on display when all they want to do is sleep and see "their friends," and the TV version of a happy home looks nothing like where you live. It's hard, no doubt about it. Then you add to that the reality of life and questionable judgment that led to a poor decision, and it seems to spiral out of control, until you land on your back looking up, so now you have to choose to get up or get out.

I started out by telling you that I witnessed the most horrific exchange between two people who, I suppose, at one time promised to honor and cherish each other. Now, due to the length of time or lack of love or broken promises, they are a hate-filled, ugly shell of the person they used to be, unrecognizable to all who see them, who at one time loved them and are completely blown away by who they have become.

As I pushed my cart away and went down another aisle, I began to wonder what would have happened if instead of "showing out," they had quietly agreed to disagree, or perhaps even end the relationship without spewing the verbal hate that no one deserves to hear after a day, a month, a year, or a lifetime of love.

I've got to think that the most hurtful words in the English language are *I don't love you anymore*. I can't imagine how that must feel, as those words are coming out of the mouth of the one who at one time you couldn't wait to kiss, the mouth that promised *in sickness and in health*, the mouth that rang with excitement and joy at the birth of your child.

And today, that person seems to speak a different language, words you've never heard them say to anyone, much less to you, which are coming forth like a torrent, and the sheer volume of words washes over you that for years were unspoken, and you never expected to be said and I'm sure you pray you never hear again.

If this conversation is going to take place, let me ask you to rethink the impending damage. I'm going to assume that all involved know that their hearts are very distant, so there is no need to shout to be able to hear each other.

In fact, if your anger is going to cause you to speak a different language than the one your spouse or family or parents are used to hearing you speak, then rethink your outcome because the damage that it will cause will most likely never be healed or forgotten. And when kids are scarred at a young age, you've done a lifetime of damage, and no kid deserves that, least of all from their parents.

And I'll add that no parent deserves to be treated with disrespect and hurtful words by their children. They brought you into this world or chose you to be their child. (And kids don't come with a how-to manual.) They did the best they could with what they had and who they were, so back it down before you break their fragile, aging hearts because when parents are deeply hurt, they carry that with them to their last days, and no parent deserves that, least of all from their kids.

Ladies and gentlemen, if the end is going to be what it is going to be, then be gentle. You can break the heart without crushing the spirit. For most people, the heart can heal, a crushed spirit, not so much.

If you are going to make life-changing decisions this year, show a bit of respect. Find within your hardened heart some measure of basic decency and kindness and be very careful with your words.

Ah, friends, in good times and bad, I think the world would be happier if we gave people a bit of our heart rather than a piece of our mind.

Made in the USA
Middletown, DE
29 May 2021